1089 nights

To Mary,

Happy Travels!

AN ODYSSEY THROUGH THE MIDDLE EAST, AFRICA AND ASIA

Ann von Lossberg

iUniverse, Inc.
New York   Bloomington

1089 Nights

An Odyssey Through the Middle East, Africa and Asia

iUniverse books may be ordered through booksellers or by contacting:

iUniverse
1663 Liberty Drive
Bloomington, IN 47403
www.iuniverse.com
1-800-Authors (1-800-288-4677)

ISBN: 978-1-4401-0520-3 (pbk)
ISBN: 978-1-4401-0521-0 (ebk)

Printed in the United States of America .

iUniverse rev. date: 11/10/08

To my father and mother

The Book of One Thousand and One Nights (Persian: Hazār-o Yak Šab, Arabic: Kitāb 'Alf Layla wa-Layla, Turkish: Bin Bir Gece Masalları; also known as *The Book of a Thousand Nights and a Night, One Thousand and One Nights, 1001 Arabian Nights, Arabian Nights,* and simply *The Nights*) is a collection of stories compiled over hundreds of years by various authors, translators and scholars. An original manuscript has never been found, though several versions date the collection's beginnings to 800-900 AD.

What is common throughout all these editions is the story of the Persian shah Shahryar and his queen, Scheherazade (Persian: *Sahrzād*) that frames the larger body of work and the tales themselves. The king takes a beautiful new bride but is devastated to discover her infidelity. He executes her, declaring all women to be unfaithful. He marries a succession of virgins only to execute each one the next morning. Scheherazade is the next virgin. On the night of their marriage, she tells him a tale—but doesn't finish. He must keep her alive in order to hear the riveting end the next night, when she immediately begins another tale. So it goes for a thousand and one nights, a period in which Scheherazade bears the king three sons. King Shahryar realizes he has already fallen in love with Scheherazade and cannot deprive his children of their mother. He repents and makes her his wife. (*from Wikipedia Free Encyclopedia, with amendments and additions.*)

Scheherazade reminds us of the power of storytelling, to which she owes her life.

Contents

PROLOGUE: LEAP AND THE NET WILL APPEAR[*]

Men go abroad to wonder at the heights of mountains, at the huge waves of the sea, at the long courses of rivers, at the vast compass of the ocean, at the circular motions of the stars; and they pass by themselves without wondering.

Saint Augustine

I'm betting on nature, not nurture. That wanderlust comes with us. That someday scientists will find a gene, a travel gene that predisposes us to itchy feet. And that other catalysts triggered in the environment conspire to get our feet moving. I figure my molecular mandate kicked in about age twenty-nine.

Before that, I was along for the ride. Nothing I can put under a microscope from my very ordinary childhood presaged wanderlust or remotely massaged it—no models in the family, no traveler friends who transported me with their stories, no inspiring teachers. I even hated geography in school.

---

[*]   Zen saying, anonymous.

Other than an occasional trip to Ocean City, Maryland, my family lived at the neighborhood pool one block from our house. By age sixteen, I had become a hopeless homebody.

Had my hard-earned babysitting money not gone into it, I would have reneged on a trip to Colorado Springs with a high school group. I waved goodbye to my parents from the departing train, suppressing the urge to bawl. I looked up to see an overhead bag teeter and fall on my head, giving me the excuse I needed to let it all out.

In the end, I loved that trip, the edginess of it. Again and again, fear morphed to wonder, summoning every cell to life. I was more surprised than anyone. *You're really doing it*, I said to myself.

But I get ahead of myself; the Colorado trip was the second catalyst. The first catalyst got the whole physiology stirring— thanks to a man who I never met or saw. I am forever in his debt. I like to think he was a young, handsome encyclopedia salesman trying to put himself through college, not one of those creepy men who sold hairbrushes door to door.

I was about thirteen. The suburbs hugging Baltimore city had begun to flourish. Out of a sea of middle class homes in the community of Lochearn, he schlepped his bag up two sets of steps and knocked on our door one sticky summer afternoon. My parents purchased a set of encyclopedias from him.

The pictures were so beautiful, I figured the books had to be expensive for my parents. My father worked the graveyard shift at Procter & Gamble in the day when unskilled but diligent employees making soap on the floor could hope to run the production floor years later. My mother was a homemaker, like most mothers in those days, who stood on her head to feed me, my brother and sister on my father's modest salary.

I pored over the encyclopedia pages for hours, seeking out the colored pictures of exotic landscapes and golden temples and leopards perched in African trees. Whatever I knew least. It set off such a longing in me.

The longing was the visceral knowledge of a thing not yet known. I took my imagination to bed where it tantalized me into the night. The wee hours became a magical time, as the pictures indelibly imprinted in my head came back to life. I never transposed myself into those distant lands or dreamed of walking on the wild African plains. Such a leap would have been too great, my sense of myself too green. That those images stroked my love of beautiful things and introduced me to new and mysterious people and places was enough.

As unassuming as that day may have seemed, I realize it was a hallowed day—not just another hot, steamy cookie-cutter summer day. A germinal had bud; people and events began to gather to it, moving surely and inexorably towards their mandate. And as genes are wont to do, like them or not, these indelible moles and ticks and traits define us. Even afflict us.

When my itchy-feet gene blossomed full force sixteen years later, arriving on the heels of the demise of my marriage, the last thing on my mind was travel.

I felt as destitute as a person can feel. How could I have known that this unspeakable sadness was a prelude to events beyond my reckoning—events that would begin to unfold one frigid night months later.

Enter Jim Hudock, the last catalyst. Another ordinary kind of person. Before I'd even known him, Jim's reputation was legendary among my circle of friends. Everybody loved this guy.

He had never married. We became friends after the breakup of my marriage. A good friend with a gentle, disarming manner was just what I needed. He had a beard then, as he does now, though it was hippyishly long in the Seventies. His broad shoulders that tapered down into a tall, slender frame were easy on the eyes too.

Born in New Bedford, western Pennsylvania, population six hundred-plus, Jim descended from a long line of Slovakian farmers and grew up on his grandfather's farm. Three generations of Hudocks worked in the steel mills. Despite a degree in international economics from Oberlin College, he started a landscape contracting business with a friend in Maryland—the pull of his grandfather's legacy, I always thought. He found something inherently wholesome about working the soil.

A man of few needs, Jim was the consummate non-consumer who would have made a fine ascetic monk. So unassuming, so uncaring, so unconscious was he about things like houses, cars and clothes, left to his own devices, he'd happily live in a teepee, drive an old rusty car and become a nudist.

I'd known Jim for months before he mentioned his trip to Asia. In passing. We sat on my living room sofa in front of the fireplace one very cold winter night. I listened entranced as he retraced a journey nine years prior that spanned Europe, Turkey, Iran, Afghanistan, India, Thailand and Hong Kong.

My ailing Volkswagen bus was the link. "Sure, I know VWs well from a trip across Asia," he had said. He had traveled overland in a VW bus with two friends the summer preceding his senior year of college. Their destination had been southern India. I couldn't believe that someone I knew had done such a thing. As he spoke, his eyes held the light as I'd never seen.

There were so many questions. How had he been content to stay put all these years? I wondered. But foremost: "Why didn't you mention this before?" I asked.

He shrugged his shoulders. "I guess I didn't realize you'd want to know."

"How about our other friends? Do they know about your trip?"

"No. It's difficult to explain to people. It just doesn't fit in most conversations, you know?"

Working long, demanding hours as a legal secretary in the Maryland Attorney General's office, I couldn't possibly manage such a trip. My job consumed my life, and I resented the precious few hours I could call my own. I felt as if I'd been duped into giving up the best years of my life.

Jim's landscape work was even more grueling, with long hours. At age twenty-nine and thirty-one, we were like-minded souls—already under-whelmed with contributing to the gross national product. Time was the greatest good for both of us.

That night in my living room gave me my first case of wanderlust and bridged a pivotal divide, neatly separating everything that went before from what was to come. A faint voice rose up inside me, scarcely audible since it came so far from the past. I opened my mouth to give the words life, as Jim turned to the window and laughed. "Oh no, look, the sun's coming up!"

I leapt up. "I'll make some coffee." Fortified for the trip, Jim took me on his return from Asia back to the US. I began to see myself in these places and gathered information like a person leaving on a trip. "How much did it cost? How did you always find accommodation?"

I hugged my legs. Despite the lack of sleep, I was very much alive that morning. Jim's words dizzied me, made me feel out of breath. The prospect of actually doing these things excited me and terrified me. If I were to travel, I figured, I'd need to learn from a seasoned traveler. And who better than Jim, since I was already smitten?

I wore the idea for days until that distant voice, stronger now, surfaced again. "What do you think of teaching me the ropes, traveling together? Going for as long as we can afford to? I want to see everything, especially Asia." And then I shook a bit.

I think I shocked him, which had nothing to do with convincing him. It was years before I realized I had been a catalyst for Jim too. And I couldn't help but wonder: if he brought me to the end of a path twenty-nine years long, poised as I was on the brink, ready for that last little nudge, is it possible for a gene not to become a full-blown case? If Jim had never mentioned his trip—if we remove him from the picture altogether—would I have traveled the world anyway? I have to believe I'd have found my way, though finding a companion is paramount. How many lifetimes does it take to meet a person willing to quit their job, sell everything they own and just go— precisely when you're ready to go?

I wonder too: would Jim have traveled again if I hadn't challenged him? I think not. The co-owner of a growing business, he'd already resigned himself to the American credo to stop when you drop. Nothing in his life had rivaled his earlier trip to Asia, yet he never gave himself permission to do it again.

In short order, I gave notice at my job and Jim put his business into the hands of trusted employees. The dream to consume the world whole would sustain some snipping and paring. We traveled for three months to the American Virgin Islands, an exotic yet easy English-speaking destination for my first trip. The Thai temples and Afghani mountains would have to wait.

I sold my house and wrapped up the loose ends of my divorce, whittling down the sum total of my earthly possessions to a section of my parents' basement. I had no appreciation for how much the liquidation of my former life would leave me completely adrift. Racking doubt began to pierce my bubble; was I really prepared for this trip? Since all plans were firmly in place, I buried the thought six feet under. Unprepared was not negotiable, I told myself; and I would love it when I got there.

We set off in July, 1976. The plane ride to Puerto Rico en route to the Caribbean is indelibly set on my spiritual template. I quickly realized that my intuition had been fully intact: I wasn't ready. And there was no falling luggage this time.

My convincing performance evaporated when the ride became turbulent. In my exuberance to run away from a shattered marriage and run towards the independent person I wanted to be, to finally take stock only in myself, I'd made a clean sweep of my past, never affording myself a safety net.

What was I thinking? I was light years ahead of myself. The cabin suddenly seemed too small, the air too thick to breathe. I coached myself to relax and take slow, deep breaths.

Even if I wanted to go back home, I had nothing to return to. I'd quit my job and sold my house. My precious dog Jodi and cats were gone. So many things that I loved and brought me untold pleasure were farmed out to others, or gone. Feeling bone destitute, I wrapped my arms in a thin airline blanket and sucked in as much oxygen as possible.

Jim turned and smiled as he looked out the window, in his element. I couldn't bear to disappoint him or become a burden, much less scare him away. The mere prospect of telling him I couldn't go through with this made me worse.

So I went through the motions of beginning this trip we'd planned for so long. When we reached our room in a guesthouse in San Juan, I began to implode. I begged Jim to please take a very long walk so he wouldn't see me having a nervous breakdown. I felt as if I were falling apart. In retrospect, I was only rearranging.

Jim steered me outside, not knowing that few things work their magic on me as the night does. An other-worldly din unlike anything we'd ever heard emanated overhead. Hundreds of little *coqee* frogs that live in the trees in San Juan sounded their name. It was like a Disney production; the animals heard and knew and cared. We sat and listened for a long time until they stopped. One night was all I needed that night.

A month of camping and snorkeling at St. John's Bay in the American Virgin Islands rehabilitated me. With backpacks ready, Jim and I hopped the ferry to St. Thomas to catch the ferry to the British Virgin Islands, our next destination. At the last minute, we sat on the dock, wavering.

British Tortola was just another pretty face with beaches and tourists. I wanted more—more culture, more difference, things I couldn't fathom, things that left me breathless. The ferry to Tortola arrived and tied up. Should we hop on or not? We consulted our map.

"I know! Let's go to Trinidad and Tobago, the islands off the coast of Venezuela. A friend at work loved them," I said. The exotic ring of the capital's name—Port of Spain—that alone seemed reason enough. Why not? We watched the ferry leave without us.

A warm breeze kicked up. The blinding white sun reflected like prisms on the water and unearthed another first for me. The unknown could be delectable. I felt like the seagulls wafting on the air overhead. Never had I done anything so spontaneous on a whim. And having nothing more than a backpack to my name felt oddly liberating. I was giddy as we climbed the plane ramp to Trinidad that afternoon. "You know, I'm beginning to savor the veil of anonymity too," I said to Jim.

He smiled. "You sound like a veteran."

That day was a turning point. I was committed to travel. For another three months, Jim and I toured Trinidad and snorkeled in Tobago until we were water-logged. We were becoming pretty committed to each other too.

"I think I'm ready for the round-the-world trip now," I announced on our way back to the US. We realized that a larger trip would mean cutting loose a lot more and selling Jim's landscaping business.

And then fate would conspire against us with a vengeance. We hadn't considered unloading a business at the height of a recession. Each passing week without a sale presaged the final showdown: the business or the trip; financial security or the dream of a lifetime. We were itching to go. Jim didn't waffle.

He gave up on finding a buyer and liquidated all his company's assets.

Two weeks before our departure date, Jim asked if I wanted to go skydiving with friends. I couldn't believe it; I asked him not to go. No one needed to tell me when the insistent telephone rings came. He had broken his leg in two places and would be laid up in a cast for six months.

My first instincts were homicidal, which gave way to the maternal caregiver because Jim was in pain and totally incapacitated for weeks. That fate thumbed its nose at us only strengthened my resolve. My anger and grief came full circle. The hiatus enabled me to complete my undergraduate degree full-time while we both worked to save more money. Every moment of planning towards our trip was delectable.

We figured our journey might take a year, more or less, and span Europe, the Middle East and Asia. Our parents were supportive, though the whole notion seemed too abstract to take in. As it was for us. Traveling the world with no set plan and no set time schedule was like trying to fathom light years. That our four parents still had each other, enjoyed vitality and good health was assurance enough for us to go.

More than a year after the first false start, we stood at the port of Baltimore and waved off the Volkswagen van we'd refurbished and painted ourselves. Screaming red and shiny bright with yellow curtains, it fended for bonny England atop a large container ship. Just about the most beautiful magic carpet I'd ever seen.

We would not join our van as soon as planned. At the height of the recession in 1979, my parents, Jim and I sat in long gas lines hoping to get enough gas to drive two hours in bumper to bumper rush hour traffic to Dulles Airport in Virginia. We always flew the discount "standby" fare in those days. Two times, our names were not called to board, so we returned to Baltimore to begin the whole process again. The third try was the charm and everything happened at breakneck speed. Kisses were grabbed and we set off, our interminable two-year wait for this moment finally ended.

On the road with our VW bus, we traveled through seven countries in western Europe for five months, settling for the winter in Berchtesgaden, West Germany, an alpine recreation facility for vacationing US military. I worked as a maid, a *zimmer madchen*, at a tourist hotel; Jim was a restaurant manager at a ski resort. Our co-workers were southern Germans and travelers like us from around the world.

Camping across Europe had saved us pots of money, avoiding expensive *pensiones*. From early morning until sunset, we ticked off a formidable list of sites—a composite of castles, basilicas, museums and green bucolic landscapes. A hitchhiker made me realize one day what we missed: interaction with the natives. In some respects, the van bogged us down. We always picked up hitchhikers; I listened to them talk with great interest-turned-envy. They clearly enjoyed a much freer lifestyle. I soon concluded that hitching was the *real thing*, not traveling in a van.

And then fate intervened again. The Iran hostage crisis made traversing Iran less feasible. Since Americans were no longer welcome in Iran, we scrapped our plans to move eastward by car. Selling the van in Germany, we relied solely on ground transport and hitching. Plan B was to head south into Turkey, Syria, Jordan, Israel and Egypt, and continue south to Kenya where we'd sail aboard an ancient Arabic *dhow* that catches the prevailing winds from Lamu, an Arabic seaport on the coast, eastward to India.

This is when traveling really started for me: when we left Germany *sans* van. The East wafted on the air—first in southern Italy, then Hungary and Greece. The world seemed more intimate and alive. Our submersion was complete in Turkey, as if we'd come home. The story *Love in the Desert*, and our Palestinian friend Abdul, best embody the romanticism of the East.

We eased into hitchhiking in Greece and Turkey, setting us free and ratcheting up the whole experience. We saved money too.

Another group I watched with clinical fascination was women traveling alone, a prospect that struck terror in me. I soon decided this was the ultimate real thing. The major difference between these women and me was between the ears. They knew they could do it; I did not. Jim and I parted ways for a day or two now and then, once for various days, enabling me to try on this new lifestyle for size.

I concluded that poets and introverts make the best lone travelers; at least these parts of me embraced solo travel. The first forays were sublime, especially the sheer I-did-it-ness of it. But having passed that travel rite, I concluded that sharing experiences was preferable. And that made me realize how ideally suited Jim and I had become as travel mates.

To begin, our naiveté was mutual. We had both planned to tick off every country in the world. The rest was spot on. We presumed to think that our modern-day odyssey could be no less extraordinary or life-altering than Ali Baba's journey across the desert. That our odyssey, like the classical ones of literature, would mirror a vastly larger, inner journey. We sensed this trip would be unlike anything we could ever do, like a birthright or coming of age.

We never called our trip an odyssey aloud; it seemed too presumptuous. But it was always our odyssey.

The *how* of things was infinitely less romantic. Guidebooks for Europe were prevalent then, with slim pickings for the Middle East, Africa and Asia. The Internet was embryonic in the early Eighties. We targeted towns and cities of interest and created an approximate route, always reserving the right to change our minds at any turn. Since we began to change our minds with frequency, we lightened up on the research.

One of us read up on a country and made recommendations to the other. As a complement, we often read literature or

nonfiction indigenous to the country. Research and travelers'
tips formed the bulk of our decisions. But whimsy reigned
supreme. An inviting photo, a curious name, a fork in the road
that seemed to pull more from one side enticed us most.

The average stay in towns was about three days, cities
about a week, countries three to four weeks, sometimes more.
Each country deserved its due, we felt, so most countries
hosted us for a month. Turkey, Kenya, Thailand, India and
Cambodia held us in their keep longest. Jim was the voice of
reason, always suggesting we slow down, stay in places longer.
Being the born-again travel convert with only a lifetime to
take on the world, I preferred to plow ahead. He indulged me
but complained loudly at times. Fair enough; then we would
stay put for awhile.

If extended travel came with operating instructions, they
might say: Shed all responses learned in the world of standing
still. Take your cues from the heart, not the head. Since
guidebooks create the beaten path, get off it now and then.
When there's no accommodation to be found, try the closest
roof. (For the asking, we slept in the home of Tibetan peasants
in Nepal, a Sikh temple floor in Dar Es Salaam, a jailhouse
bunk in South Africa and a Catholic church in Mozambique.)
Finally, ready or not: plan to have your former self rearranged.
Then throw away all instructions.

I never realized how much I resisted rearrangement,
probably because it asks us to give something up. The closest
I come to abandon at home is yogic-type meditation which I
invariably do in neat blocks of time with one eye on the clock.
Abandon in drivels.

Travel taught us abandon like nothing else can. I always
thought it was the sights and the people that draw us back
again and again. Now I realize it's more than that, something
more elusive. It's how travel changes us, makes us softer and
satisfies something soulful. How it promotes the most personal
kind of peace.

The kind of change I speak of won't happen on a two-week vacation ordered by travel agents, guides and tour buses. The fixed itinerary and time constraints from the world of standing still continue to haunt you like a pesky mosquito.

Time is at the heart of it, the largest difference between the traveler and the tourist. It takes days for the senses to come out of hiding. The drone inside the head doesn't disappear for a week. Shedding the personal and cultural layers of conditioning that stand between us and what we see takes months, enabling us to view people and actions in their own light. For some reason, the developing world's feral edge, its ready access to our primordial past, delivers that full immersion best.

Jim and I also agreed on travel modes and style of travel. Traveling light became an essential, not a preference. I carried what looked like a baby pack with a sleeping bag. He carried a larger pack with sleeping bag, small cooking stove and tent. Our packs always stayed with us to prevent any mishaps or long waits for luggage. Now we use large shoulder bags or totes on wheels. Clothes in tow covered one climate at a time. If we needed more, we bought them; beggars inherited any castoffs. Like gypsies, we washed small items in the hotel room sink, hung across a plastic line we carried and tied helter-skelter across the room. Local laundry ladies got our business for the rest.

Curiously enough, money was never discussed. It didn't have to be. We both knew that money was the currency of a longer trip. The more we saved along the way, the farther we could venture. When the money ran out, the trip ended.

Our first surprise was how incredibly cheap traveling turned out to be. Divested of the fixed expenses of a mortgage, car, utilities and insurance, moving requires far less outlay. Like a sleuth, I tracked every centum; in two and a half years, we each spent only $2,500, including car shipping, airfare, gas, rooms and food.

Everything was local fare; local hotels, local transport. We liked that the cheapest mode of transport benefited the little guys—the rickshaw, the *tuktuk*, the *jeepney*. Though the crush of humanity, bags, vegetables and goats in third class seemed gratuitously tough at times, the experiential paybacks were huge. There were no regrets. Being with the locals always felt right, and the best way to see them up close, watch them interact with one another and talk to them ourselves.

For seventeen months, we toured Europe and the Middle East. We spent another thirteen months in Africa. When we arrived in Kenya, the prevailing winds meant to blow the Arabic *dhows* east to India weren't prevailing. Since *dhows* have no mechanical power whatsoever—not an engine, not even an oar—we would not be India-bound. By then, we were so smitten with Africa anyway, we continued overland to the far southern tip, the Cape of Good Hope, and back up another route, eleven countries in all.

Something happens when you plod on for years, long after others have left. We were like onions, shedding layers of our former selves. The overland descent into Africa took most of us. For months, we wrestled with loss of control, then finally relented, realizing that Africa's conditions are unequivocal. We stopped working so hard and gave up control, removing our watches and trusting in caprice. Travel was no longer some kind of job, a set of disparate choices that dwelled outside of us. Our surrender was complete, like a draft of wind that lifted our legs and enabled us to continue.

We trusted that a ride or food or help would come when we needed them, that we'd somehow manage. And we did; we always did. For one place in time, the bubble that was Africa taught us to leap, and the net always appeared. Curiously enough, we unlearn this each time we stand still, but relearn it when we set out again.

More surprising, more confounding than the change within us was its effect, which seemed to conspire in the world around us. Once we relented, experience found us. Events we couldn't have imagined inexplicably took us in their fold. In my memory, the events set in Mozambique, the story *The Train to No Man's Land*, still seem like a dream. They couldn't have happened. Things like this just don't happen to people; yet they did to us. The language that filled my journals, and my stories here in *1089 Nights* years later, gave way to something richer and transcendent. All because of surrender.

Much like the ancient tales the title brings to mind, the stories of *1089 Nights* that draw from Turkey to Mozambique to Indonesia tell us of wonder—the wonder that is the world around us. We've always known it, though the media makes us doubt it each day. The world is a resplendent place, not a terrible place at all.

Once Jim and I headed north from South Africa and retraced our steps, our pace slowed. As much as Africa gets into your blood like no other place on earth, it also tests your mettle, picks at you and wears you down. My intestinal parasites had nestled in to stay. I thought I could never tire of travel, that my enthusiasm would always outlast our money. But after twenty-seven months on the road, almost overnight, I didn't think I could live out of a zippered pocket another day. I day-dreamed about my next home, the nest I'd create, how I'd fix it up with Turkish rugs and African *khangas* arranged on the walls—the house that expressed everything I loved.

As much as the rich and exotic landscapes and cultures of the developing world fed our deepest longings like nothing else could, we needed to quit it. I was bone tired and had lost over fifteen pounds. Jim's and my relationship was travel-worn as well. Our over-zealousness to take on the world came at a large cost to ourselves. We had become alter-egos of each other, spending virtually each waking hour together, finishing each other's sentences, vying for the attention of each person we met. It wasn't normal. We couldn't continue living as one.

And then in Zimbabwe, news of my father's heart attack quickened our pace north to Kenya, where the only affordable return fare to the US could be found. We pushed ourselves to reach Nairobi.

It's no small wonder that we both sustained rocky landings back on US soil. In retrospect, a thirty-month trip had been too long. We didn't want to become like other travelers we'd met who couldn't seem to stop, who couldn't go home.

I landed home first, leaving Jim behind in Nairobi in October, 1981. He traveled on to Uganda and central Africa for another six months, experiencing the pygmies of the Eturi forest in Zaire, the mountain gorillas of Rwanda and a volcanic eruption in Zaire—leaving me chartreuse green with envy. When Jim returned to the US in mid-1982, we soon found ourselves planning the rest of our incomplete circle around the world, working and saving our money until we could set out again.

A thirteen-month trip in 1984-85 to Europe and Asia began our love affair with Asia. We married in Thailand in 1985, a most unconventional wedding told in the story, *Unholy Matrimony*. Jim's career in microfinance with an international relief agency in Baltimore continues to take us to Southeast Asia regularly. I return to the beach town of Sihanoukville (Kompong Som) in southern Cambodia every year or two to visit schools participating in the foundation I started there. *The Young Green Grass* tells the story of Ra, the first student I placed in a Cambodian-Khmer school and English school.

Jim's and my original master plan to travel to every country in the world amended itself. The fifty-some countries we've visited seem woefully short of the UN's official list of one hundred ninety-three. Another plan to travel the greater world first and bounce around the US later in an RV wanes in favor too. We're still too smitten with the developing world.

For years, my travel journals beckoned me. In 2004, I finally unearthed them from the basement. I was homesick for the experiences that formed me as much as my own mother. Dusting their covers, pulling stuck pages apart, I tried to decipher the scribblings often made by one candle power at night. It was an emotional reunion. We communed for hours—the many people and places tucked away in a hallowed place in my memory.

It was a verdant garden for the picking. I finally set pen to paper, eliciting the spirit of Scheherazade as I went. Her stories saved her life, spanning a thousand nights and one night. My stories enabled me to find my voice, spanning a thousand nights and eighty-nine.

So sit down here with me, please.

Relax and prop your legs up. Have a *chai,* the drink of the earth that makes everything right. Open my picturebook album with me; let me tell you of my fine friends and adventures that have simmered and seasoned these many years. Oh, but the sights outside our door are wondrous. It's a heady ride we'll take. You can see for yourself; the camels are always waiting.

But hurry; you mustn't tarry; there is an urgency. The world changes so quickly. I have seen the villagers in the bush of Africa crowd inside a tiny shack by night, an eerie blue aura bouncing off their child-like faces. The young girls in the remote reaches of China who dress as we do here at home. The developers who scarf up the ancient rice fields of Bali because the young won't till them.

Hurry, they are all telling us, the world passes us by faster than we know. If we don't catch it soon, the airwaves will immutably wash over us in the same likeness. And we will become as one.

TURKEY: DESERT FEVER

*Then awake! the heavens look bright, my dear; 'Tis never too late
for delight, my dear; And the best of all ways to lengthen our days
Is to steal a few hours from the night, my dear.*

Thomas Moore

The hospitality of the Turkish people is unlike anything we've experienced. You might even say they love you too much.

The *Qur'an* tells believers to give their guests the very best, the eye of the goat. We much prefer the figs and over-sweetened *cay* we've received. *Cay* (chai) graces every social setting in Turkey and somehow immobilizes its drinkers. In towns and villages, the *cay* shops fill up early morning until closing. We can never seem to pull ourselves away from them.

After five weeks, Turkey feels like home. Jim and I sit in a *cay* shop in Nevsehir, Cappadocia, in central Turkey—a late morning start at the end of June, 1980. "It's good to be among the living again," he says.

Just yesterday, we moaned and groaned in unison on opposite hotel beds in the room closest to the bathroom.

Dysentery. "It was kind of fun being sick together, don't you think?" I coo and blow on my *cay*.

We try to divine who slipped us the vermin. "It had to be that water vendor in Goreme," Jim says. Those glasses. Dressed in traditional garb, suede skirt with tassels over white pants, a colorful vest and red fez with large minaret-shaped water dispenser on his back, the water vendor wiped out a glass and poured the water. Against our better judgment, we drank since we'd just climbed off a virtual mountain.

Next to seeing Istanbul, the region of Cappadocia where we are now was Turkey's main draw for us. Part of the arid central Anatolian plateau, Cappodocia connected the trade routes from China and other eastern cities to western ports in ancient times—known as the Anatolian Silk Road. The desert has a timelessness about it, especially when a camel passes. The occasional crumbling *caravanseri*, the stopping-off places for ancient caravans, recall centuries of weary travelers.

Cappadocia looks like a mushroom village in a fantasy world, a Disneyesque kind of limestone landscape formed by the wind, the rain, volcanic eruptions spewed across the Anatolian plains, and the various peoples living here since the tenth century. Known as "fairy chimneys," they resemble tall white-gray icing peaks. Stories of houses and chapels with ancient frescoes are hidden from view inside.

We wave to Pascal, a French traveler friend, to join us. Since the din makes conversation almost impossible, we all sip our *cay* and feast on the sensory overload. Quintessentially Turkish, awash in dark monochrome colors, the shop packs them in—olive-complected men with steel-black hair, wearing Turkish fishing hats and skull caps, long-sleeved shirts, and *salvar*, the dark baggy pants with deep crotches that fall into folds. Little white cloud puffs billow in the light above the smokers lounging in old leather chairs. Drawing on *hookahs*, tall brass smoking pipes, the breathy bubblings rumble when the fervor dips. But the sounds I love most that rise above the din like sprinkles of glitter are the *clink-clink-clinks* of tiny metal spoons against glass.

A little girl would delight in the doll-sized utensils. About two inches tall, the *cay* glasses taper into a curvaceous waistline in the middle. With miniature tongs, Turks pile sugar cubes to the top until they melt. Jim and I follow suit to make the black tea drinkable. The pitfalls of endless tea-totaling are evidenced by men with stained or rotten teeth who appear toothless at first glance. The women who labor in the fields all day, I notice, don't have these dental problems.

Even in the morning, the *cay* shop bustle resembles a pub atmosphere—animated, often raucous and consummately male. The waiters are all men too; perhaps an occasional owner's wife. But usually, I'm the only woman.

Of course, I felt out of place the first time. Jim and I looked around to realize I was the only female, my pallid skin and sun-bleached white hair illuminated against the dark swarthy landscape. I smiled uneasily as all eyes turned. Our table filled up, and our table mates bought us one *cay* after another. They seemed as accepting of me as they are of Jim. I think the men make allowances for me since I'm a foreigner.

When Jim, Pascal and I stand up to leave the shop, the protests come. "No, you must stay, one more!" and pronto, more prepaid *cays* appear. As if we have nothing else to do all day, we plop ourselves back down and talk some more.

Well, to say we talk is a misnomer. Between our guidebook Turkish and Arabic and their halting English, maybe ten words flow among us. Two or three risk being worn into extinction for overuse. The word *good* deserves distinction. Where would we be, how could we describe our pleasure or travel in Turkey without *good*? *Guzel* tea, we tell them. *Guzel* food. *Guzel* Turkish cigarettes in little tins. Everything is *guzel*.

After an hour, you'd think this would grow unspeakably tiresome. No one seems bored with speaking monosyllabic gibberish. We are all content to share the same poor air. The fact is: we are smitten, all of us—we with them, they with us—with how delectable difference can be. Their guffaws, their smiling blackened teeth, their generosity and entreaties to stay tell us that these are good people; salt of the earth people. Though we may not remember their faces in a week, each exchange counts for something. Something staid in the movement of time remains.

This time we must go. Half the *cay* shop waves us off while Pascal remains rooted to his chair. Jim and I hurry down the streets of Nevsehir to the bus stop that will take us to the fairy chimneys. A spindly young boy with brown-rimmed glasses, spanking white shirt and navy Bermuda pants uniform watches us, smiling, then comes running over. He looks very studious since glasses are uncommon in Turkey.

"My. Name. Is. Cemil." His eyes beam, he seems so pleased to practice English. We tell him our names. "Look!" He shows us the names in his English book. "Jim and Ann!" He revels in the joke.

"The bus to Goreme?" I ask. When.. is.. the.. bus.. to Goreme?" He dances a bit, as if he has to go to the bathroom.

"Please. Come. To my house." Jim and I look at each other, conflicted. "Please, you see my fam-i-ly."

More than any place we've visited, people in Turkey take us home. Mostly truck drivers who give us rides invite us. Families in nice cars pick us up too, but we rarely go home with them. Perhaps they're bashful about their English or we aren't a curiosity to them. It's invariably the people who can't afford to who adopt us.

The back streets of Nevsehir narrow into scratchy dirt roads lined with tired little bungalows. Two adults in tow, Jim and I are feeling very much like the trained bears the gypsies lead around for money.

If only we could know what he yells to his parents as he bursts through the front door. ("Mother, Father, I've brought some *yabancis* (foreigners) homeee!!!") We deposit our shoes at the door where four pairs of plastic sandals sit. A wide-eyed father, mother and two sisters round the corner and greet us warmly. The father wears the traditional *salvar* pants and is short, no taller than his son, though muscular and fit, his striking dark blue eyes lined with dark lashes. Dark-haired cultures always harbor these errant recessive genes. Alexander the Great must have passed through here too.

The mother is fair-complected like her son and plain with small eyes. Her dark blunt-cut brown hair meets a white blouse, tucked in and belted with a long dark skirt, not a stitch of makeup or jewelry. The two sisters are small and willowy with long, straight hair, maybe nine and eleven. Though quiet, they seem very precocious and keep a close eye on me.

The home is clean, small and Spartan, a tattered woven rug on the floor, an uneven pale wash on the walls. Two brown-edged pictures of women and a Turkish calendar bearing a smiling Ataturk hang on the walls. Jim and I sit in the two upholstered straight-back chairs. The family conversation is animated. Cemil puffs up with pride, relishing his role as translator. Clearly, without him, communication would be at sea. "Your fa-ther." He smiles and starts again. "My fa-ther, my mo-ther, coming you …to…to the dinner." He stamps his foot. "Please, can you come to the dinner?" and smiles.

The parents are probably Jim's and my age, early thirties. The older daughter offers *cay* first to Jim, then me, the father, Cemil, her mother and sister. The mother whispers to her and she slips out the door to the market. Daughters are veritable indentured servants.

The younger daughter offers a golden-colored cologne, a custom we first encountered on Turkish buses. I unwittingly held out my hands and the ticket man drenched me but good with cheap *eau de cologne*. It covers a host of airborne ills. All I could smell for hours was myself. "No thank you," I say, smiling, hoping I'm not seeming rude.

Garlic and paprika fill the air, followed by the smell of baking bread. The father directs us to sit on the floor around the small circular family table. Mum and daughter number one serve a most lavish, memorable Turkish meal shared from large communal plates—red lentil soup, *kofte*, a spiced lamb, salad and roasted eggplant scooped up with Turkish flatbread baked in the stone oven. We eat with the right hand in the Muslim way. Everyone uses the long tablecloth, too large for the low table, as a napkin in the lap.

Cemil explains with some difficulty that his father is a construction worker. His father seems proud of his son's language skills and encourages him to play host. "Jim! What I am calling this?" Cemil asks, pointing to Jim's beard.

"Beard," Jim says.

"My father say very good beard! *Guzel!*" The father nods and smiles, stroking his cheeks with his hand. Everyone has a good laugh, and it is as if we have sat around this table with these people many times before.

Mint tea, pistachio pastries and Turkish coffee finish things off, a veritable feast. When it is time to depart, they give me a box of fancy soaps and Jim a tin of imported candies.

They ask us to come back the next day. We decline, to save them from financial ruin. We must head to the next town, we say. But we aren't ready to leave their warm fold either. Dragging our feet, exchanging addresses with vows of keeping in touch, we finally rip ourselves away.

A day later, still in Nevsehir, hospitality Turkish-style steps up a notch. Ahmed accosts us on a street, his small, thick frame virtually bouncing off of Jim. About thirty-something, Ahmed is short and swarthy with a mustache. He talks like a hyperactive child.

Locals latch onto foreigners for a host of reasons. I suspect Ahmed's reasons are part friendship, part wannabe tour guide, part *Hey everybody, look at my good friends the foreigners.* We collect various brothers and sisters and go to places Jim and I have already seen, which we mention in passing. Never mind. "*Guzel*," Ahmed says with a thumbs-up sign.

Jim and I had planned to move to our next destination that morning. After a long, claustrophobically-scheduled day with seven of us squeezed into his brother's '67 Chevy, our cheek muscles hurt from trying to return Ahmed's manic enthusiasm.

Turning down an invitation is rude in the Muslim tradition. If your host offers the eye of the goat, you eat it. Only when you decline an offer three times is it considered sincere. So we respectfully decline three times in the Islamic tradition. The problem is, Ahmed isn't counting.

He lives, unmarried, with two brothers, a wife and a younger sister (we think) in a tiny detached ramshackle bungalow. Since other family members, cousins, whomever, are always joining us, we can never get all the relationships straight. At night, the living room looks like a bad dream: four anemic whitewashed walls, an old dark sofa and chair, both torn and filled with crumbs and whatever, lighted by a single anemic lamp. My heart drops when Ahmed retrieves a large thick album.

"Here is Paris," he tells us, "here is Budapest"... and Sofia and Istanbul—excursions out of reach for the average Turk. Jim's insipid smile mirrors my own feelings: we are hostage. No one can possibly divine the locales of the places in the photos; Ahmed could have been anywhere. Each photo captures one subject only—a smiling Ahmed standing next to a column, a sleepy-looking Ahmed sitting on steps, a stooping Ahmed on a beach at sunset.

Then we see the scores of photos of other *yabancis*, all taken here in Nevsehir. "Here is German," he says, "here is Dutch, here is Australian. And look, here is Amedicans!" Smiling for a street photographer today in this precise spot in town, our mugs will no doubt be enshrined here as well.

Ahmed announces our full schedule for the next day and Jim and I realize we've played out this relationship. "Oh, too bad, we really have to go in the morning," I say.

"No problem," Ahmed says. "But you must stay one day more. We plan all the things." Their faces are downcast like funeral mourners. "What is it to stay one day only?" his moustache asks in a deep inverted comma. Jim and I look blankly at each other, trying to glean a plan. Taken as acquiescence, Ahmed cheers. They all cheer with thumbs-up signs around.

It's wonderful to be wanted, but not too much. We've unwittingly become the chattel of an extended Turkish family. The prospect of how a morning departure with more pleading might play out is too awful. So we decide to take the cowardly way out.

Six of us sleep on the concrete living room floor (thank God for our sleeping bags). At sunrise, Jim and I dress quietly and leave a note written on the back of a rumpled envelope. (*Ahmed: Thank you for everything. You and your family were so wonderful to us, we'll never ever forget you. Please forgive us, we really must go. Your best of friends, Jim and Ann.*) Who knows, maybe the note will join the album too. Then again, perhaps our untimely departure will relegate us to a fallen status.

Tiptoeing over open-mouthed, snoring sleepers, arms and legs sprawled across the floor, we slip out the door. Mohammed would have frowned.

I close the outer screen door which bangs as it hangs off its frame. Like true infidels, we slither down the street quickly, certain the family will waken, come running out and tackle us or something. We're really too old to be doing this. "They were sweet," I say to Jim, my face flushed with humiliation and guilt. Ahmed is definitely crazy enough to come to the mini-bus station looking for us. To get out of town fast, we hitch a ride with the first truck. Packed with locals and vegetables, two goats, a pig, and men and women, they all look like long-lost family to me. When the wind flattens our hair, we know we're free again.

The women smile at me. This is the closest we've come to women in Turkey. Some wear the *hijab* because this region is more traditional. *Hijab* means "veil" or cover in Arabic; depending upon where you are, the veil can be a simple colorful head scarf with hair showing or the full *hijab* habit found in orthodox Islamic countries covering the full face and head with a black free-flowing gown. The rural women wear the *salvar* type pants like the men, except print colored, with long white kaftans that extend down the back.

In cities, women wear no head cover at all or modern colorful scarves. In Ankara, the capital, most women dress like women in the US. Social custom in Turkey is much more relaxed than other Muslim cultures like Syria, Iran and Saudi Arabia. The Turks take great pride in Ataturk, Turkey's first president, and his legacy of a secular society. Ataturk replaced *Sharia* law with a Western code of law, banned women from wearing the veil and encouraged them to dress like Western women and enter the workplace. Women also got the vote and held office in parliament.

Yet for most Turks outside the cities where we find ourselves, life within the family and community remains very traditional. The two sexes operate largely in separate public arenas. Women move about in the streets for a discrete purpose without tarrying or talking to strangers.

As a foreign visitor, I don't need to cover my head, I talk to men on the street and sit in *cay* shops—all the things women who live in towns and villages don't do. But I dress modestly, wearing long pants or a skirt, though my arms are usually exposed. Only at the heavily touristed seaside venues are standards completely relaxed.

To make life easier, Jim and I also tell people we're married. Most of the men we encounter are older *cay* drinkers, truck drivers and shopkeepers—unemployed or service sector people. Since they treat me like Jim's wife—welcoming and kind and inclusive—I think they see foreign women as exempt from Turkey's social conventions.

Which isn't to say that all the men have been completely courteous. Turkey is a youthful country and the sexual energy of the under-thirty guys, if harnessed, could heat the country through a bitter winter. Much like the deer-rutting season at home, the air is heavy with musk.

Before we set foot in Turkey, traveling on the Orient Express, Turkish men came onto me as soon as Jim's head was turned. They find foreign women a novelty, I figured. Foreign women are also a free ticket out of poverty. But most confounding was they didn't seem to respect that Jim and I were a couple. Wouldn't they have a problem with someone coming onto their wife?

The more we talk to young men, the more we find marriage to be the number one topic of conversation—how they yearn to marry, but can't. I cannot imagine any young guy in our country fretting about getting married.

The customs of Islam have inadvertently created a lot of sexual frustration. Many young men don't marry because they can't afford to. Marrying means planning years in advance and accumulating a dowry for the bride, often a sizeable investment. Of course, saving for the dowry, or *mahr*, means having a job, another problem. And since dating is done only as a precursor to marriage, young men without a job or the requisite bride price can't hope to date. It's tough to have sexual relations when you don't come in contact with women.

Lacking opportunities to have normal relations with women, young men appear to have three options. They can use the services of prostitutes. They can practice bisexual sex. Or they can get their kicks in illegal parlors where Western soft porn films are shown. In a town outside Konya, we saw one of these "parlors" one night, through the window of a storage-type building packed full of men glued to a flickering light.

Their whoops and hollers reached such a frenzy, one could only assume the local police were paid off. Or in attendance. Jim and I had to laugh. We peered in to see them watching *Saturday Night Fever*, that bastion of lasciviousness!

It all makes sense now. Gyrating, made-up women in tight, skimpy clothes reinforce the belief that Western women are devoid of morals. At worst, they are all whores. At best, they lack the high standards of their own women and are easy targets—the opinion, no doubt, probably extended to me and most tourist women. Turkish men can't possibly see me through different cultural lenses as I thought, because religion is absolute, not relative to other cultures. Proper behavior for women can't extend to some and not others. I realize that men have been telling me this with their actions all along.

It wasn't until years later that I learned that respectable Muslim men would never talk to strange women on the street; more so, respectable women wouldn't dream of answering them. With each answer, I inadvertently reinforced their poor opinion of me.

So consider the opportunities for young horny Turkish males when a real live, dirty dancing woman from another country appears in the flesh. Pavlovian. The instant Jim would move out of view, our newly-acquired, touchy-feely male friends hovered. Some of them, in breathy, feral-like tones straight out of a D-grade movie, would invite me to rendezvous at appointed hours and places (*You come with me tonight, yesss? yesss?*). The whole of their limited English vocabulary was borrowed from those soft porn movies for these moments. And it goes without saying that all foreign women stand by wringing their hands for the moment we might be approached. How women respond is irrelevant, I learned. No one was listening. So preoccupied and so over-wrought were they, nothing could temper their fervor.

Let's be honest. Did I dislike all this boyish attention? Not all the time. Turkey is a country where all the good ones are not necessarily taken. And the good looks of some of these guys defy the laws of nature. Only perhaps Mother Theresa would not be tempted for an instant to do something completely stupid and irrational.

A local bus takes us to Konya through rugged mountains with patches of pale grassland, juniper and thorn trees scattered here and there. Konya sits three thousand feet high on the Anatolian steppe and was once the capital of the powerful Seljuk empire that ruled the land from present-day Turkey to India in the eleventh century—the major cause of the first Crusades when Konya was reclaimed. The city was also the birthplace and present-day home of the Whirling Dervish sect, the mystical Sufi offshoot of Islam.

A new friend, Atol, a modern, well-spoken shop owner with excellent English skills shows us around Konya. The narrow, retail back streets are a hodgepodge of big-small-high-low brilliantly colored signs. Freshly-baked oven bread and fried olive oil waft on the air as the dinner hour approaches.

We stop at Atol's shop, which is closed, to admire fine tribal carpets through the window. Two men who command the narrow street with their presence approach us, their formal red and white *kefiyah* head scarves and white *jelabiyah* pajama-like gowns signaling them to be Arabs, not Turks. They move as if they own the street, as if they may mow us over if we don't move. Perhaps they are here because they trade in carpets, as Konya is famous for its fine Seljuk and Kilim carpets. Our friend's face brightens. He knows them and greets them warmly, introducing all of us. Jim and I smile and extend our hands.

As I shake the hand of one, he digs his middle finger into the center of my palm—what I have come to call the itchy finger—which registers through my nervous system like an electric shock, reminiscent of those stupid trick buzzers my brother used when we were kids. I am paralyzed, hot and limp with humiliation. I finally look up, perhaps after minutes, surprised to realize that my personal cataclysm has not registered through the group. Idle chatter continues. I can't look at my suitor again and can't say how long they stayed. And then the imposing white presence of the two moves across our path and is gone, the air sweeping their *jelabiyahs*.

How could such a small, unnoticed stimulus to the hand delivered in broad daylight make me feel so violated? Who dreamt up this disgusting gesture? Clouting him might have conveyed the right message best; he certainly deserved it. But making a scene sends off alarms in my head, especially in another culture. I can only hope that giving him no recognition whatsoever deflated him most.

Days later, I convince myself I've overreacted. I must be mistaken; it must mean something else. I muster the courage to ask a Muslim woman I have met. Her horrified, contorted face gives me my answer before she speaks. "This is such a terrible thing, I cannot even tell you what it means! I am so ashamed! Who did this to you?"

My one-woman cause is born. I explore how best to convey the golden words that will spin the perfect message and redeem Western women—the very next time a man mistakes me for the female lead in his last porn flick. I turn the words over in my mind, edit and practice them just as I will say them to my suitor. But lacking any command of the Turkish language, I realize, my words are powerless.

The men of Turkey did not inspire fear in me for one moment. The younger ones are more like frantic puppies in need of obedience training. As tiresome as their advances can be, they are stuck in their social milieu, born into a monastic life they didn't agree to. If they can't hope to meet girls in a normal fashion, it follows that they would be over-sexed and woefully backward in matters of love and courtship. The world has always advocated for the rights of women in Islam. I never considered that men of few means might need advocates too. Living in a kind of suspended animation, they are stuck in that gawky pre-teen stage of inexperience for years—maybe even a lifetime.

The next morning, we hitch towards Antalya on the southern coast. Hitching is excellent all over Turkey since trucks provide the main form of commerce. Most truck drivers we meet are in their thirties or forties (taking into account that most are younger than they look). A short ride takes us out of Konya. Then a young guy with an old, beat-up truck hauling crates of green-striped watermelons stops to pick us up. His name is Dorsun. Another truck driven by Dorsun's friend, Ramadan, follows behind us with two passengers and more watermelons.

A bit younger than Jim and I, I'm guessing late twenties, Dorsun has an unassuming, quiet manner. About five feet, seven inches, an inch or so shorter than I am, he is taller and fairer than most Turkish men. Plain looking with a square face, brown eyes and brown hair with cropped bangs that stand up a bit, he wears regular jeans-type pants, not the traditional Turkish *salvar*, and resembles an American farmhand, fit and muscular in his T-shirt. He speaks no English, matched by our limited Turkish. But then, we're finding, relying less on language makes you more adept at picking up on nonverbal cues.

With room for three in the front seat, I always sit in the middle next to the driver. As we bounce down the rutted dirt roads, Dorsun sings to the Turkish music on the radio (he's pretty good). When the road becomes flat and straight, he turns towards me, catching my eye, for the purpose of stealing a look. Our eyes meet for a second and he smiles ever so slightly, a rolling effusive sexual energy filling the air. When he does it again, I pretend I don't notice.

I wonder how many times a young Turkish truck driver meets a Western woman and sits smack next to her. Probably rarely if ever. I look down and realize my skirt leg touches his pants leg—an intimacy unheard of in Turkey. And then the bottom of my leg is exposed too. I never appreciated before how rife with temptation these innocent truck rides must be for a young guy. Despite the blasting dry season heat and cramped front seat, I hug Jim's side, putting nearly a foot's length between Dorsun and me. He doesn't attract me in the least, so I don't feel complicit. I keep my gaze out Jim's side.

In a short while, Jim hops out to make a pit stop. I slide to the door on the pretext of rolling down the window further for air. As soon as Jim is out of view, Dorsun reaches over and puts his hand on my leg, just places it there like that's where it belongs. What is he thinking of? I suspect he isn't thinking at all. I push his hand away and say "Get off!" Registering no expression, he turns and faces forward.

Hours later, as Jim retrieves something from his pack in the back, Dorsun does it again, a tighter hold this time. "GET OFF!" I say in a low threatening growl, the sentiment of which he has to glean. With Jim so close by, Dorsun's blatant bravado confounds me most.

I jump out the door as Jim walks along the side of the truck and catch the look on Dorsun's face. As flustered as I am, his expression haunts me, melts me through with its sweetness. He is like all the others, a pubescent man. There is no relationship between the person I demonize that moment and the child-like vulnerability in his face. Later that day, as we make conversation of sorts, I point to my own ring on my left hand. "You? Married?"

He smiles and shakes his head no. *"Ah hayir, hayir."* He points to Jim and me and looks quizzically.

"Yes," I smile proudly like a new bride. I realize we've just had our first real exchange.

I hope that resolves the problem. I'm certainly not worried enough about Dorsun to mention him to Jim, much less bail out of this ride. Even if I felt compelled to tell Jim, I doubt my concerns would sound credible as Dorsun is all-business around Jim.

We now pass through the Taurus mountains and the rough terrain requires Dorsun's undivided attention. North of here, the Taurus mountains stretch more than twelve thousand feet high. We pass far fewer trucks on this stretch. The roadbed becomes more narrow and broken with eroded edges. All eyes remain glued to the road.

We sight the lower valley far in the distance, which means we will descend the great Anatolian steppe before day-end. The scenery remains stark and pallid. In the mountain valleys, the road makes large circles around wide hills of rock and sand, an occasional goat bleating from on top. Dorsun dips his head down and points up to our right. A large stone castle, gutted like a skeleton with no roof, overlooks the valley, still imposing, still grand.

"*Hacli, hacli,*" Dorsun says, making a cross with his fingers.

"I think it's a Crusader castle," Jim says, sending a chill through me. We over-dosed on castles in Europe, we saw so many. And this one looks like a European castle. But few monuments still standing go back to the eleventh or twelfth century. For me, nothing instills a greater sense of history and the ruggedness of that time than this lone castle perched atop a valley of rock and sand. I ask Dorsun to stop. Set against the afternoon light, the silhouette has a haunting effect. I turn to watch as the outline disappears out of view.

Our two trucks stop to eat at a little roadside restaurant Dorsun must know. The owner's wife cooks up a robust Turkish meal, replete with oven baked flatbread, a pepper-tomato-egg mixture, cooked potatoes and salad. "*Guzel!*" Dorsun exclaims. He insists on treating his guests, Jim and me. Three dinners have to be expensive for him. We top off the meal with over-sweetened *cay* in the little girl glasses.

When we set out again, lively music comes from behind—more folksy, less Islamic—which I assume to be Ramadan's radio. Dorsun watches his rearview mirror and smiles, pointing for us to look behind. Ramadan's two passengers sit on chairs playing a Turkish horn and drum in the back of the truck while Ramadan waves and dances in his seat. Dorsun laughs an odd almost girlish laugh which makes us laugh.

The air feels more humid and the terrain more hospitable as Dorsun eases the truck down off the great Anatolian steppe. Color is welcome; even the scruffy pale greens. I sight some olive groves just beginning to bear fruit off the road.

Then we get a flat tire—and lose an hour. To reward us for our troubles, Dorsun stops to swim in a barely perceptible river that flattens out into a small pond to one side. I would love to get wet, I feel so grimy. But donning a bathing suit in front of Dorsun or getting my clothes wet aren't an option. Jim skinny dips, while Dorsun and the others put on a great show. Bathing in their underwear, they lather up all over like four abominable snowmen, wash their hair vigorously with soap and brush their teeth with their index fingers.

Jim and the others remain in the water as Dorsun walks back up the rise towards the truck, where I sit and watch. He dons a clean shirt and the same dirty pants, a little lift to his step. I feel no alarm but raise my guard just the same. He looks to be in deep thought, smelling the length of something he moves under his nose. Looking up, he hands it to me through the window. *"Kekik,"* he says. The leaves are long and narrow, light green-gray like thyme. It must be some kind of thyme, I figure. I break a leaf and smell it.

"Yes, thyme," I say. *"Kekik?"* I ask again.

He nods. *"Yaes, kekik."*

"Kekik guzel," I reply, to see him staring at my hair. I turn my head, hoping I haven't encouraged him.

He retrieves a small towel to dry his hair and combs it back with his fingers. His skin is remarkably fair by Turkish standards, with freckles lining his nose and brow. I haven't seen a Turk with freckles. His manner can be so disarming. I also suspect he may be younger than I thought.

He walks around the front of the truck towards my side, looking over his shoulder towards the others. I sit above him in the truck seat, the side door open. He faces me straight on, intent, and takes another step forward. I put out my foot to distance him, ready like a she-cat. "GET AWAY!" I hiss.

He turns and keeps moving with head down. Jim walks up from the pond now. Shaken, I breathe deeply. Jim deserves some explanation.

The next moment, everything is as before, our sweet regular Dorsun diddling around the truck. He makes me doubt myself, wondering if he'd intended simply to walk around the truck and do nothing at all. Not likely, I decide. I long to bridge this cultural chasm that separates us, to help him understand what foreign women are really like. But what are the chances he would understand even if we spoke the same language?

Surely this guy has a tapeworm. Only a couple of hours down the road, we stop again to eat as the sky turns mauve— this time, *lahmacun,* Turkish pizza. We certainly aren't roughing it on this trip. *"Guzel!"* Dorsun proclaims.

"So what are we going to do about sleeping tonight?" I ask Jim.

"Don't worry, I think we might get to Antalya tonight."

We walk outside to find the valley around us enveloped with mist and grope our way back to the truck in the dark. Ramadan says goodbye and heads off, his friends waving from the back. Dorsun turns on the ignition; the truck lights flicker and weaken. He opens the hood, then slams it back down in a minute and yells "kaput!"

The truck inches down a narrow winding hill in the dark with no headlights. There are no stars to help. If this continues, we will surely meet our end off this embankment. I am about to announce my plan to get out when Dorsun shuts off the engine, pulls up the emergency brake and says something in Turkish. I point to the ground. *"Schlafen hier?"* I figure he might know some German since so many Turks work as guest workers in Germany.

"Yah," he nods and smiles. Jim and I retrieve our sleeping bags from our backpacks, the first time we've used them in weeks.

Sharp, jagged little rocks along the shoulder make us reconsider our idea to sleep on the ground. We unload watermelons from the back of the truck for half an hour to sleep on the wooden bed. *Why doesn't Dorsun just stretch out on the front seat?* I wonder. As we ready our sleeping bags, the thought occurs to me: We don't *really* know this guy; he could knock off Jim in his sleep and kidnap me or something. But that's as much energy as I can give it; I don't believe it for a minute.

Though the night is uncomfortably humid, Jim and I sleep with my body spooned inside his, his arm around me. I finally told him that Dorsun was bothering me, if he hadn't noticed already. He listened quietly and nodded. Jim is hardly the volatile jealous type. And it's not like this is a new problem.

I hear Dorsun settling down on the back side of Jim. As we all lay quietly waiting for sleep to come, I hear the ocean in the distance and realize we are closer to the coast than I'd thought. The stars command more of the sky now, countless exquisite pricks of light shining through a low moving gauze of clouds. In a matter of minutes, Jim snores softly and shifts to his back, leaving me feeling vulnerable. Left to my own devices, I secure my sleeping bag over my shoulder and zip up the side like a mummy in a sauna.

I hear Dorsun moving on the other side of Jim, followed by a nudge on my shoulder. *I can't believe it! What in the hell is he up to? And what should I do?* I decide to ignore him and lay there listening, wide-eyed. More rustling. He nudges me again. I wait and turn my head ever so slowly to try to glean peripherally what he's up to. His dark form hunches over Jim, breathing unevenly. He says something in Turkish, then enunciates it again loudly as if I might comprehend it this time. I slowly turn my head back to the side, scarcely breathing, close my eyes and wait.

Dorsun moves again, gets up and jumps off the truck. I follow his footsteps, breathing shallowly, as they come around my side and stop. A latticed wooden wall separates us. Though I cannot see the features of his face, he stands in front of me and says the words again. I inhale, not moving a muscle. He leaves, his footsteps moving back to his side, climbs up and takes an interminable length of time to settle down again. I finally exhale. *What was all that about?* I suspect his little charade was a coup, a show of power that he could have taken advantage of a situation, but chose not to. I'll never know.

We awake to a showy sunrise, a mist hugging the shore in the distance like a steam bath, the Mediterranean ocean glorious and sparkly in the sun. "Antalya," Dorsun points to the mist. For breakfast, Dorsun cuts open a beautiful, deep red watermelon. We will be in Antalya in less than an hour, I should think.

We coast the truck down the hill and jump-start the motor, arriving in Antalya around eight o'clock. As a parting gift, Dorsun gives us figs. He seems very comfortable with us now.

The Turks who have loved us too much these past six weeks populate my memory like a grandstand full of people cheering us on. Few people on earth have endeared themselves more. Dorsun will always punctuate the crowd. If I got through to any of the over-sexed guys just a bit without the benefit of language, it would be him.

We ask him to write his address. But I realize Jim and I will never see him again. This small measure of time, a truck ride that bumped along a road for two days, our monosyllabic conversations, some good meals, and a close call are what bound us. Now that they are finished, nothing else will quite work. I resist that truth but it is nonetheless immutable.

The image of Dorsun in my memory will always be that vulnerable look I saw in the truck. And his last knowing glint: the knowledge that something had transpired between us. I felt emotional when we parted. He was in his prime, but his life wasn't as it should be. So many lives weren't as they should be. That's what all those little Dervish dances had been about. I really liked Dorsun; he helped us out so much and was generous beyond his means.

"Assalamu Alaikum (goodbye-peace be with you)," I say.

"Wa'alaikum Assalam (peace be with you also)," he replies, smiling with approval that I know some Arabic. He smiles easily now. I want to hug him, but realize this would be a complete mistake and undo all my hard work. I think I've furthered the cause, given him some pause for attacking the next female traveler he will surely go out of his way to pick up. So we shake hands.

Mohammed would have smiled.

SYRIA: LOVE IN THE DESERT

We grow accustomed to the dark, when light is put away either the Darkness alters, or something in the sight adjusts itself to midnight, and life steps almost straight.

Emily Dickinson

Jim and I wouldn't have bumped into Abdullah that day, had we not lingered in St. Peter's Grotto in Turkey. He'd have remained faceless, lost in the crowd of people whose troubles we'd never know.

Instead, Abdul latched onto Jim and me like Whirling Dervish Flypaper, holding fast for thirteen days through Turkey and Syria, and making us believe we'd somehow always known him. Our little soirees began with *shi* (chai) in the evening, adding breakfast over *shi*, and slowly filling in everything between. But as quickly as Abdul appeared in our lives, he left us, slipping into the past and leaving his enigmatic mark.

In August, 1980, we met Abdul in Antakya, the ancient Antioch of Syria, as rich in history as cities come in the world. Through the lens of history, the tiny speck that is Antakya shines like gold, a deep rich patina worn by centuries of life under the Greeks, Romans, Arabs and Crusaders.

Why do extraordinary events always seem to pair with extraordinary places, blurring the edge between person and place? Abdul and Antakya have become as one, transcendent in my memory. Do extraordinary places conspire through people to leave their mark on us? Did Antakya render Abdul larger than he was, or Abdul, Antakya? Whichever, I cannot say. But the memory of them warms me on even the coldest days.

Jim and I decide to head to Antakya in Hatay, Turkey, in early August in the height of the dry season. The Hatay province forms the small eastern handle of Turkey east of the Mediterranean. The higher altitudes and the prospect of air that moves will deliver us from the sand-baked heat of central Turkey.

As we near Syria, still in Turkey, small differences strike me. The cadence of the words on the street is less rhythmic and seems to catch in the speakers' throats. The *hijab* is more prevalent among women. Secular Turkey gives way to the traditional Muslim Middle East; the spoken word is now Arabic. Leaving Asia Minor behind, we now enter the land of the Arabs, the Arabian peninsula.

The next morning, we visit St. Peter's Grotto, a small grotto and altar with a beautiful white stone façade, reputedly the first Christian church founded by Peter. The Crusaders identified the site during their rule of Antakya and built a lovely three-windowed facade. The Romans later Christianized Antakya, which has remained a Christian island in a sea of Islam. Church steeples dotting the landscape replaced mosque minarets. Anybody who was anybody in the Bible passed through here. Even a heathen would be impressed.

I take in the grotto silently, trying to imagine who else stood where I stand, when a little man I mistake for a child begins talking incessantly to Jim, asking questions and destroying my reverie. He says his name is Abdullah. "What is your country?

How long have you been in Turkey? Did you see Cappadocia? Where do you go next? Is this your wife?"

Abdullah has the gift of monologue. His stories continue as we walk from the grotto to a Turkish *lamacun* shop up the street. I beg off, returning to the hotel to nurse an upset stomach. Though Abdul fasts for *Ramadan,* he brings me a gift of *homos,* yogurt and pita bread to the hotel room. "Verdy good for the stomach," he says, patting his midriff.

"*Shookran, shookran* (thank you)," I tell him.

Abdul is in his mid-forties, I'd say, more than ten years older than Jim and I. Small framed, standing scarcely five feet, he consumes little space in the world. I could probably pick him up. His hairline recedes a lot for his years and the dark hair that remains is flecked with gray. A fine slip of a moustache lines his lip. He always greets us with a disarming smile and a little separation between his front teeth.

A Palestinian Muslim, Abdul's father was among many Palestinian heads of household rounded up by Israelis in 1948 when Israel became a state. Abdul was about thirteen. Sent to Lebanon in the night, his father was never seen again. "He was very good, my father, like the, how do you say, *qidis* (saint)." A sleeve wipes an eye, a long wipe like a little kid would do it. "All he is caring about is us. When he leaves, he is telling us not to be angry." After living in a refugee camp for a year, Abdul and his mother were able to move to Jordan with her brother.

"We are staying with my uncle one month," he continues. "Then we are on our own and my mother is working long hours like the *mamluk* (slave). I am asking you, is this better than the refugee camp? At fourteen, I am my own mother. This is not the way of our people, to leave the child. But I cannot blame my mother."

Abdul later served in the army in Jordan and enjoyed a fairly good life as an officer. When the Middle East crisis heated up in the early Seventies, all Palestinians in the Jordanian army were interrogated about their allegiances. Abdul refused to pledge that he would fire on fellow Palestinians if commanded and was ousted from military service on the spot. No longer allowed to work in Jordan and watched by the Jordanian military for six years, he fled to Algeria to live. I never asked if his mother was still living. And from what I gleaned, he had been married at some point.

A Syrian man joins us for *shi* one morning. I hold my breath. Abdul likes to argue and his favorite topics are Islam, the Arabs and women—all with whom he has not made peace. His banterings start out friendly enough; that's how he lures people in. But they all end up the same. Abdul greets our new friend in Arabic like an esteemed guest, fawns over his needs, pours his *shi*. A robust flow of conversation rises and falls between them, affable enough. In ten minutes, Abdul raises his voice and waves his head, the veins in his neck popping. Their parting seems civilized, though perhaps premature.

"So what were you talking about?" I ask casually.

"Oh," he sighs, a contrite sigh, I thought, "a sutra of the *Qur'an*, about the life after the death."

"You disagreed with him?" I say, just guessing.

He turns slowly, defensively. "No. *Inshallah* (God willing), I am just saying my piece, not arguing," he argues.

Abdul's recurring theme, his countless failures with women, is not self-deprecating humor as I thought at first. "What is it I do wrong?" he implores the heavens. Even if someone steps forward and braves an answer, it's difficult to imagine he would hear. Listening is not one of his strengths; he likes the limelight too much.

We can forgive Abdul's frustrated rantings because they somehow help him to make sense of an unjust world. Jim and I don't believe the overwrought Abdul anyway. His eyes conceal a different person: the soul of a poet. With the drama of an accomplished Thespian, he recites lines from the *Qur'an* and Rumi and Gibran. Recovered now from the last brush with the Arab, he turns to me. "Poetry is love, you know? To me, it is like the breath." He loops his hand in the air.

> "I am from there, I come from there and remember,
> I was born like everyone is born, I have a mother
> and a house with many windows. I come from there.
> I return the sky to its mother when for its mother the
> sky cries, and I weep for a returning cloud to know
> me."

"Who is that?" I ask.

"Mahmoud Darwish, the poet of the Palestinian people."

What I appreciate most about Abdul is his respectful treatment of me. His fussing over my needs makes me uncomfortable, but the sentiment wears well. "Is it too hot for you there? Look, this chair is better." Today he buys little sesame candies for me and picks me flowers. Unlike some of our past friends-turned-suitors, Abdul has never come onto me when we were alone. Jim seems very comfortable with him too.

Abdul knocks on the door of our hotel room now, a small bag of things thrown over his shoulder. "I am leaving Antakya today," he announces soberly. Only the fourth day since we first met, it seems like far more; it has been an intensive four days with Abdul. My feelings vacillate and jumble, this seems so sudden. I will definitely miss him. I won't miss the heavy remnants from the past.

"Where you will go?" he asks Jim.

"Damascus," Jim says.

"Inshallah, I go there too! Which hotel?"

We all vow to meet up, though Jim and I don't put a lot of faith in seeing him again. *"Assalamu Alaikum,"* he says with a wave.

Jim and I head to Damascus, the capital of Syria, the day after Abdul leaves. The Antilebanon Mountains to the west and a sea of beige sand to the east define Damascus, one of the oldest urban settlements in the world, some say the first. The city's borders abut the desert abruptly as if drawn with a line. The Baruda river, which means "seven rivers" in Arabic, made settlement possible in this desert oasis.

Time moves slowly in desert cities. Little has changed for centuries—the landscape, the cobbled streets, the camels, the beans and rice, the *hijab* worn by the women, the *jelabiyah* worn by the men, the call to prayer. You need only to breathe it in; Syria's rich history stretches before you.

The third day in Damascus, we return to our hotel to find Abdul sitting in the lobby, cigarette in hand. Most of the time, he wears Western pants and shirt. Today he dons the traditional white *jelabiyah* with white pants underneath and black and white checkered *kefiyah* head scarf, the Palestinian colors. Most men in Syria wear the red and white *kefiyah*, tied many different ways. (My personal favorite is the *kefiyah* tied at the neck, the ends tied on top of the head toothache style.) Abdul keeps track of everyone for us. "Many people here are not Syrian," he tells us. "That one is Jordanian...that one Saudi.. Kurd.. Iranian.. Iraqi."

The three of us set out for the old *souq*-market, the ancient, covered market that sells everything from *hookahs* to nuts. I wear a skirt and long-sleeved shirt packed for cold weather. Though my head is covered by a large scarf I bought the day before, I still stick out no matter what I do. Some women wear modest Western dress that covers the arms and legs and a colorful scarf on the head. Most prefer the *hijab*—fully clothed in black, the head covered and the face framed. A few wear the full *hijab*, the *burka*, with a slit for the eyes or thin veil covering the face. Abdul says these women come from the villages and are pilgrims from Iran.

The average Syrian or Arab has gained about twenty pounds since we left Turkey. "Syrians have more money than Turks," Abdul tells us. They obviously have more cars too. The streets seem hostile, no longer the domain of pedestrians. New shiny black Mercedes move too fast and honk too much.

Something else is missing in Syria. I realize it's the throngs of people. We miss the people of the streets who retire from public places as a country becomes developed. Teaching English isn't a priority in Syria, so our usual cadre of English students aren't to be found either. Gone are the invitations to dinner, being adopted out for the day, an insistence that we stay. We interact more with middle class, educated and moneyed Syrians, still the men. Though people we meet are pleasant enough, a cool formality characterizes their exchanges. Some even act wary, particularly government officials who can be downright mean.

People in most countries don't see us as an extension of our government. But let's be fair. US-Syrian relations have been tepid at best for years and strained further by the Iran hostage takeover, in its ninth month. Naturally Syria sympathizes with Iran. And if we consulted the State department's travel advisories at the time, Syria would be among the countries considered unsafe for American travel.

Everyone forgets their troubles today because the moon has been sighted. This night marks *Eid,* the end of *Ramadan,* the Muslim's month of fasting. Spirits run high and the streets are filled with festivity, good food and fireworks. Abdul has fasted since we met him, rising at four in the morning to eat without taking food or drink again until sunset. "Only when our stomachs are empty," he tells me, "can we understand the suffering of the poor."

"Is that the *Qur'an?*" I ask.

"No, it's Abdullah." He smiles cleverly.

"Very pithy."

"What is this pithy?"

"Oh, let's just say wise like Rumi."

He likes that, so much so that the same smile seems to crease his cheeks for hours. I doubt I could have pleased him more.

The *adhan*, the *muezzin's* melodic call to prayer proclaims the greatness of God and winds its way through alleys and streets in search of supplicants. *Allahuuuu Akbar. Allahuuu Akbar.* We follow Abdul to the Omayyad Mosque, one of the oldest mosques in the world dating to the eighth century. Foreigners can enter and observe.

A rectangular building, the Omayyad looks more like a church inside and out, suggesting that the first mosques followed earlier church designs. Reminiscent of many great cathedrals, two stories of columned arches flank both sides of the prayer hall. Warm rosy tones filter through the rows of windows, giving an ethereal feel to the room and drawing the eye up to Allah. Long chains supporting great weighty chandeliers lend a grandeur. Hundreds of crystalline glass pieces ablaze with white light add an unexpected garish touch. Islam is so full of surprises.

Natural-toned decorative tiles, modest in number, defer to the exquisite architecture. Except for a few pastel panes that accent the clear windows and the deep red oriental rugs, color is minimal in the prayer hall.

The energy is palpable and mounts as people pour in. Believers pack the long prayer hall, probably because of the *Eid* that night. They kneel and prostrate the earth, the great oriental rugs cushioning their brows. A chill runs through me. The unified effect of hundreds bowing the same moment and the sense of humility are wondrous. We've unwittingly walked into one of the greatest mosques on earth, on one of the most important days in the Muslim calendar.

After *salat,* Abdul takes us to a café he's frequented for years, he says. We drink *shi* and eat too many sweets, as Muslims do to reward the flesh for its sacrifice after breaking the fast. Abdul orders *arak* for Jim and me, a colorless, vile-tasting alcoholic drink made from anise. He pours himself a glass too as he talks with his friend the waiter in Arabic.

"This man is living in a refugee camp for Palestinians," he turns to us, his eyes wide and dark, like they are when he wants to pick an argument. "In the Syria, there are ten camps. You see. He is taking the orders, preparing the food and serving it, sweeping the floor and closing the shop every night. And for what?" he motions wildly and waits for effect. We squirm uneasily. "For nothing! Like a beggar," he jerks his hand up. "The Palestinian people live like nomads and gypsies in their own land!"

Our celebration threatens to lapse into more Abdul soliloquys. He chain-smokes expensive cigarettes and refills our glasses. As the *arak* flows, I'm relieved he doesn't drink more and settles for parody—mimicking his first wife, King Hussein, our hotel clerk—people he regards with affection, or disdain. It's easy to tell which.

The three of us set out early the next day to find the streets astir with life. I am glad to find Abdul his old self. It's market day, he tells us, the weekly market when people pour in from the hills. And a good opportunity for us to see the rural women. The women from distant villages mill about in faded black from head to toe. "Are there Bedouins here?" I ask Abdul.

I've only seen pictures of Bedouins, the nomadic desert people. "Yes, they come." He points with his chin and raises his brows. My heart bumps up a beat.

A curious dark blob commands half the road ahead, a mass of dark skirted cloth and eyes. Each woman wears the dark *hijab* with a colorfully printed fabric draped on top of the head, perhaps the design of the family. Some wear thin, dark face veils—some colored—drawn across the nose to the temples with only the eyes exposed. Gold trim lines their head pieces and dresses and flashes of gold catch at their ears.

As they approach, eyes turn to steal glances at me. I count nine women. Are they sisters, sisters-in-law, mothers and daughters? Do they all live together? The mystery of them holds the three of us in place. They exude an earthy sensuality, reminiscent of the gypsies.

"Is that a tattoo I see on a chin?" I ask Abdul.

"Yes," he says. "On the cheek and top too," he says, pointing to his forehead.

We are like the people in the hinterlands of Turkey who seem dumbstruck to find us on their soil. The Bedouins are as if from another time. If only they wouldn't move so quickly; if only they'd just stop so I could take in everything at my leisure.

Aware of our stares, the women quicken their step. Witnessing ancient tradition incarnate is deeply humbling—these primordial links to our distant past that still see the light of day instead of rotting in museums. With time, the traditions of our ancestors can no longer serve us. But something priceless in our human history dies when tradition dies, something no less dear and immutable than an endangered species we can never hope to gaze upon. I can't imagine an earth without these Bedouin women.

I want to bridge our worlds with some small overture. If only I could penetrate those public facades with a glimmer of recognition. And I snag one. In the row closest to us, the lovely eyes of a young woman covertly meet mine and widen into a smile. She speaks to the young woman next to her who turns and gives me a smile as well.

The irony strikes me as they pass. The most concealed ones are more mysterious and alluring by far. Their silhouettes cut figures of pride and sensuality, precisely what this abundance of cloth was meant to cover. The full-length dresses tucked at the waist fall into deep folds and flowing lines that ripple and sway as they walk. The air about them gives me goose bumps.

The three of us linger, hoping for a crumb that might fall. And Allah is willing. Another young one, perhaps an adolescent, drops a parcel. With a little chortle, she wheels around to retrieve it, mutters something, and flashes us a full uncensored smile. She is stunning. I smile back, elated. This is the best we could ask for.

All this sexual energy must be driving Abdul nuts, not to mention Jim. They are transfixed too. "Oh my goodness, did you see that beauty?" I raise my eyebrows to Abdul.

"Yes, but no thank you," he says. "The Bedouins will kill you for two things only—touching their land and one of their women, *especially* a virgin."

If Abdul doesn't adore women, he certainly makes a convincing case, since he dwells on the subject day and night. I sometimes wonder if he's more smitten with being in love. Try as I may, I can't picture Abdul beyond the courtship stage.

We have an ongoing argument about women's rights in Islam. "Mohammed is protecting the place of the woman," he tells us. "In his day, women were not treated like this. These tents that women are tripping over, the *burka*, these are the laws of men, not Islam."

"Then why aren't the men advocating to change the laws?" I ask. "If you don't change things unfair to women, people have a right to take you for your practice." A soccer ball careens out of nowhere, smacks Abdul soundly in the arm and off he goes after the kid. End of discussion.

He has a keen sense of what's right and grows impatient with others who don't see things his way. His between-the-eyes honesty can be refreshing or humiliating. Take the young boy who just smacked him. Granted, some of these boys playing on the streets can be downright unruly. OK, like little hoodlums. But I feel for the kid. I can see the scene when Abdul catches up with him. Like a man having a vertical grand mal seizure, Abdul will deliver a thorough dressing-down of the kid and his friends, the father and mother, or anyone who dares to challenge him. He will be out of control, but I guarantee he won't swear. He's not one to complain about how basic civility has gone awry, as we might: he's here to ensure that it doesn't.

If Abdul thinks someone charges too much when we're shopping, he protests, "Are you taking our clothes too?" When kids won't leave us alone, he tells them "sell us and buy another"—in other words, get lost! When all else fails, the really annoying kids get a solid whack on the side of the head. Corporal punishment by complete strangers seems perfectly acceptable in Islam.

"The reason I like the Arab people," I say to Abdul one day, "is because they're passionate, idealistic people. Maybe too passionate and idealistic, actually." Abdul doesn't deny being passionate, but don't call him an Arab.

"Just because I am speaking the Arabic, I am *not* the Arab!" He wags his head. "I am the Palestinian. The Arabs are the goat-herders from Arabia. Finding the oil under the feet and being in the right place, they are still the goat-herders!" He strikes the air for meaning.

"OK, OK," I say, "so you aren't an Arab!"

He folds his arms in conciliation, and says gently. "My heart is Palestinian and from the heart comes the sweetness of every sweet thing." Coming down off the trough of the last wave, he is humble pie again—this time, pining for the love of a woman. I wonder sometimes if he is manic-depressive.

"I cannot be free man until I find a wife. *Inshallah,* I will treat her like a queen. She cannot find another man in the world who will love her more!"

More than anything else, Abdul is an incurable romantic, what I like about him most. Perhaps he's brainwashed me these many days together, but I suspect his love could rival his hope. I only wish I could be around to see him a contented man.

As the three of us make our way back to the hotel, an Oum Kalthoum song wafts down the street. Though she died in 1975, Oum's voice is more ubiquitous than the call to prayer anywhere in the Middle East. Abdul joins in, singing to me and making me laugh. With hand to heart, his face contorted with the pain of unrequited love, his voice follows the difficult ululations as well as the master herself.

Kouli farha eshtakha min kablak khayali	*Every happiness I was longing for before you*
Eltakaha fi nour a'ainaik kalbi w fikri	*My dreams they found it in the light of your eyes*
Ya hayat kalbi ya aghla min hayati	*Oh my heart's life, you are more precious than my life.*
Leih ma kabilni hawak ya habibi badri	*Why I didn't meet your love a long time ago?*

"What is *habibi?*" I ask him. "So many songs I hear have this *habibi* in them."

"*Habib* is love, my love, my sweetheart," he explains with hands punctuating. Abdul always delivers up the simplest utterance with his hands, raises his eyebrows and over-forms words to ensure his meaning.

We are almost in sight of our hotel when the call to prayer sounds. Abdul searches in vain for a free piece of sidewalk to call his prayer rug, falls to his knees and blocks the narrow walkway while prostrating himself. Undaunted, people step over him. In Islam, this is not an oddity. Jim and I wait at the side on the dirt border, smiling sheepishly as people pass. "There are hundreds of ways to kneel and kiss the ground," he says when he catches up.

"The *Qur'an?*"

"No, Rumi."

In a bustling *shi* shop the next day, as if Abdul isn't intensity incarnate enough, we make a new friend named Hasan, a Syrian who drives a bus between Damascus and Baghdad. Hasan worked for the British military during World War II and speaks excellent English. He has six kids and entertains us with stories of his jealous wife. Since she's Christian and he's Muslim, she fears he'll take another wife without her knowledge. Hasan and Abdul become fast friends. And since Hasan is an Arab, he can take on Abdul's perennial arguments about the Arabs.

Jim and I have noticed that Abdul turns down joining our sightseeing ventures. We get his history lesson following each trip, but he never makes the trip. And then it dawns on Jim—the reason Abdul travels, why he seeks out new friends and dresses up handsomely in his *jelabiyah* and *kefiyah* when he goes out. "Abdul is not a tourist at all!" Jim says wide-eyed, leaning in though no one can hear. "I think our friend is wife-hunting!"

I ponder this for a moment. "Ahhh, yes, I think you're right. It all adds up."

I waste no time asking Abdul. "Yes, it is so." He sighs, and explains why he must go to these lengths. It's not acceptable to talk to a strange woman in public in towns and cities, so he must network through contacts and ask others about marriageable women they might know. Then he meets with the woman's father or brother or uncle, whoever her guardian is.

I can only guess, but father interviews have to be infinitely more demoralizing than job interviews. "So you're talking to anyone who has a marriageable daughter?" I ask, blushing, realizing my poor choice of words.

"But of course not. I am having my standards." He sits up erectly. "I am asking many questions to my friends. It is not the young one, not the beauty I seek. I am seeking the beauty inside." He touches his chest. "Perhaps the oldest daughter," he says, nodding his head for emphasis, "the one who is not yet marrying. If she is having the love in the heart and, how do you say, the sparkle in the eyes, the eyes that dance, no problem," he says with a resolute flick of the head and hand. Then turns directly to me. "Like you." In the balance, that was probably a compliment, I tell myself.

"*Inshallah*, all I want is to marry before I die. Is that so much to ask?" he implores the heavens again. "There is no salvation for the soul but to love," he says in his theater voice. "Only from the heart can you reach the sky." It must be Rumi, I won't even ask.

"So love will make everything, right?" I ask.

"Yes, but of course. Love is all we have."

Abdul and I talk of little else at *shi* the next day: tactical wife planning and Abdul grooming. Jim loses himself in the *Syria Times*. Abdul and I plan the gifts he will take, what he will say, the poem he will quote. We roleplay; I am the daughter who asks the questions. When we're done, he is so polished, I can't stand it. Not slick; just right.

He makes me smile, impersonating the last father. "Sometimes they are having more hair than me!" We both laugh, though it really isn't funny.

"Are the fathers likeable?" I ask.

"Yesss," he answers carefully, "they offer the *shi* and the candies in the Muslim way, they are respecting. But they are having a job, you know, not always the nice one. No problem, I understand."

"How many interviews have you had in Damascus?"

"Three," he says. "And only one time am I meeting the daughter. They are not even appearing." He waves his hand. "The problem is, I am not having enough money for the father!" His cheeks flush with indignation.

Abdul needs a break and it seems he'll soon get one—a woman whose family is friends with Hasan's family. In her late thirties, the daughter comes from a working class family and everyone speaks highly of her character. Hasan promotes Abdul's good character. And the dowry, Hasan expects, will be more accommodative, more in keeping with her modest beginnings. Could this be the one?

Jim and I spend the afternoon sightseeing but think of little else, wringing our hands like anxious parents as Abdul meets the family. Upon our return to the hotel, Abdul is nowhere to be found, so we reluctantly eat dinner without him at our favorite *homos* restaurant. Just as we're ready to leave, a dejected, downtrodden Abdul walks in. He can't eat, he says, but sits to reenact the full drama for us. And everyone in the restaurant.

"I am meeting the daughter this time," he begins. "She was very beautiful, ohhh very nice. And she is liking me too, I can tell." His voice rises, taunting. "But not the father. He is *not* liking me, and he is the only one who matters."

"What did he tell you?" I ask.

"At the end, he says 'the hunter is under the sun and the bird is playing in the shadow.'"

"What in the world is that supposed to mean?"

"It means everything is not as it should be."

"And it doesn't matter that the daughter liked you?" I ask.

"No, it didn't matter," he says. "She was crying when I left."

Again, it was money, Abdul says, not enough. "It's always the money!" he moans. With arms flailing, he rails to Allah. "Islam is a great prison. The men are not free to do as they please and the women are bound by their father's wishes! I will marry a goat to show Islam that it is cruel and unjust!"

The bride price, he tells us, amounts to tens of thousands of dollars in the bank and covers prescribed purchases that include a small treasure of gold jewelry and all the items needed to outfit a household. Perhaps Abdul shops in the wrong country. Surely Syria's brides come at a higher price. Jim and I strongly suspect he also competes with an age bias.

Abdul grows increasingly morose, so we say goodnight. At the moment, our charming, singing, poetry-reciting friend isn't the least bit romantic or elegant. And I can't bear to watch. We are all damaged souls, but Abdul seems irreparably damaged.

I want to believe the human spirit can surmount anything. That a fatherless child with no country who's been relegated to wandering and never fitting in can find love. Would a Palestinian homeland have made the difference, I wonder? Or two parents? Or just more money? Watching Abdul's quiet desperation from this distance is painful enough. I know he must question whether he can ever find love.

His rejections may be about money on the face. But anyone can see that Abdul's longing is as vast as the desert. The depth of his despair weighs on everything he touches.

At *shi* the next morning, Abdul, Hasan, Jim and I plan an outing to a restaurant Hasan knows outside of town. And then I notice. The sound of our little foursome rings hollow, as if something is wrong. Not once have Abdul or Hasan joked or laughed. Jim and I, the ready audience, aren't laughing either. Something seems amiss between them; maybe something to do with the last bride meeting? Perhaps Abdul is angry at Hasan? Or Hasan feels responsible about the rejection?

Abdul lavishes little presents on Jim and me, plying us with things to eat. Then as smoothly as he slips in a line from Rumi, he wields the blow that could only be delivered with drama. "Tonight will be our last night together," he says with hands folded on the table. "After we are eating the dinner, we must say goodbye."

Of course, this event had to come. Who goes first is immaterial, I tell myself. It's not like he's betraying us. He's no different than countless others who have said goodbye before, I tell myself. I will miss his spirit more than I can say. To compound his bad news, he seems to pull away from us, as if we have already lost him.

We drive in one of Hasan's buses, four of us in front with all the other seats vacant. The road winds through the desert, climbing the hills where the seven rivers of Damascus originate at the Feeje river. White linen tables with old stains sit atop a concrete slab under large shade trees next to the river, a refreshing change from the desert.

We all watch quietly, letting the river's jetties and bubbles transfix us. I look up to see a large odd object rounding the bend, making its way to us—the deteriorated carcass of a dead sheep. I suppress the urge to allegorize. Everyone in the restaurant watches blithely, turning back to their meal as if the grotesque bloated form was nothing more than a bottle bobbing downstream.

Abdul pays for everything. Yesterday, Hasan paid for everything. Even in Syria, these are not small sums for people of little means. For a few *lira*, Abdul asks some gypsies to dance for us and tell our fortunes. Abdul will find love, the young gypsy with furtive glances and jingly gold jewelry tells him. I resist having my fortune told in case she says something ridiculous. I want to preserve her bead on Abdul.

We walk along a path through groves of olive trees to take in a panoramic view from the hills overlooking Damascus. I shudder, the starkness is so extravagant. Except for green patches of olive groves, the valley is colorless, a jumble of concrete mid-rises and beige desert stretching to a flat horizon. The evening hues soften everything. The sunset washes the buildings and desert floor in a soft pink as far as the eye can see. The air blows warm and dry on our faces. I cannot fully fathom that I stand in the heart of human history.

Jim runs back to the restaurant to the bathroom and Hasan goes to retrieve the bus. Abdul has been very quiet, but turns to me abruptly, seemingly breathless, and takes my hand.

"I am ashamed to call this love human and afraid of God to call it divine," he says with intense, pleading eyes. "Your fragrant breath like the morning breeze has come to the stillness of the garden. You have breathed new life into me."

He has never touched me except to shake my hand each time we meet. Even in the shadow, I sense it. He is different; he looks at me differently and that was not his Thespian voice. I remove my hand and smile uneasily, going along with the joke.

"Rumi, right?" He registers no response. I hug my arms. "Ah, you see, I recognize him now."

He looks back, then turns on me quickly, his face contorted and sad. "Ahn, please. Go away with me, marry me. I will treat you like a queen. No one in the world will love you more. You cannot even imagine how happy we will be." Surely he forgets that I know all this by heart.

He has never addressed me by name; when he says it, it doesn't sound like my name. His words move me for an instant, this little man who'd have to stand on a chair to kiss me. Who wouldn't want to be happy beyond imagining? Is such a thing possible?

My disappointment in him colors his words most, that he would betray Jim so easily. "Abdul, Jim and I are engaged to be married," I lie.

"But Ann, I will love you more than Jim can love you. Come with me, you will thank Allah every day." He turns to check for Jim and Hasan.

The empty bus with Hasan and Jim suddenly bounces down the drive. A crazy Arab hangs out the window waving like a lunatic as if he's just rescued us in the desert. We hold our ears as the brakes screech and the bus stops.

Abdul takes a deep breath, smiling proudly, vulnerably, back in check. The door swings opens. He motions. "After you."

JORDAN: THE PINK SCAR

And the night shall be filled with music, And the cares, that infest the day, Shall fold their tents, like the Arabs, And as silently steal away.

Henry Wadsworth Longfellow

What is it about the Bedouins that so captivates us? Our brief encounter in Damascus turned me into a groupie. Every day, I still pan the jumble of faces on the streets for another glimpse of one. "The place to find the Bedouins is Jordan," Abdul once said. Though he didn't share my interest (Bedouins were the *first* goat herders), he always helped me scout them out. "Look, there's some," he'd say as we walked, or "over there," nodding towards a black tent encampment on the desert floor—maybe half a dozen sightings all told over two weeks' time. A mere tease.

"Are there less of them now?" I asked Abdul. He pondered carefully and tilted his head.

"Yes, it is true," he said, "there are far less living like the real *bedu*," the Arabic word for nomad. "Sometimes we cannot recognize the ones in the city."

Jim and I resolved to find the real nomads before they all became sedentary, and Petra, Jordan, one of the wonders of the natural world, provided our first encounter.

We camped high atop a rock promontory among the pink sandstone cliffs of Petra valley. Our vantage point overlooked the entrance to the valley to one side and, to the other, a small settlement of Bedouins. Under the moon's diffused silver veil, Jim and I and the Bedouins' dark shadows moving across the sand were the only inhabitants of the ancient Nabataean valley at night. Perhaps the authorities let them stay there in exchange for keeping an eye on things.

By day, their black tents were less romantic—a collage of fabric with canvas, cardboard, whatever, overlapped helter-skelter on top with lines drawn in various directions. A desert shantytown. Large plastic containers and tins, buckets, blackened pots and other junk were scattered outside. Young children with wild hair and dirty clothes ran barefoot across the hot sand while tending to the goats and pitching stones with sticks.

A Bedouin explained that the tents are woven out of goats' hair and pieced together like a quilt. In the dry season, the fabric sags and separates, creating fissures that breathe and ventilate the air inside. In the cooler wet season, the fabric shrinks and keeps out wind and rain. "The holes are catching the wind," a Bedouin man told us a bit defensively. "We are not poor people." I hadn't even inquired.

One early evening after the tourists had left and the valley was ours again, Jim and I drew pictures in the sand with Bedouin children. A Bedouin man motioned from his tent for Jim and me to come. Filling a teapot with water, he greeted us and gestured towards small stools in a section open at the front of the tent. His heavy brown *jelabiyah* and red and white *kefiyah* headpiece seemed remarkably clean for a place where water is scarce.

I guessed he was in his late forties, though his face appeared older. Many Bedouin men have weather-beaten faces, the older ones reminiscent of *shar peis*, those strange Chinese dogs with deep furrows of skin. Presumably, the women in the desert age better since they venture out in the sun less. But then we haven't seen enough to say.

The tent was about fifty feet long, though some in Petra valley were larger. Bedouin tents are divided into two sections, we learned—the public area and the women's area. The public area receives guests by day. By night, the flaps roll down for warmth. The women move about freely in both areas, though their section to the right remains closed. No one outside the family can enter and other women pass only by invitation.

Our host heated the *shi* in an old black Arabesque pot over charcoal coals on the sand. An efficient column of smoke billowed to the top of the tent and found its way out. We sat on mattress-type seats on the ground and sipped our tea in glasses that took a long time to pick up, much less drink. Once Jim and I exhausted our greetings and thank yous in Arabic, we were adrift for conversation. Our host gave his undivided attention to poking the coals. We blew on our tea and smiled a lot.

Which was just as well to me. I reveled in the rare opportunity to survey the inside of a Bedouin tent. Unfortunately, the light at the entrance flooded the area where we sat, enshrouding everything else in shadow. I squinted to see better. Cellophane packages, cloth bags with Arabic script and strewn boxes— mostly consumables—lined the edges of the living area. The lack of furnishings and permanency interested me most. A small blackened oil lamp hung from a horizontal post and, behind it, a deep peach-colored fabric, airy and light. *Where would a Bedouin woman wear that?* I wonder. I longed to see her.

An errant breeze stirred within the tent, brushing my skin before it billowed the tent. The goat hair walls expanded like lungs taking breath, and the beautiful fabric lifted and danced. Our host looked up and smiled as if a family member had entered.

These were real *bedu*. I realized we would smother in each other's environments and customs. His distant past was still tangible for him, while I could never hope to have so much as a glimpse of mine. I envied him, though I'm not sure why.

An old picture frame with no glass held a curled, faded paper with ornate gold Arabic script, a sutra from the *Qur'an*. A keepsake, no doubt, one of the precious few items that occupies space from venue to venue. Someone stirred in the other tent section, though she never surfaced.

We rose to leave and thanked our host. *Shookran*. Pleas to employ a guide, a camel or to buy something never came. How nice; we had been the guests of genuine Bedouin hospitality. An Arab friend told me later: The hospitality of Islam began with the Bedouin who holds the guest in the highest esteem. As his guest, he holds you in his protection. For the time you sit on his rug, he is responsible for your life. The mere possibility filled me with love. Our host didn't convince me he was prepared to save our lives. But in fairness, there wasn't a rug either.

That experience only whet our appetites. We needed to drink more *shi* on real Bedouin rugs and test our host's meddle. Wadi Rum to the southeast sounded like an excellent place to find the Bedouins in their natural element, the desert depths. T.E. Lawrence, the famous British officer, made Wadi Rum famous. Based there during the Arab Revolt of World War I, Lawrence stayed in Wadi Rum a total of eighteen months and came to love this place. In 1918, he wrote, "divinity is here. Wadi Rum is magically haunted ... vast and echoing and God-like". The Peter O'Toole *Lawrence of Arabia* movie was filmed in Wadi Rum too.

Apparently all Bedouins were once *bedu*. They called themselves *arab* and claimed most of the Arabian peninsula's interior. The harsh desert environment created a passionately independent life of raising goats and sheep, and breeding horses and camels. But the desert's limited food supplies meant moving and constant war-faring with neighbors along the way. Today, Bedouins are replacing their camels with pickup trucks and jeeps.

Three Bedouin tribes dominate the area in and around Wadi Rum, about twenty families. Each has lived on the Arabian peninsula for generations and claims to descend from the Prophet Mohammed. The Huweitat tribe, semi-nomadic today, was well known to T.E. Lawrence, who reported: "Of all the *bedu*, none were so jealous of their personal integrity as the Huweitat—every fourth or fifth man considered himself a *sheikh*."

A half moon and Venus below come into view as the night slowly consumes the last vestiges of day. The truck we've hitched a ride with approaches our destination. At least I sense it's Wadi Rum anyway. Scruffy, monochrome desert images have undulated out our window for almost two hours. We can scarcely make out the landscape now. But it feels different, as if we crossed a threshold. The desert's inner sanctum. It's the sand, the way it holds the light from the heavens. The sand is finer here.

Wadi Rum takes in a hundred and fifty mile radius, the largest *wadi* in Jordan secured within the vast chasms of the Great Rift Valley. Astronauts on space missions speak of picking out the Rift Valley's three thousand mile scar on the earth's surface that extends all the way from northern Syria to central Mozambique in Africa.

The road swings back inland along the main road south; our truck stops for no apparent reason. We turn to the driver. He points for us to follow a sand road we never would have found on our own. Never. We can't believe it's a road at all. I want to run after the truck as he pulls away.

On pure faith, we walk. The sand makes our packs seem heavier. As we approach a small rise, a broad flickering light signals civilization. A dark figure with *kefiyah* approaches. As he comes into view, wearing a striking uniform lined with red, I realize he's a policeman. The Desert Patrol gets my best looking uniform award, hands down. A deep tawny-brown *jelabiyah* with white pants underneath is belted securely at the waist with a wide red leather strap that crosses at the chest to the shoulders. The *kefiyah* head scarf is red and white with a black *ekal* band on top to secure it, a round metal insignia in front. Very fetching. A gun holster bears no gun. "Wadi Rum Desert Patrol?" we ask. The policeman nods and turns around to deliver us there.

A few hundred meters over a rise, the so-called fort with Jordanian flag comes into view; figures stand around a fire. A squat white building reminiscent of an old foreign legion movie sits below. It's difficult to imagine how such a small building could keep anything out. Surely T.E. Lawrence didn't work here.

We try to convey to the policeman that we want to pitch our tent. "OK, OK, camping," he says, nodding, and takes us behind the fort to a flat area downwind from the camel corral. I love camels; I've always wanted to have the opportunity to see them closer and touch them. But not cohabitate with them.

We suggest a spot farther away, upwind. "How about here?" Jim asks.

"OK," he nods. "Camping OK."

The town of Rum hugs one riverbed. *Wadi* means valley or dry riverbed, until the rains come for a short time each year. Wadi Rum holds many subsurface springs inside its rock recesses, drawing countless peoples into these valleys for more than three millennia. Primitive inscriptions on rock faces tell the stories of those who lived and passed through—the

Thamuds, Safaits, Nabataeans, Greeks and Arabs—often trading spices and frankincense.

Besides the fort-police station, the town of Rum is only half a dozen buildings and a school. The Jordanian police, we learn, are all Bedouin. The tribe of the Desert Patrol must differ from the tribe that lives here in order to maintain authority over them. Makes sense; because allegiances are always to the tribe first. The Bedouin are also found in the combat units of the Jordanian army. Most of the inhabitants of Rum live in Bedouin tents within the village vicinity.

We join Bedouin policemen around the campfire in front of the fort. I notice all their gun holsters are empty. They invite us to eat Arabic bread and coffee with cardamom. Who would think you could make bread in the desert? On the desert actually.

The baker clears a shallow bed of red hot coals off the sand and lays a *khoubiz* flatbread dough on the hot sand. He covers the bread with sand, laying the coals and ashes on top. When baked, the bread is pulled out and beat against a mat to free it of sand and ash. We find it quite delicious.

In the coolness of the early morning, Jim and I set out to walk across the desert that is Wadi Rum. We stick out like *khawaagas* (foreigners) in our sun glasses which, oddly enough, the people of the desert don't wear. Even when we think we're doing a good job of blending in, we probably stick out most. Jim dons one of my bandana scarves and I wrap my head in a large scarf *kefiyah*-style.

We walk straight out into the valley to view the extent of the corridor, the most pristine, exotic landscape I have ever seen. Deep mauve-colored sands line a level-flat desert floor set against vertical mauve rock groups that meet a pale blue sky. There is nothing else, life of no kind—not goats or sheep or people stirring. We feel like the only people on earth. The beauty and desolation of this moonscape hold us in that spot.

And this is only a small piece of the yawning Arabian desert. The corridors of Wadi Rum run north and south, with one large intersecting corridor. Our corridor appears to be a mile or two across and various miles deep, hemmed by vertical rock cliffs of sandstone and granite called *jebels* to the sides. A rock climber's paradise, Jebel Rum is the highest at 1750 meters. The *jebels* closest to us are widely spaced, the ones in the distance long and rambling like mini-mountain ranges. A small, lone *jebel* sits in the middle not too far away.

The rocks are stratified with color and uneven as if hot rock was affixed in layers like clay but cooled before melting together. Feeling whimsical, the artist topped off the whole thing with odd, bulbous-like stacks, pillars as they're often called. Over the millennia, sand and wind have added to the sculpture by raking and scoring the rock faces with horizontal lines, some with dramatic gashes that open up into vertical chasms. A smooth surface or uniform color is not to be found.

The pink sandstones and deep beige granites, we learned, were the marriage of fire and water when the molten granite formed during the earth's infancy. The sandstone became layered under water millions of years later. Humbling. Inside the visible lines that separate the two rocks, hidden springs can be found. Millions of years later still, the fault line running between Africa and Asia shifted and created the Great Rift Valley.

We noticed a Bedouin policeman watching us pass earlier, another dark, swarthy, classic-good-looks Arab dressed in uniform with *kefiyah*. He hurries out now to meet us. "Why you are walking all the way there?" he asks. When we don't answer right away, he says with a dramatic nod of the head: "I am telling you, it is verdyyy far." He squints against the glare. "Where do you go? To Lawrence's Well?"

"Yes," Jim says, nodding.

"Ohhh," he says as if in pain. "It is more than ten kilometers to Lawrence's Well!" Ah, another Thespian.

Jim points to the only rock face in the distance perpendicular to the valley. "Lawrence's Well is close to that rock, right?"

"Yes, yes," he says, "but you are needing the transport! In a few hours, it will be forty degrees Celsius! Let me take you with my horses, I finish work in ten minutes. Please. Come with me." You would think if a Bedouin who's lived in the desert all his life told you it's too hot to walk, that would be enough. But we're stubborn, and skeptical. Correct information, we've noticed, is often compromised to ensure the sale.

We look at each other, in sync. Our guidebook says eight kilometers; we don't believe it's more than ten. And even if it is, we can manage. It's still early. "We're OK." I smile sweetly to convince him of our well being. "We have water. We have food. *Shookran.*"

His jaw stiffens, he cocks his head to the side, closes his eyes and swallows his pride. "As you wish." When we distance ourselves, he yells, "OK, OK, then, paying what you want. It is not good to walk." This shakes my resolve a bit. Is he really worried about us? I follow Jim's lead, who plods on without looking back.

"*Assalamu Alaikum,*" I yell back.

About ten beats, he yells back, "*Wa'alaikum Assalam,*" defeat in his voice.

The desert floor stretches out like a nondescript landscape before us, slowly taking form as we walk. Scruffy, pale green grasses and bushes dot the valley. On closer examination, the desert floor actually abounds with form. Billions of rippled tiers run across the sand *ad infinitum*, mirror images of each other, with knife-like edges cut by the wind. Tiny animal tracks cut lines across some of the ridges, underlining the impermanence of it all. It's difficult to imagine a desert could support life in the dry season.

We walk slowly without talking, the sound of our feet mushing through the sand. As the sun rises to the east, washing more sand and rock in light, the *wadi's* colors take on lighter beige hues. The blue sky fades. Though we're both in good physical shape, the sand tires us. In two full hours, we've reached the *jebel* in the center that looked so close. Not impressive progress.

I survey the corridor with different eyes, realizing the scale of things isn't at all as it seemed. I recall a cartoon I once saw where a guy flies a kite and the kite is way off in the distance, it's so small. He plucks it out of the sky instantly because it's actually a tiny kite at the end of a short string. The valley plays the same trick. The levels where I'd expected to see people walking against the rock are maybe fifty feet high. They would be giants. In reality, we would scarcely see the people. I strain to see a barely perceptible lower strata of people and their animals moving like bugs against the face of the next *jebel.*

As we round the other side of the *jebel*, a buff-colored camel with no apparent tether stands quietly in front of us chewing like a cow chews cud, his lower jaw moving with a mind of its own. An old man with a large walking stick approaches us from the right. A Bedouin shepherd with a staff? But where are his goats?

A light gray beard stands out against his dark, tawny skin. He wears an old tattered sports jacket and red and white *kefiyah* with black *ekal,* the sides of the *kefiyah* tied around the neck. He motions for us to come, gesturing towards the camel, presumably to ride. "No, no," we say, smiling and waving. "We're OK. *Shookran.*"

He comes closer. A small framed man, he must be seventy or more. Dramatic furrows and crevices etch his eyes. The dry white skin on his nose and brow looks irreparably damaged. Jim extends his hand and they shake. "*Assalamu Alaikum,*" I say and extend my hand too. He slips me the itchy finger in the palm and I pull my hand back. Jim gapes at me. I want to let out a shriek to fill the desert.

Making conversation about how beautiful the day is, Jim points to the sky. I just want to get the hell away from this man. How could he, *especially* after I evoked the name of Allah. I shoot Jim a look. "Could we go, *please?*"

He offers Jim a rolled cigarette, the tips of his fingers hardened and orange with nicotine. Since Jim has been trying to quit without success, he accepts. The Bedouin lights both their cigarettes with a Bic lighter. I'm trying to quit too, but I notice he doesn't offer me a cigarette. They stand there smoking together, a man moment. Jim, the eternal goodwill ambassador, extols the virtues of Arabian tobacco, enunciating loudly, "Very niceee!" His cigarette hand punctuates the air like a Sixties Marlboro commercial. Why is it that if we enunciate and speak loudly enough, we figure others will somehow divine our message? The Bedouin smiles approvingly. Tea and coffee and cigarettes are the great equalizers. If only I had some.

We walk another hour in the open valley in pursuit of the next *jebel* to the east, half our water supply drunk. We break out the long-sleeved shirts from the daypack. The sun looms overhead and we get the real thing, the stark desert sun and blinding reflections off the sand. The dry punishing heat has turned up maybe thirty degrees Fahrenheit since morning. Mirages waft and glisten in front of us. Bodily fluids shrink.

We finally reach the second *jebel* and follow the narrow band of shade hugging the rock. The first Bedouin policeman told us about pictographs we could find here. Jim discovers some figures—four people in a row about six inches tall, and two camels, nice dromedaries. I wonder how old these are and which people made them? What were they saying? Perhaps they're a memorial to the dead. Or an ancient family album.

We should have gotten a damn guide. The fact is, areas not well touristed like this tend to have under-whelming guides. It's more frustrating to anticipate learning a lot and then realize the guide is making it up as he goes. Or he follows the local folklore with little historic fact.

I recall the guides who accosted us last night and this morning, a guy with horses and the other with camels who said he knew where to find all the inscriptions. They were both too expensive and seemed more like opportunists, not real guides.

The rock that leads to Lawrence's Well doesn't look far now, though they never do. Since it's almost twelve o'clock, we should be close. On this good note, we make a digression to eat lunch out of the sun, following a narrow shard-like opening between two vertical rock walls. Jim's pack brushes the rock, the sides are so close.

Since I lead, I see it first. "Green!" I squeal. "Remember green?" Our first bona fide desert oasis! We sit and eat lunch in a mini-garden, very mini, a few young green plants and an old stubborn tree. Water has to be here, though we can't see or hear it. When I put my hand down the crack from where the tree grows, it does feel cool and damp. Finding that spring would be nice right now, as we must ration our water like it's gold.

Jim finds another pictograph close to where we sit, a snake design with a symbol next to it, as big as a fist—perhaps a religious or burial symbol, or an early coat of arms. The rock where I sit is smooth with use. I wonder, did a Nabotean family stopping to eat here, too, decide to leave their mark?

In the spring time, I have read, the sand comes alive with hundreds of flower species such as poppies and red anemones and irises that lay dormant the rest of the year. As we join the open valley again, the Bedouin shepherd we met approaches from the north on camelback, walking slowly. No creature belongs in this landscape more than a camel. To think they almost became extinct thousands of years ago, used only for their meat. Once people began to ride them, they realized that the camel could bear great loads and sustain long distances without water.

Rider and camel break into a slow gallop towards us. The gangly neck and legs move almost at odds with each other. Set against a white desert backdrop, the Bedouin's colorful *kefiyah* accents the picture—another moment when I can't believe I am in this place and witness to these things. The Bedouin motions for us to sit behind him on the camel. He must be joking. "Over my dead body," I say. Jim smiles and waves goodbye.

On the other side of the valley, we find an oasis bigger than our mini-garden, also subterranean. Subterranean this time of year anyway. Nothing is sign-posted in the desert; we can never be sure if this is Lawrence's Well. We find another group of pictographs which makes our day feel quite productive.

The sun and heat seem more oppressive, the air more stagnant in the afternoon. The full extent of the valley, the rock faces and the sands are washed in white. The shade provides no refuge from the glare. Our shirts stick to our backs. I wish I could take my clothes off. Wet and pink, Jim's face seems to glow. Dark perspiration marks run down his pants legs like he wet himself.

The heat melts my brains and pounds in my head. I am not thinking clearly. I see the policeman's face, his pleading face, and hear his warning. I'm thinking a person could die here in a very short time if they didn't get help. I'm thinking we may not make it back. How can we possibly make it without enough water? There is only stark whiteness and indifference here. No one would see and no one would care if we died.

I'd even go with that disgusting old man now. I look around for him and his camel. *Please, please come back and offer us a ride again.* Jim has stopped in front of me, facing me. "Are you OK?"

"Yes," I lie. "Let's just reach that *jebel* in the middle again." But I don't think I can reach the *jebel*. "I'm sorry, Jimmy. Can we rest again?" I plop down on the hot, open sand, as limp as a *kefiyah*. I have stopped perspiring.

When we finally round the rock, the camel sits where we he was before, looking unspeakably beautiful to me. He lets me touch his head. The Bedouin yells from above and motions for us to come up. The climb is steep and jagged. "You go," I motion to Jim. "Just let me die here."

But I am like the Bedouin women; I have no choice in the matter. Jim pushes me from below while the Bedouin pulls from above as if I were a ragdoll.

The stark beauty of the desert from the summit washes over me, working like a salve. The valley to the west stretches as far as the horizon, meeting the last sliver of the sun as it sets. The rose light permeates the air we breathe, dense and nurturing like a mother's soup, rendering the desert benevolent again.

We stand in a cozy campsite the shepherd has created to wile away the long hours. I sit down on a rock and croak a long mortal sigh, a little like a camel actually, letting the diffused sunlight seep into every cell. Slowly, the desert gives back what it took. The Bedouin offers us *shi* that cooks on a flatbed of coals and we marvel at our good fortune since we're out of water. I even feel affection for him.

After two glasses of tea, I say to Jim, "So that guy was right, wasn't he? It was more than eight kilometers." I smile broadly, unspeakably happy.

Jim isn't conceding as quickly. "Maybe," my former eagle scout says. "At least the way we did it, it wasn't."

And then we spot goats in the desert, the Bedouin's goats, their little stick bodies silhouetted by the sun. So that's it, I realize, he watches his goats all day long from here. The shepherd retrieves something to his side and looks through old binoculars, probably T.E. Lawrence's binoculars left behind. He hands them to Jim.

"Ahhh," Jim says, "look out there," and hands them to me.

"I know, I saw, they're goats."

"No, just look," he says. I look and see goats! "Do you see what else he's watching? I look all around. And then a young girl comes into view. Dressed in full dark *hijab*, she's basically the female counterpart to the Arab men—a loose dress with pants covering the body and a fully covered head, forehead and neck.

"You mean he sits up here all day and watches her?" I say. "He's not even a damn shepherd?"

"No, no," Jim laughs. "I think he's a shepherd all right. I'm sure those are his goats. I think he sits up here to protect the girl and the goats."

"Really? I'd say the girl needs protection from him!"

"Look there," and his eyes point behind the Bedouin where a rifle sits.

"Yeow. I think I forget where I am sometimes."

We empty the Bedouin's teapot and thank him profusely before climbing down. We figure the police station will take another couple of hours. I hope the moon comes up tonight because it will be dark otherwise. At least the temperatures are bearable and we're somewhat revived.

In a short while, our shepherd comes upon us yet again on camelback, presumably on his way home too. Patting the space behind him, he smiles and makes a last plea to take a ride. I don't think he even cares about money. The camel looks down on us, his bulbous brown eyes relaxed, his mouth pursed in indifference about the matter. I never noticed how extraordinarily long camels' eyelashes are. He lets me touch his face and pet him.

More than anything else in the world now, I'd love to ride that camel and not take another step, to be lulled high above the ground like a baby all the way back as night sets in. There are few times I've wanted anything more.

"Jimmy, are you willing to sit in the middle?"

"No, I don't think so," he says.

"Well me either. I'm not interested in being sandwiched against him. I don't trust him."

Walking like a very old person, my pride in tact, we make our way back to the encampment and watch the exquisite silhouette of the Bedouin and his camel moving elegantly as one before us.

EGYPT: THE INSHALLAH FERRIES

The night has a thousand eyes, and the day but one; yet the light of the bright world dies, with the dying sun. The mind has a thousand eyes, and the heart but one; yet the light of a whole life dies, when love is done.

Francis William Bourdillon

Our steamer ferries putter tentatively up the Nile. I want to say down the Nile because south always seems downstream to me. But the water's strong resistance confirms our ascent; we're definitely headed upstream. Jim and I take in the verdant green palms and lush bulrushes that frame the small settlements south of Aswan. As a child in Sunday school, this is the Nile I'd always imagined Moses floating down.

We are two barges lashed to one ferry, side by side, the ferry being three levels high. *Inshallah*, we'll spend one night on this sorry excuse for a vessel, arrive at Wadi Halfa the next afternoon ("there isn't anything there except the train," is all we know about Wadi Halfa), followed by a two night train trip to Khartoum.

These are the ferries that you read about each year, the ones that sink and drown hundreds of people. It's easy enough to see why. We brim with humanity and illicity, maybe two times over capacity with no life preservers in sight. We resemble a refugee boat more than a ticket-selling mode of transport. Blackened wood floors for sitting and sleeping would be second class. Mounds of mattresses, boxes, makeshift bags, pots and pans, clothes and food litter the deck. The traders are the ones who look like they move entire households.

It gets worse above us in third class where the deck is open to the sun. At least we have a roof overhead and enjoy the light sitting close to the edge. Below are first class "stateroom cabins," a misnomer, for very pricey closets.

The lower level, our English-speaking Sudanese neighbor tells us, contains the engine room and the place where food is served. Toilets are in the hold. "Sometimes you are seeing the animals down there too," he says, pantomiming with his fingers. "What do you call it in English?"

"Rats?" I ask, grimacing.

"No, no, the little one."

"Mice?"

"Yes, that's it," he says and laughs. Just so there aren't any roaches crawling around me at night is all I care about. The roaches in Africa should be classified as rodents, they're so big.

An air of industry fills the deck as everyone goes about the business of mapping off their territorial home for two days. But with floor space, as with international affairs, sovereignty is a matter of careful vigil, lest you turn your head and a neighbor annexes your space. Many learn the hard way. Jim and I are protected by our foreignness; no one would dream of encroaching on the *khawaagas'* space.

I step and pirouette over bodies and legs and bags, and descend two stairways to check out the legendary hold in search of the boiled water that hotels and restaurants in Africa customarily provide. The air in the lower level feels stagnant and close. I open the first door. The squalor and heat take my breath—it must be a hundred and twenty degrees in here and so humid it should be raining. A grimy, blackened abyss greets me with smoke, enshrouding the human forms that move like apparitions in and out of view.

A loud metal-on-metal clanking makes communication impossible and tells me I'm in the engine room. Yet people line the floor, blinded by the light I've brought in. They blink like little moles roused from sleep. Welcome to the fourth class, the bowels of the earth, the bolges of hell, rich fodder for writers like Zola and Dante, who surely traveled on an Egyptian steamer ferry in their day.

A smiling, sweat-drenched man wearing a dirty bib-apron and a sleeveless soaked undershirt motions to come in, mouthing something and extending a steaming cup of liquid. It looks to be very black tea. *Or perhaps this?* he is asking, pointing to a large pot while ladling up a cup of what looks like hepatitis stew. Blue-white flames leap around the bottom of the large black pot. "No thanks." I smile and wave, and skedaddle.

Jim and I have a spot to call home and ample food we've brought with us. When the morning mist lifts, we enjoy some views, shelter from the sun most of the day—and some movement of air. Everyone seems in remarkably good spirits. An animated haggle breaks out, and all heads crane to see, probably an incursion of space. But that's the end of it. A sense of resignation fills the air for the long haul.

In five short hours, early afternoon, we resemble a floating shantytown, vertical blinds of every invention blocking the slant of the sun's rays—scarves, towels, umbrellas, pieces of plastic tied together hanging precariously by string or plastic from the ceiling and from each other. When a rare puff of wind comes, we all cover our heads as makeshift walls come crashing down amid cries of *Allahhh!*

The Nile widens, removing us from a good view of the shores and leaving us to take in each other instead. No problem, since the people-watching abounds. Many of our boat mates are clearly Egyptian, but most are darker skinned with close-cropped, curly hair that suggests they are northern Sudanese—Muslim black Africans who mixed with the Egyptians and Arabs over time. They usually stand above their Egyptian neighbors in height. The majority of travelers are men, though we also see women and families in second class. The men wear the traditional dress, the *jelabiyah* and scull cap, and the women, the *hijab*. The women's *hijab* in Upper Egypt has become more colorful than we've seen. Some travelers don regular street clothes and we see a few black African women wearing colorful *khangas* typical of southern Christian Sudan. Few countries vary more culturally between north and south than Sudan, the root of many problems historically and today.

Our boats slip up the Nile as quietly as a small city afloat. I guess we knew this couldn't be altogether relaxing. To the backdrop of competing Oum Kalthoums crooning love songs from the loudspeaker and portable boom boxes, people mill about restlessly—talking, playing games and snacking to pass the time. Some read the *Qur'an*. Some trawl for fish. Jim and I take turns reading chapters from *The Blue Nile* by Alan Moorehead. Young boys and not-so-young men climb like little monkeys from level to level and boat to boat while a self-appointed mayor waves his arms and admonishes them to stop. Some dip makeshift cans with long tenuous strings into the Nile to scoop up water for drinking—the same water used for cooling the water buffalo, taking lathery baths, washing pots and pans, and clothes. Just upstream, a man stoops at the water's edge, looks up to see two ferries coming, splashes water on his bottom and hurriedly pulls up his pants.

Some people cook on kerosene burners, undoubtedly a violation on any other boat. The smell of fried meat wafts on the air. The friendly Sudanese family who sit beside us carry food in stainless steel *tiffin* stacks with dinner spread out like a picnic in the country. Is it possible that the British learned the fine art of picnicking from their colonies? They share dates and sugar cane stalks with us. The husband looks remarkably cool and crisp in his white *jelabiyah*. They are returning to Khartoum after visiting a relative in Aswan, he says. We have a smiling relationship with the wife who seems very quiet, perhaps because she speaks no English. The two young daughters turn away when I smile at them.

The father casually asks Jim what he does for a living. This never goes well. Jim tries to explain the concept of landscape contracting. "I guess you'd say I'm a farmer. I plant grass and trees and plants, usually for businesses."

"Oh, yes, very good," the man chirps in approval. "So it is for their goats you are planting the grass?"

Jim smiles. "Actually we plant it to make the land look… beautiful."

"Oh, I don't understand. The grass is not for the goats? How else do you cut the grass?"

"Well, people in the US use machines to cut the grass, lawnmowers. Only American farmers tend to own goats," Jim says.

Our friend looks puzzled. "Ohhh," he squirms, "but this is a very strange custom, cutting the grass with a machine! What is the sense of having goats?"

Jim laughs a defeated laugh. "Yeah, you know, I have to agree. It is a strange custom."

Our friend offers us more dates. Jim takes rather long to retrieve one and thank him, hoping to perhaps put this conversation to rest. "So you are having cows, then? Do you give the grass to the cows?" he continues.

Jim shoots me a look. "Actually, you're right! That's what we do. We give the grass to the cows."

Our friend smiles broadly and nods. "Ah, good. That is verdy good. Otherwise, what would be the sense?" He shrugs.

"Exactly," Jim agrees.

As people finish eating, banana peels and vegetable skins and vendor bags get lobbed overboard. We're relieved to see that our friend collects his trash in a bag. "Can we put our trash with yours?" I ask.

"Oh, no problem," he says. "Yes, of course." He then gathers the trash together in one bag, walks to the railing and pitches the whole thing overboard, the white bubble bobbing conspicuously downstream.

At sunset, Oum Kalthoum is drowned out by a recorded *muezzin* making the call to prayer, more like a call to wake the dead. Supplicants face the mauve eastern sky, stand and kneel, bow and stand on makeshift prayer rugs. Dinner eaten, prayers said, life settles down to a comfortable pitch.

Our little society afloat has evolved our first day out. Colors fade and meld into night; reclining bodies are strewn across the floor in every direction. Since we still get little relief from the heat, Jim and I climb to the top deck. When the stars turn up full volume—not a single source of light to compete—the moving, lilting star show makes everything right with the world again. Flawed as it is, our humble abode has come to feel familiar.

We reach the temple of Abu Simbel in the afternoon of the next day and approach the four colossal monuments built by Ramses II in 1200 BC—for me, more impressive than the pyramids. The boats list as everyone crowds to one side, followed by a passionate reprimand from the loudspeaker.

These seventy foot high, seated figures carved out of monolithic rocks were moved when the upper dam that created Lake Nassar was built. The dam displaced almost a hundred thousand people and relegated other important archaeological sites and fertile lands, mostly Nubian, to a fishy grave.

Ancient Nubia or Upper Egypt ran from north of Khartoum to Aswan, present day Egypt. The black pharaohs of the Kush Empire ruled Upper and Lower Egypt for a century and were a constant rival of Egypt. The history and cultures of both peoples were closely linked for centuries.

In the evening we approach land. This is Wadi Halfa, the loudspeaker tells us, though we can see only a single derelict shack on the water's edge. The original Wadi Halfa, we learn, was once an important Nubian center of commerce. It too became a casualty of the dam when the town was moved in 1970. Beyond the shack, the so-called port stretches into a desert of nothingness, save a few mounds of sand and a palm tree or two. Today the once-thriving city on the bottom of the lake gives its name to no more than a transit stop.

The boat springs to life! Everyone pushes and shoves towards the exits as if we're engulfed in flames, a pressed block of dark heads and arms set against white *jelabiyahs*. Stretched out on land, our numbers are staggering. Jim and I hang back as the crowd swarms like ants carrying their nests across the desert. Following at the end of the line, we eventually sight a train silhouetted by the sun in the distance. At closer range, we see the cars overflow with people: people hanging out the windows, people sitting on top and people scrambling to get on. This journey has taken more out of me than I realized. The prospect of getting on that train fills me with a slow, gathering malaise.

I dig my heels in. "I simply can't go on that train today," I tell Jim. He needs little cajoling and agrees to spend the night and take the next train tomorrow. Our packs feel suddenly lighter as we walk around. And the people-watching has stepped up a notch.

The ubiquitous white *jelabiyahs* of the men still dominate the landscape, but we see more white turbans instead of skull caps. Darker skinned, tall young men dressed in regular street clothes, probably non-Islamic Africans, are there as well. I'm most excited to see more women whose presence makes the landscape finally complete. Local custom may discourage their going out on the street, but traveling from place to place necessitates it. They wear all the colors of the rainbow—brilliant fabrics and scarves wrapped softly about the head and shoulders—so beautiful and sensual. I've missed women. I've so missed their femininity these many months. Surely Jim has too.

The people's faces are dark like Africans, but with Caucasian-like features. "Ah, and these would be the Nubians!" Jim says, raising his eyebrows. Some people are lighter skinned. I wish everyone wore ancestral nametags. Other men and women have freckles sprinkled across the nose and cheeks. I have recently read that many of the more than one hundred ethnic groups of Nubia originally came from the Arabian peninsula.

We walk towards the west to discover a few sad tin huts that constitute the town of Wadi Halfa. Someone must live here, but there certainly isn't anyone selling food or rooms for rent. "Well, I'll just pitch our tent and eat berries off the bushes before I'll get on that train," I say.

"What bushes?" Jim laughs. We eventually find a man selling steaming hot, slimy-looking okra stew on the street, the only food we can find. I pray it's too hot to sustain parasitic life.

The okra man tells us business is always good when the train comes. "What do you mean?" I ask. "Doesn't the train come every day?"

"*Inshallah,*" he says, "about one time a week. Sometimes eet tees taking longer."

My knees go weak under me. "I'm sorry, why is it taking longer?"

"The train ees going when eet tees full."

This is not good news, and I pray it is wrong, as so much information in Africa is. We rush back to the train to find the ticket man. Yes, he tells us, the next train comes in seven days. Maybe. And no, there are no other train lines in northern

Sudan, no Red Cross planes and no camels going to Khartoum. The train is it.

We plop down under the weight of our packs to sort out our destinies. We have two no-choices. We stay in this God-forsaken desert outpost for at least a week or spend two nights on a train with no room whatsoever.

I feel like I can't breathe. The hordes of people set against the sun atop the train resemble a Medusan-type monster with waving snake tentacles. I've been a really good sport so far, but it's time to sprout wings and fly out of here. We both stand there mute, like condemned people. Being stuck, really stuck, is what I manage least well. Jim watches me closely as if I might crack and break.

Our foreigner novelty and a lot of smiling get us on the train. We step over people sitting on the iron steps and slide the compartment door open to find a seat inside non-negotiable. A piled-high entry is followed with an aisle of people and boxes and bags. "I'm sure the conductor will tell everyone this is illegal and clean this place up," Jim grins. I can't even laugh. The end of the car is filled with a family and their bags and food. Car-end after car-end, we're greeted with more blinking faces.

Survival in the desert slowly evaporates our *khawaaga* status. We are more bodies vying for space. The next car-end contains new tubs and buckets stacked in piles with no apparent owner. We decide to pile them higher and clear enough floor space for ourselves and backpacks. The owner soon returns— an Egyptian who delivers supplies to his Khartoum shop. He seems delighted to share his space and leaves his goods in our care to tend to more elsewhere. We are unspeakably happy. *Inshallah*, we will all have room to recline, even if in small balls.

The train leaves in an hour, our friend tells us, an hour longer than I think I can endure—much less two more days. In two hours' time, I am giving myself a pep talk, borrowing all the motivational sound bites I can muster about living in the moment and opportunities masked as catastrophes. We finally move. The stale, stagnant air of the humanity pressed inside is whisked out and cleansed.

The train stops frequently. All stops seem to be unscheduled, and no one ever knows how long they'll last—sometimes an hour, sometimes two minutes. Each time, men and women scramble through the high, narrow windows to quickly take a leak—the men bearing their backs, the women lifting their skirts and stooping. With a push from outside, they climb back in. Once the train moved as a yelling woman dangled half in and half out the window with no pusher from behind. Everyone rushed to her aid, grabbing whatever they could—arms, clothes and hair to get her back inside. It was painful to watch. Personally, I'll wait for as long as it takes to find a lavatory.

Two hours and many cars later, I find all the lavatory entrances barricaded and brimming with people and their belongings inside. What was I thinking? I decide to wait until it's good and dark and late before crawling out a window. Islamic modesty aside, watching a female *khawaaga* in pants stoop outside your window passes for great entertainment in the desert.

Jim and I awaken in the morning to find ourselves covered with the dust of the Nubian Desert. Our friend Abus must have slept with his other wares elsewhere. Four days without a bath, mopping up filthy floors, I haven't been this dirty since I was a very little kid. The prospect of a shower seems sweeter than anything I can imagine now.

An Om Kalthoum song, sad and pleading, plays in the next car. Abus comes to check on us, his white *jelabiyah* looking like a dirty wrinkled rag. We all share bananas and figs and groundnuts from the vendors.

Towns continue to be Islamic with basic stucco mosque structures and a few colorfully-decorated houses with child-like drawings that tell the story of the residents' *haj,* or religious pilgrimage to Mecca. My heart jumps when we see our first black African people with facial tribal scars.

"Do you think we could say we've officially entered the bush of Africa?" I ask Jim.

"Yes, I think we can."

At the next stop, Abus bids us farewell again, scales the ladder running up the car and disappears to the top of the train. Just like that. Before the train moves, a conductor in uniform enters our car-end from the outside door and demands that Jim and I pay first class prices since we're on the floor of a first class car. "You make a joke, right?" I ask.

That grills him. "No, not joking, madam!" Of course, this is extortion; none of the people or goats in this car ride first class, and he'll promptly pocket our money.

Jim and I look at one another, precisely of the same mind. "Excuse us," Jim says, "we were just leaving anyway."

We gather our gear and scale the ladder to join our friend. The top is open and airy and divine; no fighting for space up here. Abus is pleased to see us and shows us how to sit since the car bows and falls off on both sides. It's definitely a little precarious. We lash ourselves and our packs to the racks as a precaution. "You really slept up here last night?" I ask.

"Sure," he nods. I keep waiting for the conductor to appear and demand first class fare. When the train moves, the dry warm breeze buoys our spirits. Who would have thought first class was on the roof all along?

I think what I love most about Africa is the rich brown-red soil. Everything in Africa seems to spring from it: the deep brown people, the elegant golden-orange *khanga* prints the women wear, the animals on the plains—all complementary colors on a palette.

But the skies define the place most. The horizon stretches out unencumbered as far as you can see. The skies loom larger than skies should be, with starchy whipped clouds perched like mobiles. By day, they wrap Africans in deep blue and, by night, an immense canopy of pinprick lights. The people of the bush may lack material wealth, but they are rich in many ways. And I think they know it.

The landscape looks like paradise to me, slowly giving way to more and more green as we move farther south. As the last light of day fades, we hear tribal drums for the first time, signaling that we're really in black Africa. I hug my arms. More than anything else, drums are the soul of Africa, beating at night as they have for thousands of years, as organic as the acacia trees on the great plains.

I recall the words of European colonials who grieved for years after leaving the continent. Africa gets in your blood and always remains with you, they say. Back in England or Germany or Belgium, they feel forever displaced. But there is paradox in their words, which I am coming to understand. The love we all feel for Africa is not returned. It threatens to spit us out before we've scarcely begun.

We suck our sugar cane and revel in the exquisite sunset. Except for an occasional elephant beetle smacked in the head, life is as good as it gets.

SUDAN: THE CAMEL'S CRY

Most glorious night! Thou wert not sent for slumber!

Lord Byron

Khartoum has always been an exotic name for me that conjures up romantic images of the days of the Madhi. A *madhi* is a religious leader, a messiah actually, so the title isn't used lightly. And certainly not conferred upon oneself. But Mohammed Ahmed apparently didn't know that. In 1884, he proclaimed himself the Madhi of Khartoum, eventually delivering the city from the oppressive rule of Anglo-Egypt.

More than eighty years later, Hollywood decided to immortalize the great siege in the film, *Khartoum*. Let's be fair; Hollywood has always had difficulty portraying any ethnic class east of Europe. And billing top name stars is also imperative.

Still, I expected the great *caliph*—the prophet of God and servant of the Prophet Mohammed—to be a larger than life presence with a booming voice. Instead, he is of small stature with a voice that doesn't ring true. And no amount of squinting renders him Arabic-looking. When the camera pans in for a closeup, we realize the great Madhi is actually Laurence Olivier, wearing as much make-up as the women. Because the studio couldn't find a single Arab who could act?

It gets worse. General Charles Gordon, the eccentric British commander sent to evacuate the thousands of Egyptian soldiers from the capital, is played by Charleton Heston with an equally unconvincing British accent. The Atlantic Ocean must have been a great divide in the Sixties. The final blow is the throngs of honkie-American extras bearing phony mustaches, pancake make-up and thick eyeliner to pass as Arabs.

In the end, phony looks and accents aside, Jim and I are in Laurence and Charleton's debt. They first piqued our curiosity and moved us to see Khartoum for ourselves.

Khartoum bridges Arabia and Africa, east and west. An Arabic poem calls the confluence of the White Nile and the Blue Nile "the longest kiss in history." The largest country in Africa, Sudan is also one of the poorest.

As our train pulls into Khartoum station about 3:30 in the afternoon, the heat bears down like a mid-day burn. The streets and shops bustle with people just the same. It's the height of the dry season. A translucent veil of dust, a lovely beige-peach hue, hangs over the city.

We expect to see a city of stretched resources and poverty. We discover instead a worn but pleasant grandeur along the Nile's riverfront with an open, airy feel. Grand old umbrella-like shade trees and imposing stone museums and ministry buildings overlook El Nil Boulevard. Green city parklands, surely irrigated parks, seem to tame the dry, searing landscape. We have not seen rich green shades like this in weeks. Contrasting the lawns and orange-brown soil, the universal color is white. The streets are dominated by men, and the men wear white flowing *jelabiyahs* and *kefiyahs*.

The two Niles split Khartoum into three small cities—Khartoum, the capital, Khartoum North, and Omdurman, the largest suburb-city and traditional center, where we will look for lodging. The poor cousin of Khartoum, Omdurman is famous for its commerce and *souq*-market.

As we leave the river promenade, the streets become chaotic, teeming with people who mill around slowly—a flood to the senses. Streets are remarkably wide. Mostly two stories and white stucco, with some mid-rises, the buildings are flat-roofed—a nondescript mishmash heralding the tenuous and transient. Some are half-begun or half-demolished—it's difficult to be sure—but buildings that probably wouldn't pass any building code anywhere.

Open sewage runs along the street and goats feast happily on uncollected trash piles. *Khawaaga* floats on the air and follows us through the streets—often a greeting, sometimes a mother pointing us out to her child. Shop owners look up as they sprinkle water outside their thresholds to minimize the dust tracked in their shops.

Beggars *sans* arms, eyes, legs hang on our sleeves, making the hand-to-mouth motion. Omdurman seems to have more beggars than Cairo. Donkey-drawn carts zigzag around road ruts transporting people and market vegetables and fruit. Straight off, we locate our most important haunts—a *fuul* shop (beans and rice served in a bowl, Egyptian style), a fruit drink stand, a fig vendor and an Arabic coffee vendor.

But I am transfixed most by so many good looking people. The Nubians are striking people with rich dark complexions. Both young and old women have an unassuming beauty. I can't help myself; I stare with complete abandon. The women flash shy, striking smiles behind dark, limpid eyes—eyes as I've never seen. If only I could pull out my camera and photograph them; no one at home would believe this.

Many Nubian men tower above the crowds. The women wear pastel-colored scarves wrapped loosely about the head and shoulders, with more gold jewelry than we have seen in the hinterlands. Ornate gold earrings are commonplace, often three along the ear with a gold ring through the nose. Beauty tattoos, little dots and dashes on the feet and just below the lip, are permanent, not henna. Tattoos, we learn, were first worn by Egyptian women around 4000 BC, and the fashion later migrated to the Upper Nile through the Nubian women.

As if from another planet, black African men with short cropped hair and raised bubble-like scars that designate their tribe mingle through the crowds. They greet one another with a slap on the shoulder and a swift slap of the hands in a handshake.

Hotel space comes at a premium since refugees from Uganda flock to the three cities of Khartoum. "You may not be finding a room in Omdurman," a hotel owner warns us.

After searching for an hour, we give up in desperation, settling on a room inside a corrugated metal-roof building—a box with no windows. Two hard beds, a ceiling fan and a weak, naked light bulb that hangs on an electrical cord complete the furnishings—the kind of place you'd check into to kill yourself. A flickering, buzzing fluorescent light in the corner adds to the bad dream quality.

"Boy, this is some kind of record for the worst abode to date," I say. At least the sheets look clean. I'm wondering if this building was here last week. On a regular basis, we're told, the government demolishes stalls and buildings constructed without building permits, only to crop up like weeds in another few weeks.

Since we want to spend as little time as possible in our room, we walk to the ancient *souq*. The smell of leather and smoke and goat shit hang on the air with no place to go, not unlike all the air in Khartoum. Small smoke clouds billow out from a distant stall that we approach. An Egyptian man smokes a *shisha* pipe at a tobacco stall with *shisha* tobacco made from molasses and fruit—a welcomed smell.

But the smells sharpen again as we enter the animal section, which should be a shrine rather than a market, so many animals have ended their lives here. Illegal ivory fills stall after stall, followed by stalls of lizard and snake skins, then goat, sheep and gazelle hides piled high—as cheap as old curled paper. "Let's get out of here," I say. "This place is making me sick."

We pass the camelhair stalls—camelhair rugs, bags, saddles and shoes without end. No wonder camels are so testy—this is their fate after giving their milk, their meat, their wool and hides, not to mention lugging people around the desert with nothing to drink for thousands of years.

We want most to see the infamous Omdurman camel market, the live camels at the *Souq Abu Zeid,* a weekly Friday market. "What day is it?" I ask Jim.

"I think it's Friday," he says. We applaud our good fortune, but also question whether we can push our bodies any more today. Early tomorrow morning, we must begin the daunting tasks of registering with the local police station, obtaining a permit to travel south (since the south is considered a semi-autonomous region), obtain a permit to take the train and a permit to take photos—a nasty British bureaucratic legacy multiplied times three generations.

We need some coffee to think this over and return to our hotel street to visit the coffee vendor with two cinder blocks for seats. His thick, spicy Arabic coffee is as good as we've found anywhere, brewed on a charcoal burner atop a wooden crate in an old traditional Arabic brass pot.

Down the street appears Abus, our friend from the train who we left three hours ago. "Hey!" he spots us and, like a long-lost friend, runs with arms out-stretched. We tell him about our plan. "Yes, yes, you must see the camel market," he says, throwing his hands up. "I take you there!" He hails a taxi, of sorts, a rattle-trap Toyota with a back door that won't close properly. I guess this means we've decided. As we leave the city, the street resonates with *adhan,* the *muezzin's* call to prayer.

Many of the camels come from Western Sudan, Abus's home, he tells us, where a number of nomadic tribes are traditional camel breeders. The camel market is little else than a large field of sand, maybe half a football field, with men in white flowing *jelabiyahs* and long white flowing turbans wound about the head many times. Some don multi-colored or dark red scull caps. This is people and camel watching at its best. I am the only female to be found, except for the female dromedaries who stand or sit flat on their legs looking aloof and bored as they chew and chew.

A cacophony of complaints emanate from the camels as prospective buyers make them get up and down. Deep guttural peals mixed with what sounds like long belches and hisses only lend to people's lack of sympathy for the creatures. Camels are just misunderstood.

Abus loves his job of self-appointed guide of the foreigners, speaking loudly for others to take notice. He does seem to know his camels, explaining that the two-hump variety live in the Mongolian desert. The slender, buff-white camels are often bred in Dongola to the north, commanding high prices in Arabia for racing, he says. They are very loyal, intelligent animals.

We approach one that turns and promptly hisses and spits on Abus, its big yellow teeth flashing. "Do they bite too?" I ask quickly to swallow a howl that wants to surface.

Not to be upstaged, he wipes his face with his *jelabiyah* skirt and continues. "A young one of this breed is fetching a thousand pounds or more." And we all turn as an extraordinary sight in the distance catches our eye.

A camel and rider race as one across the horizon, looking like a mythical creature in a flurry of white tails whipping behind on the wind. A test drive apparently. We cup our hands over our brows to see against the sun. The camel gallops in a curious, confounding manner, its head drawn low, almost parallel to the ground. The legs reach out more in front than back, propelling the creature forward in spite of its odd posture. And then the show ends abruptly as they turn and cut back towards the market. Jim and I sigh in mutual disappointment.

Camel selling looks more like a male schmoozing-spitting-smoking *soiree* than a market. "So where are they making the sales?" Jim asks Abus.

His hand teeters up and down. "Plenty of business making right here." He looks at his watch and jumps. "Allah, it is getting late! We must go to the tomb of Shaikh Hamed Al-Nil to see the Whirling Dervishes. Come. It is close."

We arrive just as the last flash of sunlight sinks below the horizon—a sea of white *jelabiyahed* and turbaned men with tall staffs against the horizon. They surround the tomb that stands two towers high against the sky. We race across the field to join them. Much like the pilgrims who circumvent the Kaaba in Mecca, they chant and strut counter-clockwise around the tomb. *La ellaha illa Allah, la ellaha illa Allah, la ellaha illa Allah* (there is no God except Allah).

The head of the procession comes around. A Sufi *sheikh* dressed in dark robes carries a tall black flag with red trim. When the procession stops, old men dressed in white robes dance and whirl. A few tourists and children dance as well. The only women present are tourists. The sheer scale of the crowd, its voice moving slowly as one, become a kind of walking meditation *en masse*.

We stay until the last people disperse, savoring the last bit of a full evening. The same taxi that brought us returns us, in heaves and bumps, to our insufferable little oven in Omdurman city. In the dry season, Upper Sudan has to be one of the most inhospitable places on earth.

There is no relief at night inside our little room. The ceiling fan pulls down the dry, baked air heated by the metal roof all day. We turn it off; then back on. Even the geckos that flock like moths on the fluorescent light don't move. I wander down the hall in search of the bathroom.

Om Kalthoum music emanates from a partially open door. I walk by and glance in to see women belly dancing and giggling with complete abandon in a windowless room larger than ours. They are quite accomplished, singing with the music, as good as a sultan's harem, I imagine. Dressed in skirts and under-blouses, their soft jade colored fabrics fly like birds' wings. Yellow-gold jewelry jangles at their ears and wrists. This is the most wealth I've seen in Africa.

Surely I've fallen down a rabbit hole. They are Egyptian, I believe. But everything stops when someone spots me. I step away and all of them round the corner, giggling like little girls. They accost me and pull me into the room. "Come, come, please come." How uninhibited they seem.

"*Assalamu Alaikum*," I say, to which they smile approvingly. "*Wa'alaikum Assalam*," the matriarch replies. We stand there smiling, feasting on each other. They coo over me as if I were a new puppy. All of them, six total, have dark eyes and dark hair. They survey my blonde hair, my silver cuff bracelets and silver rings, my clothes—bantering among themselves while Om is left to sing to herself.

Three of the women are young, twenty-something; the youngest has the most striking smile of all. The other three women are middle-aged, vibrantly middle-aged. The matriarch encourages me to join in. I noticed before; she is the best dancer, with slow, rolling, sensual movements. She's well endowed with an abundant midriff, an essential for good belly dancing. I want only to watch her.

She coaxes me to follow her. Though I consider myself a decent dancer, this is quite something else. Smiling uneasily, I extend my arms, copy the wrist action and sway my hips. She nods approvingly. I feel ungainly and realize I haven't given my appearance a thought for months. Mirrors are rare in our budget rooms, and I've actually stopped caring about them. I can't remember when I last wore lipstick, and the single tube I brought melted a long time ago. Covering up lately has had a way of cloaking the female libido, and I can't say I've missed my vanity a bit.

But here it comes bounding to the fore again, and I am embarrassed for myself. In my pants and tailored button-down shirt, my clothes hang in folds, I've lost so much weight. Standing before these extravagantly beautiful women who are the essence of femininity, I feel like a virtual man. Where the matriarch effuses ampleness and curvaceousness, I am gaunt and flat-chested. Nothing on me could possibly jiggle.

Her dark eyes burn intensely as she sings with Om, flicking her head side to side. She knows she is beautiful. Her long, tapered nose is classic, a profile befitting of an Egyptian coin. I'm aghast at her sensuality; where did she learn these moves? The others drown out the music with their ululating peals—what the Arabs call *zaghrouteh*—the loud Arabic trills I love so much. I can't stop laughing; this is fantastic. Surely, the police will shut down our raucous party.

She takes my hand and entreats me to follow her movements as the others watch. There is simply no avoiding a performance. My teacher looks fortyish, a woman of some privilege, I suspect. Her skirt and top are silken, a deep golden orange-red. How heads would turn if she passed down the streets of Khartoum looking like this. But then she would never look like this on the street. Do most women live very different lives inside the walls of Islam?

The room seems to steam, we are so hot. The smell of bodies mixed with sandalwood hangs in the air. My partner's chest and midriff shine. The music becomes more rhythmic. The others clap as she sways and jolts her hips, jiggling her stomach to the lilts like a professional. Surely she's done this for a living before. A yellow scarf with rows of thin golden coins wrapped at her hips jingles madly like little tambourines. She anoints me by untying the scarf and wrapping it around my hips.

"I don't think I can jiggle," I yell to be heard, smiling apologetically.

"No, no," they protest and edge me on. "You must!" Oh, what the hell. I pull my shirt out of my pants, unbutton the bottom and tie the ends under my chest so my midriff shows, pushing my pants down on my hips. A flat concave stomach isn't exactly what I need. I try the stomach rolls. The girls whoop and clap; with more ululations, drowning out the music. My teacher and I look pretty good as she nods approvingly to the beat. Not bad for a *khawaaga*. But making my midriff shake is out of the question; there is simply nothing here to move. They squeal and giggle at my attempts. I'm a hopeless jiggler.

I click my hips instead. I can do that, with some body waves from front to back. They cheer me on with more ululations. All of us whirl now, the room awash with clouds of color. Speaking only the language of dance and laughter, I feel a warm acceptance from these women. They are like my girlfriends at home.

We would not envy them for the mores and veils we associate with oppression. But they are not oppressed, these women; one needs only to watch them. In the end, I envy them because they are completely comfortable in their own skin in a way I am not.

The matriarch smiles broadly, perspiration beading on her olive skin and blotching the fabric under her arms. We are all soaked, our hair matted around our faces. I jump when I see Jim walk by the door, no doubt searching for me. Wait one minute, I motion to the others.

The youngest joins us in the hall and invites Jim in, a veil wrapped across her upper body and shoulders now. We return to find the others covered as well, replete with shy, blushing demeanors. Talk about throwing water on a parade.

"WHAT is going on in here?" He smiles, marveling at the beauty and lovely energy that surround him.

A tireless Om continues to croon. Everyone sits, though we can scarcely converse, between their limited English and our pidgin Arabic. We learn their names and where they go. The matriarch is Leila. They are Egyptians, as I thought, and leave tomorrow for Cairo, the infamous Nile ferry trip. Surely they will take a car to Wadi Halfa, not that terrible train. We show them our route south on a map. Leila makes a sour face and shakes her head. Not a good place, south Sudan. They ply us with coffee from a flowered thermos, cigarettes, figs and candies. Even with Jim here, they are giggly and personable. After twelve o'clock, we say good night and search for the illusive bathroom.

Early the next morning, I dress quickly to catch my friends before they leave. I smile as I walk down the hall, anticipating the faces that will light up to see me again. An Om Kalthoum refrain still echoes in my head. I would love to visit their homes and meet their men. Pressing my ear to the door, no one stirs. I knock gently, smiling. I know the young one will answer, her eyes groggy and puffy but still beautiful.

I open the door gently and peer inside to find the room empty, as gaping as my disappointment—every remnant of the night before vanquished. Bed sheets fall off the cots, trash litters the floor, stale cigarette smoke hangs in the air. I never appreciated how ugly this room is.

They are traveling now, I'm guessing, their lovely fabrics and gold jewelry covered by their black *hijabs*. Do they ride in one of those black shiny cars with the tinted windows? Wherever they are, they are laughing and giggling.

A dot of light on the floor catches my eye. I bend to retrieve a small gold coin from the scarf of my dancing partner, and place it in my pants pocket.

SUDAN: THE BUSH IN DRAG

A man gazing on the stars is proverbially at the mercy of the puddles in the road.

Alexander Smith

Surely we could call it progress, that another train ride in Sudan doesn't fill me with dread. I consider myself a veteran of the trains now.

Jim and I continue south, a week's rest in Khartoum under our belts—this time four nights going to Babanousa and ultimately Wau. Our route seems unusually circuitous on a map. From Khartoum, the train travels west and south before heading back towards the east. "We have to avoid the Sudd," Jim explains.

The Sudd is the sprawling swampland that surrounds the Upper Nile as the river moves south. Our guidebook reports that it's the largest swamp in the world, bigger than the state of Pennsylvania… "with some of the remotest parts of Africa."

I rub the goose bumps that rise on my arms. I can't wait; or so I think. The train carries less people than before (three on a bench seat as opposed to six), but we're still at full capacity.

Few get off and then we pick up more along the way. In no time, we brim with people and look like the first train from Wadi Halfa. Jim and I are unfazed. We know how to do this now and climb on top when we need a change of pace.

Khartoum doesn't separate Arab Muslim Africa from black Christian-animist Africa, as I had thought. Men still wear *jelabiyahs* south of Khartoum, though dress slowly gives way to regular shirts and shorts with an occasional T-shirt or baseball hat. The mission clothes bags have found their way to the bush.

The Nuba mountains rise to our east. The great Nilotic plain remains flat and scrubby—inhospitable semi-desert with a few tenacious trees. The land becomes more sparsely populated as we continue south, the dwellings more organic. Brown circular mud huts with thatched roofs spring from the earth. Small compounds house various huts with separate quarters for people, their livestock and poultry.

In another time, I'd have seen these places as impoverished. *(How can you bear the poverty in these countries?* friends always ask.*)* Here, I see only a very different lifestyle; not poverty. Everyone who moves about, their cows and chickens as well, appear adequately fed. The cleanly swept red earthen compound floors, the lovely split-branch fences hugging the community convey a sense of pride. It can't be all bad when your living room is a vast blue sky by day and a canopy of white twinkling lights by night.

The change is palpable. We're in the thick of black Africa and the Sudanese bush now.

Facial bubble scars that reveal the tribe of their owners mark the faces of the villagers outside the train. Taken to the level of an art form, we see straight vertical cheek lines, cross marks, large H marks and arrows that point towards the ears.

Some people have rows of horizontal raised bubbles on the forehead. A V-line on the forehead that encircles the head, we are told, designates the Dinka tribe, often with bubbles lining the nape of the neck and chest as well.

People seem more leery of us—often shrinking with fixed stares, as if confronting wild animals. Fair enough. In a land of blue-black skin and rounded full features, faces devoid of color with sharp angular lines, not to mention straight white hair, are probably pretty scary.

Clothes become more expendable and begin to disappear. Most men wear no tops the second day out, and we see more and more loincloths. Hairstyles among both sexes resemble bird coifs that gather at the top as if held with a rubberband and stand straight up like the roof tops of the thatched huts. Others are plaited or have a Mohican-type style. But most people, men and women both, have a plain short-cropped cut.

The next day out, Jim and I are back on our perch atop the train. We are about three hundred fifty miles from Khartoum. Designated trees pass for train stops. The morning drags because the train stops so often. The driver seems to relish holding everyone hostage, whether it is ten minutes or thirty minutes or a slow-rolling five miles an hour speed, for no apparent reason.

Now, we've stopped again. People from various cars back go running into the bush. Some in the cars below jump out of windows to join them. Our new Sudanese friend Ali, who speaks decent English, scrambles down the ladder to follow. This is not going to be a brief stop. I groan and raise my umbrella to escape the midday sun.

The top of the train has now become too hot to touch. I don't know how Jim can stand it in the sun. For an hour, I sit balled up inside my umbrella's shadow, my feet protruding in the sun. Ali walks back towards us. He speaks to a man in Swahili who follows his words with long *ayyyss*.

"What was the commotion all about?" Jim asks Ali.

"There was a fight. Two men," he says. "One ees pushing the other off thee train. He breaks hees neck. When thee train ees stopping, the others are chasing thee bad one into thee bush and beating heem."

Just like that. Breaking his neck, beating him, these alien words strike my ear. I look back to the woods where the people ran and hug my legs. "They beat him to *death*?" I ask.

He nods. I hug my legs tighter. "You're quite sure?"

"Yes, that ees what they say, I did not see eet."

"And the other man pushed off the train died as well?" I have to ask, sickening myself more.

"Yes," he says, nodding, "straight away."

"Did you see either of them?" I ask, still clinging to the hope that it all isn't somehow true.

Ali shakes his head. "No, I have seen nothing."

Oh, the ready presumptions—that the one man was pushed, that the other was guilty. What if the one slipped and the other ran for his life precisely because he knew people would assume he pushed him? In the bush, all answers are clear; there is no need to question.

As we wait and wait for the train that refuses to budge, the words seep in more. I rest my head on my legs. The wood's edge keeps pulling my gaze back. The loveliness of the cool green trees haunts me, the trees that move slowly in a gentle afternoon breeze and separate us from a beaten, dead man.

Does anyone here care about what has happened? I realize that my world is really quite sheltered in the US. I read of terrible things every day, but the only dead people I've known died of causes everyone could come to accept.

But beating. Beating is perhaps the most personal and insidious of deaths—incremental and slow, blow by blow by another's hand—the mortal antithesis of family and friends gathering to honor a birth, to lift one up in song, a radiance of love flushing their faces. Surely the crazed faces and that last terrible knowledge—surely these images break the heart and make it stop.

I douse my face with our precious little drinking water. If we could only move, leave this black hole that gathers and implodes unto itself and consumes the light of day.

I feel light-headed, far warmer than the temperature is hot. I continue to huddle under my umbrella, as if to stave off this place. Jim turns to me, diminished and shaken as well. "Annie, we can't really be sure any of this is true. It could all be pure hysteria and rumor."

The train finally begins to roll and we clatter along again, a soothing warm breeze washing over us. There is no reconciling these events that come and go in Africa and hang on like malarial fever. They're all the same, and daily, found in the English newspapers in Khartoum, often back page mentions.

The "justice of the bush" stories, I call them. A man in a township steals a mango, or whatever, something of little consequence. Someone yells "thief" and the victim's flight confirms his guilt. Villagers abandon whatever they do to serve justice, to chase the evil man and stone him to death on the spot. For days these stories stay with me.

I wonder if Africans have always responded in this way. If this righteousness is indigenous or imported. And how far it could go.

"If we were ever witness to this on our own, could we hope to speak up without being killed ourselves?" I ask Jim.

"Absolutely *not!*" he yells, making me jump. Jim never raises his voice or uses absolute words like absolutely. "Don't even *dream* of reacting," he says. He knows me well.

"But Jimmy, how could we possibly stand there and watch such a thing?"

"You will have to *learn!*" he says, his eyes like a man possessed. "Just stay *out* of it unless you want to be killed!"

What are we to make of the kind, gentle faces and nods that fill our days, that allay any fears and make us at home in this place? These are the people, the same people who turn on their neighbors and strike them down.

Our perceptions are true, I'm sure of it. Africans are precisely as we see them, kind and gentle. But for whatever reason, fear and self-determination reign in the bush—answers are assured, the swings to action more accessible. Anyone wields power and absolute power disguises as absolute justice.

Jim and I climb down off the top to find a place to sleep on the car floor. In the middle of the night, we arrive in the town of Babanusa to knocks on the windows. Babanusa is southwest of the very center of Sudan. Everyone in town, it seems, is awake. *Shi* and snack-selling in the wee hours of the night are probably the main source of income for most people along this train line. Since travelers have all the money, they must be wakened just in case they might want to eat.

"*Mzungu, mzungu,*" a young woman calls me, knocking on the glass—a smiling infant with a red, infected-looking eye in one arm and bananas in the other.

"What does *mzungu* mean?" I ask Ali.

"Like thee *khawaaga,*" he says. "Eet tees Swahili for thee white man, thee foreigner, after the British. Swahili ees thee tongue of East Ahfrica—Arabic, Ahfricahn and Indian together."

"So it means 'white man?'" I ask.

"No," he says. "Eet ees meaning 'thee one who runs all over.'"

"How interesting. I like that name."

We encounter a curious, unendearing custom in Babanusa. Everyone—men, women and children alike—spit. And constantly, as if they find their own saliva distasteful or superfluous. The collective effect is bizarre, almost symphonic, as spittles pirouette through the air. The tacit rule seems to be that a spittle mustn't land any less than two meters away. As we settle back down to sleep, Babanusans move about in a candle-lit darkness, their voices subdued because of the hour, the sound of myriad spits smacking the hardened earth.

The people-watching just keeps getting better. As poorly as I'm feeling, adrenaline buoys my spirit. We begin to see loincloths and hunters with spears the third day out. An electric shock courses through me when I see my first buck-naked man. "Yeow," I exclaim to Jim, laughing. "I know we're really here now."

The women have skirts with fabric tops tied over the shoulder or a single garment tied at the neck and waist. Some are bare-breasted. A few wear leather sandals, some flipflops. But most go *sans* shoes, with feet and heels as hardened as leather soles.

The elders are easily recognized by their intricately carved ebony walking sticks and large smoking pipes.

While the small children seem wary of us, the older ones are curious. Like monkeys, we make funny faces that they copy, and we all giggle. Some kids laugh uproariously; others watch suspiciously and hold their ground, determined not to be moved.

The deeper we penetrate the bush, the more the tribes mimic nature. Men and women both wear jewelry. But like the male of the species in nature attracting a mate, the men of the bush catch your eye first—bearing more silver nose pieces, more beads around the head and wrist, more heavy silver bangles and anklets.

The hunters, the young men in their prime, resemble drag queens with colorful plumed feathers at the crown and colored stripes on the face. This is getting better than Mardi Gras.

But the outside world presses in, as it must. Alongside the beautiful man-birds are *the hats,* the cool guys donning the mission-bag imports. When it comes to accessorizing, the men of the bush can compete with the best of the world's divas.

We find colorful knitted hats—the full Bob Marley or close-fitting styles; baseball hats, the high standing trucker varieties or the regular Addidas or Yankees types; and women's Sunday-go-to-meeting straw hats with bows!—all worn by the men, not the women. The really cool guys, hats *and* sunglasses, beg to be photographed, especially the ones who wear bright pink or yellow women's sunglasses left over from the Seventies, with feminine upturns at the temples.

I *ache* to take a photo. But I learned my lesson well when the train stopped a few miles back. I suspected that pictures wouldn't be appreciated here, probably even feared. And then Ali warned me with a look as I raised my camera to sneak a quick one. Just a quick one.

A feathered young hunter talked to his friends, unaware of our presence atop the train. Someone else was obviously aware, though. A long thin object sailed past my viewfinder as I prepared to snap, the same time I heard the spear whistle through the air over our heads. We vacated "the penthouse" at breakneck speed, deliriously happy to be part of the crush of bodies in the car below.

The third night out, Jim and I are ecstatic to find enough room in the aisle of our car to sleep stretched out, our backpacks serving as pillows. Sometime deep into sleep, a commotion of people and a step on my foot wakens me.

I rouse to see a beautiful man-bird sitting against the wall in a corner recess in front of me. He holds his white ivory spear securely, as if ready for action.

The thin light shadows one side of his body. I sit up and look around, the entire aisle filled with people I've longed to see closer all day. I retrieve my glasses from my pack to see better, though a good view evades me still. Everyone's eyes follow me.

All heads lull in unison to the rocking of the train. A magical hush fills the car, as if everyone respects the hour. The sway and *clickitty-clickitty-clack* of the train is all there is in the universe, as sweet as a lullaby. I want only to freeze this moment in time. *Please*, I implore them, *just stay here with me all night*. A strange gurgle emanates from the sleeping Jim.

The silver light glances the hunter's high cheekbones, concealing his eyes. I'm certain he stares at me, taking me in coolly, and I him, as we try in vain to see better. There are no electrical lights in the bush, only the light of the night coming in like staccatoed flashes across his body. The slender legs of two women curl next to him, the tops of their bodies engulfed in shadow.

The hunter's lean and muscular legs stretch out in front of me, heavy silver bangles on the ankles. His skin reflects a dark smooth luster on the chest and legs up to the upper thigh. He probably wears a loincloth. A silver and beaded string attached to the hair at the side runs under his chin like a choker. Feathers behind his head are set in the shadow. His hair is matted as if in plaits and pulled back.

One of the two women scoots closer, I suspect, for the sole purpose of staring me up. She's the intrepid one, not he. Fine with me since this goes both ways; I get a closer look too. I smile, with no response from her. The light reflects silver jewelry at her ears and neck. She is older with deep furrows from the sun lining her eyes. Perhaps she's the hunter's mother. As if reporting, in an odd, almost ventriloquist tone, she mutters a cacophonic tongue that rises and falls with pops—presumably observations about me. What I'd give to hear that translation.

My eyes have become more accustomed to the dark. I confirm that everyone around us watches cautiously, not sleeping at all. Perhaps they all got on at the last stop.

Not to be left out, the other woman worms her way in and gets closest to me, her scent strong and musky. She examines my glasses and braves a touch of the hair down my shoulder, rubbing it lightly between her fingers. Younger than the other, her hair is plaited in my favorite bird coiffure. The light silhouettes a lovely profile, a long neck and strong jaw line. She giggles and I giggle. I smile and she giggles, her white teeth catching the light.

She braves a touch to my head, stroking my hair; she is very gentle. I see her eyes a bit, bright and wide in the pulsing light and an upturned smile as she cuts the silence with a loud exclamation. Both women stroke my odd straight white hair now, as if stroking a pet. I only hope this doesn't catch on with everyone else.

I wonder what they think. Children and women both like to pet me. A child on the Aswan ferryboat reached out and touched my hair, and her mother followed suit. "Good hair," the mother said.

The young woman flattens a hand squarely on my chest, moving down—I can only assume, to feel for breasts. She's feeling pretty carefully. I can't help it; I have to laugh out loud. I love her *hutzpah*, or innocence, whatever it is, and throw my head back with teeth flashing.

I've sounded an alarm. The women fall silent. The hunter pushes himself erectly against the wall, his jaw line set in the light. His head turned towards me now, I see white and colored lines on his cheeks. Perhaps he's a warrior, not a hunter at all. What would a warrior in Africa do these days? And why would a warrior ride a train? I sit back on my pack to allay their concerns as we all continue our watch fest.

The assumption with *mzungus* goes that we have more reason to be afraid of them. I know I'm no threat. I don't carry a spear and I'm civilized, right? I live in a civil society that enjoys a host of laws to prove it.

But he thinks the same thing. We marginalize his society, though it's just as complex. Maybe he isn't an aggressor at all; maybe he only carries his spear for protection because he can't be sure who's a threat and who isn't.

I think he's more justified to fear me. Not just my frightening appearance with teeth flashing in the night. But my kind; the kind who buys the rights to his oil or his forest or his diamonds, with no regard for him or his way of life.

Sitting there with his impotent little spear poised, he could never know where the real threat lies.

I put my arm under my head for support to watch him, to await the morning light. *Clickitty-clickitty-clack* the train lulls us. He is quite beautiful, my man-bird; the male of the species. His body rocks and sways, as his eyes close slowly.

The train screeches to a stop. I sit up, my eyes burning. Jim and I and only a few others occupy the car. A curtain of white floods the dusty aisle and fills me with desolation. The space where my friends sat lies empty, stark, as if the night was just a dream. My throat tightens. I feel like bawling, really letting it out like a child.

All I wanted was for the sunrise to come, to finally gain a full glimpse into my hunter's face, to see his eyes and the colors of his feathers.

SUDAN: THE OTHER AFRICA

*Things are as they are. Looking out into the universe at night,
we make no comparisons between right and wrong stars, nor
between well and badly arranged constellations.*

Alan Watts

There is another Africa that lies beyond the stark beauty of
the *National Geographic* pictures, the idealized pictures
of a sunset taken in the early morning when hues are soft. Only
hours later, washed in the blinding light, the same landscape
reveals a scratchy moon-like desert, anemic river beds, a terrain
that annihilates anything with wheels, an invisible universe of
parasites and an unrepentant justice of the bush.

When I find those pictures in magazines now, I see them
through different lenses: truer lenses that penetrate the shadows
and frame the starkness as much as the beauty. Because the
starkness defines Africa most.

Sure, there were presentiments of things to come aplenty
before Jim and I went to Africa. Health books catalogued
pages of diseases, poisonous snakes, mosquitoes, ants and
parasites unlucky travelers could contract or meet up with.

Why does anyone travel to Africa? we asked ourselves. The inoculations to last a lifetime and a veritable medicine cabinet of prophylactic pills would have deterred most people.

But travelers are wagers, betting on the odds that the rewards will exceed the risks—which they do; they always do, even when things don't go as planned. For some, the journey is made all the more delectable by the risks. And you soon forget all those nasty diseases.

On the second leg of the African trip, as we stepped off the steamboat from upper Egypt and met the train brimming with people in Wadi Halfa, Sudan, signs appeared like great airplane banners trailing the sky: *Africa is more than you bargained for. You don't belong here!* I saw them all right, and they were there again at my back for the long train ride in the bush when the men were killed.

The only way out was south at the time, the way we were going. We were quite stuck and I doubt we'd have left Africa if we could. Hanging off trains, baking in the sun, going without proper food and water in order to get where you're going is the way Africans do it—must always do it. In the end, amidst my loudest complaints, it always felt right to be close to them. Our presence was a kind of solidarity to endure life as they did and not whine about it, at least publicly. But I never dreamed we'd endure hardship at that pitch for the whole trip south into Kenya.

The train arrives at its final destination, four days and six hundred miles from Khartoum. Wau is the second largest town in southern Sudan. Blazing through hundreds of miles of inhospitable bush to find so many people in the middle of nowhere takes me by surprise. Wau exudes friendliness, an unassuming, small town feel. Large green shade trees line the main road up to the Jur river market.

An inauspicious history contributed most to Wau's large, one million-plus population. Once a Dinka-tribe stronghold, Wau later became a Muslim enclave, a military camp of commercial slave traders in the nineteenth century. The French and English later turned it into a fort and prison. Today, Wau remains ethnically mixed with a strong Catholic church presence.

African "high life" music fills the streets and buoys us, envelopes us, a welcome island-type beat. Wau is lovely, our first black African community. Instead of a verbal hello, people greet each other with both arms raised vertically. To the curious "tsking" sound our fellow train riders have brought with us from northern Sudan, presumably an Arabic gesture, we now hear a "clucking" sound made with the tongue in the back teeth when acknowledging something.

Three guys we met on the train, two Aussies and an American, walk with us to the Wau youth hostel (a youth hostel in the bush?) where we find five more travelers—from Germany, the US, England, New Zealand and Canada—two more guys, two girls(!) and a sixty year old Brit. They've all been trying to get the hell out of Wau for three days, they say.

A brilliant fuchsia bougainvillea bush at the front of the youth hostel somehow gives me hope. A pawpaw tree next to it reaches for the sky, big bulbous yellow-orange fruit ready for picking. Out of hardened cracks in the earth, they thrive. If they can do it, we can do it.

Our abjectly basic rooms with screenless windows look like heaven. Jim and I check the mossie nets for interlopers inside. Mosquito nets are standard fare everywhere, more standard than bedsheets, which our beds lack. The draped, fine white gauze box makes me feel like the Queen of England and is one of my favorite things about Africa. We slip into the pocket sheets we've brought from home as fast as we can—a single sheet folded and sewn up one edge—and sleep soundly through the afternoon. Surfacing in the early evening, we enter the courtyard to find our new friends pooling resources for the evening meal. They invite us to join their smorgasbord of canned fish and beans, local veggies, fruit and bread.

In fleeting moments, we resemble friends gathered at home, congenial and lively as one. But left alone in our private worlds, The Quandary—being stuck in the thick of Africa—presses in on us. We don't resemble free people, which is apparent in our slow, measured movements, our sighs and distant stares. We all dig deep to hold it together.

There are exceptions among us, to be sure. Ben the New Zealander and Katie the Canadian are a romantic item—and judging by the way they can't keep their hands off each other, quite recent. Their tanned good looks, her long blonde hair, his wavy mop of hair could land them the leads in a movie, they're such a fetching couple. Since they've progressed well beyond the smitten stage, they go missing in their room for long hours, cooing over each other when they finally surface. They make Jim and me feel like an old married couple. Jim confesses he has trouble watching them too.

"What's the love hormone called? Dopamine?" I ask Jim. "The least they could do is share some of all that dopamine."

Then there's Wes, another dopamine monger from Australia who got religion and brought it along. He serenades us with cheery Christian songs on his guitar day and night (yes, he travels overland in Africa with a guitar). And he's just learned to play, he says, figuring there would be plenty of time to practice on the trip. When he doesn't sing, Wes is a man on a mission. On the pretext of a friendly discussion on religion, he works you over like an African plying his *ugali* before he eats it. I give Wes a wide berth.

In the balance, the ten of us are a remarkably good match and the rest of us forgive Ben and Katie and Wes for not being miserable. With nothing else to do but wash clothes and catch up on journal-writing, we talk out every subject under the great African sun, change partners and do it again, volley a badminton birdie with no net and play games of our own invention.

I walk past Henry and Wes and catch bits of conversation. Henry says in his most proper English accent, "No, I wouldn't say that at'tall. I don't see "these people" as pagans. Animists actually worship the spirit of God in everything, don't they?" I bend to retie my shoe. "Isn't it rather lovely to consider a tree spirit or a river spirit?" Henry muses dreamily, a few beer bottles at his side. Wes returns Henry's thoughtful comment with a vacuous stare.

Later I pass Ben and Katie and Wes to hear Ben say, "Yes, but who are we to impose what we think is right on other people?" Man, Wes just can't give it up.

The guys drink heartily at night, save Wes and Jim, who's too cheap. Fortunately, neither Jim nor I care much about beer. Though inexpensive here, beer still raises the budget exponentially. The array of vegetables to be found in the market is limited, but you'll always find plenty of beer and bars to go round, a colonial legacy.

After two days, we realize Wau may not be the African mecca we'd choose to be stuck in. The town is dirt-poor with an erratic water and electric supply at best. Staples like canned milk and beans, tea and sugar are completely unaffordable for the locals, collecting dust on *duka*-shop shelves until desperate *mzungus* like us pass through.

But there's a coffee shop in town which makes everything else better. A restaurant serves goat and *ugali*—the mainstay of East Africa brought by the Arabs—a firm, porridge-like cornmeal formed into balls and dipped into meat essence. No one seems to eat greens. Jim and I live on canned sardines and sorghum bread, a local grain-staple, complemented by a couple of sad potatoes purchased in the market and cooked on our little stove. Hot tea, another colonial legacy, always rounds the meal off.

I'm still not rational about the subject of crawling another twelve hundred miles overland in a truck to Nairobi. Locals say Red Cross planes land in Wau to drop off medical supplies and sometimes take passengers. If only we could wing our way out of here and watch that long dusty road pass from above. If a plane doesn't come, the prospect of living out my life and dying in Wau sounds better in comparison. Rides being what they are in Africa in the rainy season, we could be here for weeks, the locals say.

If anyone questioned what in the world they were thinking when they came on this trip, it has to be Henry, our most unlikely travel mate. A small, gaunt, chain-smoking Brit who loves his "cuppa" (tea) as much as his beer, Henry is quintessentially British, with flashing white hair and white bushy eyebrows that make him look older than his sixty years. There's a roguish handsomeness about him. In search of a little adventure, he says, he is making his way to Zimbabwe to visit his sister and her husband.

We all muddle through the hot sticky days, switching off books, walking languidly around Wau. Then the rain keeps us indoors. The more it rains, the bleaker our prospects for land transport become. The weekend approaches and the Feast of Easter has begun. No trucks are moving and all municipal offices are closed for four days. The southern road, we're told, is closed due to flooding. This was the scenic, tribal and animal-filled route we wanted to take. A three to four day trip on the other road could take a week or more.

Henry and I slip away from the youth hostel and find a pediatrician in the medical clinic who we ply with questions about the illusive Red Cross plane. When will it arrive in Wau, what are the chances we could get on; what would it cost? Definitive answers are rarely forthcoming in Africa. The plane brings supplies, he says. It *should* be coming soon, but they don't know when. The last one came several weeks ago. Or maybe it was a month. But as long as the rainy season lingers with heavy downpours in the evenings, the plane can't land on solid ground.

The prospect of a lifeline that might deliver us from this cloying dampness and mud, and the prospect of a worse trip south consume me. If a wish in earnest ever single-mindedly materialized an object from nothingness, it should be mine, so fervent was my plea. "So what are you thinking of doing?" I finally broach the question I've been afraid to ask Jim.

"I want to go overland. That's why we came here, right?" he says. "But look, Annie, it's fine if you want to fly to Nairobi. You could relax and do safari research until I get there."

Equally obsessed, looking like birders, Henry and I walk around town with eyes and ears lifted to the heavens—the very stuff that religion is made of. Henry and I are bound by our mutual faith and supplication. Another week of this and we'd be prostrating ourselves before some graven image of a plane, and Wau would be witness to the apotheosis of a red piece of scrap metal.

The two of us walk back to the youth hostel while debating the benefits and pitfalls of marriage. Why, I'm not sure; but we always debate. A confirmed curmudgeon on the subject, Henry argues the pitfalls which probably accounts for his protracted bachelorhood.

We join Jim and share a can of English stew Henry has lugged hundreds of miles from England. It's amazing what tastes good in the middle of nowhere. I usually hate almost anything canned. Jim and I even enjoy canned spinach now, which looks like an abomination. We top the meal off with a hot cuppa, imported Lorna Doone cookies and some homemade Sudanese beer to go with a Frankenstein movie at the Barbara Hotel—all in all, a good evening that makes us forget our troubles.

Something's astir at the youth hostel the next day. Wes and Peter and Sofie, the German girl, gather their things to leave. The afternoon of our sixth day, the other group's ninth, a truck has arrived at the garage where trucks pass through town. "If you want a ride," Peter tells us, "go and talk to the driver at the coffee shop."

Henry, Ben and Katie, and Paul and Mark, the other Americans, sit with the driver in the coffee shop when we arrive. He speaks pretty good English. The truck is a UN truck filled with wheat headed to Juba, the largest town in southern Sudan. We are to pay him for our ride, he says, and all ten of us can fit. He will leave in about an hour. Mark and Paul run whooping and yelling out of the shop, turning heads as they go.

Matters with the rest of us are more complex. Ben and Katie huddle in discussion while Henry and I look at each other. I feel strangely inert. The earth moves too quickly on its axis. From my side, Jim watches me: "So what do you want to do, Annie?"

"What are you going to do, Henry?" I ask.

He shrugs his shoulders. "I dunno," he practically whispers. I weigh my non-options. The Red Cross plane could be weeks away, or not come. Another truck could take weeks as well, and I might be in for a horrible time traveling alone.

As we walk back to the hostel, a breeze stirs and the air suddenly cools. We look up to see the sky darken ominously, sending down torrents of rain that don't relent through the night. The cloud spirit has lent us more time to think.

In the faint pre-dawn light, seven of us stand ready at the garage with backpacks and gear in tow, Wes with his guitar case. At least we all got a good night's sleep under our belts. Henry and Ben and Katie keep the faith, opting to await the plane that I've begun to think never existed, that's just an African folktale or something. Ben and Katie are so in love, they won't even notice the passing days. Henry unfortunately will.

The sunrise is glorious, the air fresh, as we climb up and claim our spots on the large flat bags of wheat. Two locals accompany us and a man carrying a rifle. We are ten in the back, the driver and the "turnkey" guy in front. The "turnkey," we note, basically provides anything that's needed by the driver, mechanical or otherwise—another set of hands for the trip. The driver looks our age, early to mid thirties, and is shorter and lighter skinned than most Sudanese. The turnkey is young, maybe twenty, and tall and sinewy like most Africans. Jim and I figure he works for the ride south, maybe meals too. Both are men of few words.

"What's with this guy with the rifle?" I ask Jim and Peter.

"The government requires vehicles moving in certain areas of southern Sudan to be escorted with an armed guard," Peter says the driver told him. "Due to the Ugandan raiders at night."

I am touched. "Isn't that nice that the Sudanese government wants to protect us?"

Mark smirks. "I think our guard is meant to protect our cargo!"

"But wasn't the war in Uganda over last year?" I turn and ask Jim.

"Yes," he says, but the unemployed military who still hold guns continue to create havoc."

Alarm sets in. "Oh gees, and you knew this before we came here?"

"I knew it was going on in Uganda, but not really Sudan," he says.

"The driver told me it's bad. The Ugandan raiders are poaching, stealing and killing at night," Mark has to add, a remark that suppresses all further conversation.

Everyone sits quietly pondering the raiders. By now, most of us have had some experience with the justice of the bush. The truck kicks into gear and the lovely cool breeze clears my head. There's no sense in worrying about those raiders now, I tell myself, though I know they'll haunt me like departed spirits for the rest of the trip.

I look back at the sky over Wau, fully expecting to see that damn plane swoop down as we ride off. It would be just my luck.

The scenery looks like a spaghetti western: flat, unchanging, with sparsely spaced acacia trees on both sides, white secretary birds hovering in the branches like vultures. The truck bounces and waddles across large, interminable ruts that are more like a construction site than a road. We weave back and forth and round the larger holes, though there's no avoiding many of them. I'm grateful to our driver who slows for his human cargo before the blasting blows that nothing can cushion. Sofie and I hold our heads as if they might break.

Our protector with the rifle inspires no confidence, and even threatens to do us in. His rifle bounces wildly up and down next to him, the barrel pointing straight at my head at times. Jim and I move to the back of the truck, a much bumpier ride. But we're thankful that the sun hides behind the clouds most of the day, making the temperatures quite bearable.

A late afternoon rain drenches us like wet dogs, but clears off after an hour or so. The wheat begins to smell. The potholes in the road fill with water, which means the driver can't gauge their depth. Paul starts the frenzy of pulling wet clothes from his pack. We all join in until the back of the truck is strewn with patches of color.

After twelve hours, we stop to camp. Jim and I cook up some veggies on our little propane stove, brought from the Wau market. Night comes early close to the equator so we all roll out our sleeping bags after we eat. The driver motions for us to sleep under the truck, presumably for our protection. I situate my bag parallel to the truck; I'm not sleeping between any wheels.

The next day, the sun sends down full solar power unencumbered by a single cloud. Before nine o'clock, long sleeve shirts come out. In another hour, we look like *sheikhs* of various persuasions, donning turbans, bandanas and baseball hats with skirted bottoms. Peter takes off his shirt. We pass suntan lotion around, but I notice no one shares their water.

Water is life in Africa and the bush teaches you how dear it is. African women carry water on their heads from the river or in heavy tins hung from shoulder yolks, often for kilometers. Few things reinforce conservation better. As we cross bridges, women often congregate below at the river's edge, talking and laughing as they wash clothes, pots, hair, whatever, during the hot midday hours. *"Jambooo* (hello)," we yell. *Ayyyy,* they smile and wave.

Our elevation must be lower. The road becomes flowing streams with intermittent breaks of land. Then we ford a small river. Only the trees at the side can tell the driver how the road follows. Swirling jetties of water signal a deep hole. The truck stops, and the turnkey hops out to check the depth, descending into the hole, the water hugging his thighs. Some ruts seem to swallow us. The engine strains and we lunge and skid. Many times, we tip so far that I'm sure we're going over.

I feel like a rodeo rider. Sitting on the wheat bags with no exposed railing makes it impossible to get a good grip. Some of us manage to secure two fingers under ropes that latch the bags in. We hold onto each other too. Paul grabs the Sudanese woman in mid-air as she nearly careens out.

I raise my guard. We are days from civilization if anything were to happen. Even the medical clinic in Wau, two days away now, would be hard pressed to help with a life-threatening need. "What would we do if anything happened to us out here?" I raise the question to no one in particular.

"Oh, no worries. I've heard there's a Red Cross plane in case of an emergency!" Peter laughs.

All eyes hold fast to the road, brows drawn, jaw lines set. I look over at Peter, who always makes me forget myself. The unflappable cowboy, he meets my gaze with a silly expression of incredulity. "Bloody hell, this is dangerous, isn't it?" He giggles.

"Oh nawww," I yell over the whining engine in my best Aussie accent, a pathetic one actually. "What makes you say that?"

It's consummate Africa, thrilling and terrifying.

Right on cue, we approach the bottom of a truck, an over-turned truck on its side up ahead. It seems like half an hour before we reach it. It happened last night, the locals tell our driver; someone was seriously hurt. The passengers were taken to a village some distance from here. Empty beer bottles en route to a brewery sit on the roadside on a small dry spot, piled high in crates.

We can only pass to the left of the truck where the road falls off and the water flows more heavily. Undaunted, our driver does what he has to do. He jams the floor shift into gear without waiting for the turnkey to test the waters and revs the engine. We crash into a hole, leaning us so far to the left that I come face to face with the water, poised to bail out. The engine whines and whines as we skid and shimmy. The only thing that saves us from tipping is the mud that holds our wheels like glue. The truck defies the laws of gravity, leans more still, then rights itself, whipping us about like rag dolls.

We are finally royally stuck. Jim, Mark and Peter jump down to help. The driver instructs the rest of us to stay put. The turnkey and three local men wade into the yellow-brown water and push from behind. The engine screams as the truck lunges and stops, lunges and stops, the rest of us watching from atop the swaying elephant like the colonial ministers of the Crown or something.

We shimmy back and forth in the mud with no apparent gain. Like watching an hour hand move, we ease around the over-turned truck. Our truck must be part bulldozer. At the first dry spot, the damage is assessed: a flat tire and a bent wheel well that probably caused the flat. For more than two hours, the turnkey beats the damaged tire off its rim, repairs the inner tube, fills the tire with air from the hydraulic brakes and bangs out the wheel well with a hammer. Great theater. A family of baboons watch, blinking and chewing from the trees on the roadside while the *mzungus* sit baking in the sun like potato chips.

When our comrade finishes, we all applaud the wet, greasy, mud-strewn likeness of him that he must wear until we make camp that night. But we presume too much; we aren't leaving yet. The engine grinds, catches then stalls, grinds, catches then stalls. Water in the fuel tank, the diagnosis passes back, and our turnkey begins siphoning out water with a tube in his mouth. Jim explains to me that diesel fuel floats on water so the tube siphons from the bottom of the tank until the water is removed.

"Isn't that dangerous?" I ask.

"Uh, yeah!" Jim says, just as the turnkey coughs and spews diesel fuel.

Few jobs can rival the thanklessness of this one. We all stand up and applaud him, for what that's worth. *Asante sana, Asante sana* (thank you). The motor sputters and starts without incident. The baboons have gotten braver, edging closer and picking up strewn objects as if looking for food. I can't even contemplate what life might have been like if this truck hadn't started.

The sun weakens with the afternoon hour, still warm on sunburned faces and hands and legs. We are all burnt and parched and out of drinking water. Moving at such a snail's pace today, I'd be surprised if we've covered ten kilometers.

We camp later than the night before just outside a village. The driver and turnkey leave to retrieve a new supply of drinking water. A walk into a village sounds like the cultural highlight of the trip, but we're all too whipped to go. Some local women dressed in brilliant gold and wine-colored *khangas* wander into our encampment bearing fruit and snacks for sale. Their white teeth flash like lights against their dark, almost blue-black skin and brightly colored fabrics.

They unload rattan baskets from their heads to show us their offerings. A young, wide-eyed girl with plaited hair parted down the middle sells Jim bananas and cookies with crème filling, the first real sweet we've seen in days. The women speak their own dialect and also talk to the driver in Swahili, the common language of East Africa. The dialect has probably changed many times along our route.

The younger women eye the *khanga* I wear. One encircles me to view the print that came from a shop in Khartoum. They're also interested in the way I've tied it. Most African women tie their *khangas* at the side. Mine is my own double-knotted-designed-not-to-come-off tie secured in the front, obviously not the *right* way to do it.

Khanga designs and colors, even the way one ties the fabric, have become artistic expressions of tribes and villages. Words printed along the border often convey a proverb or place of origin. *Khangas* are probably the most useful tools in Africa. After their lives as a skirt or headpiece, they are slung around the shoulders to carry babies, food from the market, firewood, whatever. I often sleep on mine or use it as a beach towel.

Jim and I can't be bothered to cook tonight, so we eat our mainstay, canned beans and sardines. We each polish off a whole package of crème cookies with tea, wiping out tomorrow's supply, and clean up for bed. I am almost giddy with the anticipation of resting my bones.

The cool, smooth feel of my sleeping bag, the exquisite star show overhead, the mere prospect of sleep wash over me like love. I let out a sigh, a slow soulful sigh. The rifle man shoots me an odd glance. "*Lala salama* (good night)," I say to him.

"I ask you," I say aloud. "How many people can enjoy such pajama parties?" Stretched out flat in my sleeping bag, face to the heavens, I am smiling a shaman-type half smile that is sublimely content.

As exhausted as I am, adrenaline surges through my ears. The star gazing in the middle of nowhere is as good as it gets.

So I take in the night canopy which seems larger here, the stars more crystalline, the Milky Way closer. As I finally drift off, the *pop-pop-pop-pop-pop* of gunfire sounds in the distance, an automatic weapon-like succession.

"Jim, did you hear that?" I whisper. Everyone is asleep. A few minutes later, an animal cry in the distance perforates the quiet. It's a veritable Wagner symphony out here. I close my eyes. *Let them all come and get us, the raiders, the animals, whomever, I don't care.*

We all awaken in the morning to arms and faces riddled with mosquito bites. Jim holds the record for the most. The third day brings renewed river-fording with another stop to beat out wheel wells and siphon out the fuel tank. Clouds follow us all day and deliver up a monsoon-like rain in the afternoon, the first time we've experienced this kind of downpour. When the rain finally breaks, everything comes out of our packs, our clothes blowing in the wind like laundry flags.

Ah, the irony. Jim and I dragged our feet for weeks way back in Turkey and Syria to avoid the flooding in Africa. Though the rainy season was supposed to be finished last month, we can safely say that it's still very much here.

In the late afternoon, we stop on the outskirts of a village while the driver and turnkey load up on gas and supplies. Jim and I and Wes decide to go into the village. I feel depleted and light-headed as we walk. People move about slowly and take great interest in us without gawking. In town, young boys run alongside narrow bicycle wheels, *sans* tires, pushing them with long, thin sticks held in the wheel rim. These recycled toys—wheels and little trucks bent out of wire with moving wheels and plastic bag people sitting inside—are the only toys children have in the bush.

We walk into the setting sun, everything silhouetted from behind. I look up to see people on the street part as a young boy, maybe twelve, runs towards us, yelling and wielding a long stick. He overtakes an emaciated dog in front of him, its bones protruding through its skin. I realize he is yelling at the dog. He turns and raises his stick, beating its small frame across the back, a hollow dull thud I'll never forget. The dog's submission is complete, without protest or yelp. He relents almost gratefully to death, his pathetic frame lying hairless from mange and hunger on the dirt. Most amazing: his body goes stiff with the last blow, as if he wasn't fully alive before.

Jim, Wes and I watch in horror, paralyzed. Passing locals turn with some interest; a beaten dog on the street is apparently all in a normal day. The boy's face shows no bravado or malice, as if he acted out of a sense of duty. I feel extremely agitated and begin to ask people around us if anyone speaks English. Jim is at my side, ready to save me from myself. A young man nods unconvincingly that he speaks English.

"Come, please," I say and lead him towards the boy and the dog. "Can you ask him what happened just now?" The young man has large clever eyes that consider my request suspiciously.

Looking down at the ground, he speaks to the boy, then answers to me. "The dog tees biting someone, eet tees, you know, (motioning at the head), what tees thee word?"

"You mean mad in the head?" He nods. "I'm sorry, I don't think that dog was rabid," I say to Jim and Wes.

Jim fidgets. "Annie, please, it doesn't matter."

I have seen how some little African boys taunt dogs without mercy, how they like to wield power over things weaker. And the poor creatures put up with it and put with it, perhaps for a lifetime. Or they manage to run away.

"So if a dog bites a person, you know it's mad?" I ask the boy. The young man doesn't translate. I try to relax; I know I'm scaring them. "Please could you ask him?"

"Yes," my translator says slowly without asking, "if eet bites, eet tees mad." He knows the answer already; we all knew the answer. I breathe deeply and fold my arms to my body, finally impressed with the futility of this. Jim's and Wes's faces are misshapen with discomfort. I could definitely get myself killed in Africa. At least we deal with children now.

The young boy turns and dances off. The young man doesn't move, a great hulking unease hanging on his frame.

"Thank you, I appreciate this," I manage a smile and shake his hand. "I'm just upset. Forgive me. Thank you so much for helping me."

Learning to stand on ground that constantly shifts takes some getting used to. It's harrowing actually. I consider these kids. Does the ground shift for them? They seem to know what is right already; there is no conflict here.

These are the moments I want somebody to airlift me out of here. I'm so tired. I don't want to try to understand Africa anymore.

The three of us say nothing as we walk back to the truck. It's not about the dog anymore, who's clearly better off dead. But it is about death, which influences everything and defines the way we live. Death seems to come too cheaply in Africa.

In the US, our daily diversions buffer our awareness of death, perhaps by design. Death has become opaque in Western society. But Africans know it well and live with it intimately each day. Which seems to engender a kind of fatalism.

My eyes have become accustomed to the landscape these few weeks in the bush. No, I haven't lost half my children to disease or wild animals, or watched my closest family and friends die. But we've received a stream of subliminal messages before this dog incident—the gunfire of anarchy at night, the deaths on the train, the stonings in the villages—they've become all too commonplace in our short reference.

Jim and I found something we weren't looking for. Our initial desire to be close to Nature brought us instead uncomfortably close to the nature of things—the disorder just below the veil of civility. Everything is different through this lens that I've inadvertently borrowed. There is no right or wrong in Nature, no judgment or morality or wisdom. Or pretense or virtue. It is what it is. There is only impunity in Nature.

The bush is an eat-or-be-eaten world that confirms, cries from every carrion carcass, that Darwin was brilliantly right. There is only the rule of Nature here and, those who live within it, become part of it. In the city, it is altogether different. In the city, we are removed from Nature and can speak more readily of right and wrong. But here in the bush, man's attempt to civilize his own nature rings hollow. Mores and laws seem futile in the face of it; I question how men can really live by them. It's as if someone disconnected the guy wires that underpin the values I've always taken for granted. I feel anchorless, confused, my belief system turned on its head. And it upsets me all over again that I question what I believe to be right.

It rankles through the pages of my African journals: the terrible prospect that life is insignificant. We live and thrive, or we don't. It doesn't matter. That's the way it is and life marches on. The countless animals that live to be eaten, the countless Africans taken by disease—all of us—hold no specialness in Nature.

I've watched it among our fellow travelers. We all feel it: this growing restlessness to our days in the bush. We don't laugh and joke as we did, and spend too much time brooding.

This is how insurgents psychologically recondition their victims, erase their old belief system in favor of a new one. Recruits are trained in these very kinds of places, in rural areas or the desert for extended periods—places removed from civilization where a new reality can be created outside the rule of law. A constant level of adjustment and discomfort ensure the desired change. The old ways, and the old mores, are shed. An extremely unusual person might remain unmoved, but I question whether anyone can.

The fact is, no one coerced Jim and me. We took in our environment through osmosis, whispers in our ears at night and propagandist videos by day, a world hostile to our own. Gurus and philosophers since time memorial have explored the delicate nature of civility, the edges of sanity, the illusion of self—things that terrify us, that lurk inside psychedelic dreams. I can tell you that the gurus speak the truth; self and society and civility are all gossamer structures of our own invention.

I am grateful that Africa led me along this fragile, tenuous edge, but I will be more grateful to get to the city soon. Because I am certain that all this fuss will evaporate as soon as we reach the bustle of the city, resolute once again in who we are.

We return to camp for an early night. Our clothes and packs are dry, but we roll out our sleeping bags to find them soaked. Our wheat cargo now reeks. I want to have a good cry. Not only are the dogs in Africa doomed to a miserable existence, but now we will deliver rotten wheat to starving people.

The fourth day, we enjoy the luxury of talking again instead of holding on for our lives or trying to keep dry. Bright white clouds accent a deep blue sky, but rarely block the sun. The roads are almost dry with potholes that seem prosaic. We begin to sight palm trees and some unusual rock formations. The truck moves at a good clip and the warm breeze feels delectable. Families of baboons watch us along the way, hiding in trees, then running out on the road as we pass.

We've traveled over five hundred miles in four days, almost two hundred the last day. As the truck enters the outskirts of Juba, we're all smarting from the sun and feeling a bit dotty. Even tanned Peter is burnt. I am a mess—new sunburn on top of old, burnt puffy lips that have cracked and split, a sunburned scalp and no moisture whatsoever inside my scabby nose.

We approach Juba. I think people call Juba an "urban settlement" because it doesn't measure up. A nondescript landscape of gray and tired, one storied houses and *dukas,* with spotty markets and an unpredictable water and electric supply, don't pass for a city. The concrete structures and tarmac roads we associate with cities are missing too. Juba is also one place you never forget to take your malaria pills. The open sewage system and surrounding swamps make it a prime breeding hangout for mosquitoes, flies and all things winged.

Despite its southern locale, Juba is decidedly northern in character, Arabic and Muslim, developing as a key commercial stopover for northerners. Wherever you walk, Juba looks like an African town, though its suburbs of more than eight hundred thousand people qualify it as a city. All problems aside, Juba looks like Oz to me right now. I like its unassuming character and welcome the range of hotels, guesthouses and restaurants where we can actually sit down and order a meal.

Two days later, an exhausted, disheveled Henry wanders into the African Hotel where we stay. You can't keep a good cuppa down. Henry, Jim and I have a reunion dinner at the Greek Club with Peter, Mark and Wes (a restaurant with tablecloths!) When the Red Cross plane never came, Henry tells us, he took the next truck out of town. His truck took the same road we did, but made the trip in three days instead of four. The waters had receded and road conditions were greatly improved.

Henry tells us about their trip and the hardships they endured—where he sat in the cab of the truck! I try really hard not to dwell on the fact that staying back would have been better. The men take refuge in their trip of hard knocks. As we listen quietly to Henry, I am green with envy; the men are under-whelmed.

Two days later, Henry, Peter, Mark, Jim and I depart from Juba in the back of a long, empty trailer—our most irrational act to date—which begs the question: are the short and long terms effects of jarring, rattling and pounding bodily organs over a period of multiple hours worth a single ride? For me, the answer is resoundingly no; I've had it.

"Jimmy, I'm sorry, I'm getting out of here," I finally announce.

"But here? There's nothing here!"

"I know. But there's been nothing around since the first fifteen minutes when I couldn't stand it. Starving to death or being eaten by lions has to be better than this. I can meet you in Nairobi if you want, but I'm not going on this truck." I bang on the window of the cab where the driver and friend listen to African highlife music.

The driver tells us Torit is about six kilometers down the road, if I can just hold on. Six kilometers is six kilometers too much, but OK, all right.

Jim and I get out at Torit and hug our friends who have come to feel like war buddies of sorts. Our separation comes so suddenly, and it's unlikely we'll see them in a big city like Nairobi. Henry is the hardest to leave; he has no one to mother him now. Resolute in my decision, we wave goodbye.

The terrain has become greener, downright verdant since Juba. Torit is a pleasant little town with colorful *dukas* and good markets, even a hospital and airfield. People are friendly and children run with the bicycle wheels and sticks and homemade trucks. The women wear more jewelry here, mostly beaded. Naked babies wear beaded strings around the neck, wrist and hips and colored plastic rings around the ankles and wrists.

Two little boys chaperone us to the guesthouse. They are remarkably happy kids, their bright eyes and white teeth flashing. The guesthouse looks closed, the front door locked. With a downward sweeping hand, they motion for us to follow again. Jim and I laugh and follow like obedient children. We walk to another guest house, this one smaller and derelict-looking. A policeman in a Bermuda shorts uniform walks out. "Is this a guest house?" Jim asks.

"Thees ees the police station," he smiles, and confirms that the guesthouse we just left, the only one in town, is closed for repairs. But we can sleep here under the veranda, if we like, he adds. Since gunfire rounds sound in the distance, we opt to sleep on the very hard porch instead of pitching our tent.

But that night, I am awakened by something in my sleeping bag biting me. A flashlight confirms white ants. "Since when are ants active at night?" I ask aloud. In a frenzy, I jump up, turn my bag inside out and shake it like a possessed woman. It's the ants or the Ugandan raiders. While Jim sleeps on the veranda, I pull all the tent gear out of his backpack and pitch it on the open grass, where the raiders will trip over me if they come.

The town bustles at 6:30 in the morning and we're surprised to find Torit's market nicer than Juba's. Healthy-looking fruits and vegetables abound and shops are well supplied with consumer and household goods for sale. Jim buys a pair of sandals made out of recycled truck tires.

Our guidebook tells us it's possible to go into the bush with a ranger in Torit to see the wildlife. The ranger we finally find, Ranger Benjamin, is Torit's only ranger. Their single Land Rover has been broken for three months. Even if he had spare parts, he'd first need a new battery and petrol.

The poverty of the south, the civil war and the Ugandan raiders at night have made wildlife preservation in southern Sudan impossible, he says. Illegal weapons are easy to come by and the Wildlife Administration's 303s can't compete with automatic weapons. Poachers hunt wildlife for food and commercial gain. The department is under-staffed, underpaid and lacks transport or communication—about as bleak as conditions could be. The local people have always lived off the bounty of the land and lack the education to see wildlife as a valuable resource.

As Jim and I play with Ranger Benjamin's orphaned red monkey, he tells us about a truck that moves to Kapoeta later today. We arrange a lift with that truck in town and leave in the afternoon. Though also empty, we figure this ride will be better since it's a heavy dump truck.

We soon discover this driver has a death wish and wants to take us with him. I can scarcely hold on and the mass of black and blue bruises on my legs and arms threaten to come together as one. When Jim saves me from nearly sailing over the edge, that's it.

We bail out at the next police station, wherever. The policeman there insists that we sleep in an abandoned derelict house on station property. We're on the outskirts of a drought and famine area, he says, where things happen at night. I dread the drive tomorrow, with images of hungry, longing faces clawing at the sides of our truck. There is no avoiding these areas if we want to reach Kenya. Looking back, our challenges during the train trips to Wau seem so mundane.

Jim and I eat some ground nuts and go to bed. The policeman brings us boiled water. We are almost out of food and there are no shops. The abandoned house where we sleep is riddled with bats that won't settle down. Uh, the smell of bats. I sleep with arms wrapped over my head, toilet paper up my nose (we still have toilet paper!) and breathe out of my mouth.

"Good night and Happy Halloween," Jim says, smiling.

"It's really Halloween?"

"If Halloween is still on October 31st."

"How fitting to spend the night with bats." I marvel. And how truly impressive that Jim knows what the date is. The passage of time completely evades me here. The only relevance a calendar has in the bush is to mark the seasons.

My dated journal entries tend to keep me in the real world most, though I haven't written in them these past weeks. Our days have been reduced to rise, move, eat, drop; rise, move, eat, drop. Time seems oddly foreign, almost superfluous. The bush doesn't even feel like the same planet.

As Jim snores, gunfire sounds in the distance. I stuff toilet paper in my ears too. The bush is surreal; sometimes I think I'll wake up like I did on the train, when the beautiful man-bird was gone. And until I wake up, I am sleep-walking. That

I'm not really afraid confirms it. I'm often not afraid in my dreams, because I somehow know they aren't real.

In the morning, we hitch along the roadside for a ride. By bush standards, a fair number of vehicles pass us by, but they all head north. As evening comes, just when we give up for the day and walk back to the police station, three trucks come in sequence. But they're heading north too. A fourth one with smiling *mzungu* faces approaches and comes to a screeching halt. It's Ben and Katie! *Jambo! Jambo!* We're elated to see each other, and of course they're going our way.

When I ponder it, it isn't such a great coincidence we've found Ben and Katie again. There are just so many grooves in the earth moving north and south in Africa. We share the back of the truck with three others. First, is our obligatory armed guard. Next is Francis, a Kenyan who worked in Uganda as a teacher before escaping over the border on foot, walking twenty miles a day for eight days. He seems very well spoken. Then there's Max, a Frenchman with dark, curly hair and a deviant smile, almost as if he's on drugs. He shows us a spear he says was thrown at the truck.

"Thrown at this truck?" I ask.

"*Oui*," he says, smiling proudly.

At a brief stop, we encounter half-naked warriors with spears and grimy faces who eye us up suspiciously. To break the tension, Max smiles broadly, with open arms, and expounds something in French that sounds conciliatory enough.

Jim later translates. "He said, 'dear fellows. We know it is very hot, but let us be reasonable.'" Maybe I'm wrong about Max; maybe he's actually a statesman. One of the warriors raises a spear, or perhaps he merely inspected it; we didn't wait to see. All of us, save the guard, get the same idea to drop quickly and huddle behind the truck's wooden sides.

The terrain becomes more varied and hilly, a welcome change from flat. As the sun pales and the tree shadows reach farther across the road, we stop at another police station where we must spend the night. We are still about three hundred kilometers, a hundred and eighty miles, from Lodwar and thirty miles or so from the Kenyan border.

All of us, Francis and five *mzungus*, hop out and walk towards town. The truck driver yells something in Swahili which Francis translates. "He says 'be careful of the people.'" We all look at one another. What does that mean, especially since it's broad daylight?

We are still apparently some distance from Kapoeta, as no buildings are in view. The land is a veritable desert, bleached and dusty. Nothing could possibly grow or graze in this wretched terrain. The large acacia tree canopies, covered with white dust, confirm the lack of rain. We walk over a rise to see people congregating below, maybe fifty or sixty moving about, as if waiting.

As we near them, the difference hits me immediately. Never have I seen so much jewelry in Africa. Their tribal dress, too, is as striking as we've seen and contrasts the bleakness of the land. "The Turkana people," Francis says.

The Turkana are pastoralists, we learn—tall and slender-necked and proud. The women jangle as they walk under the weight of necklaces—orange, and red and green beads pyramiding like little hula hoops from the shoulders to the upper neck. As many as a dozen little silver hoops line the edge of the ear, some with a large leaf-shaped silver earring hung high on the ear. Silver cuffs on their hands, wrists and upper arms catch the light, a coarse amalgam, but still attractive. Men and women both wear necklaces made of giraffe and elephant hair, Francis tells us.

A rose-colored, striped fabric is worn across the shoulder by men and women alike, probably the Turkana tribal design. Goat skin hides are the most common clothing. Some of the men are bare-chested with loincloths, their muscular cheeks flashing as they walk. Leather strips line the head and extend across the crown and brow. Plain thong-type leather straps are worn as sandals. No Addidas or Nike charity bags here.

The men and women also wear silver studs or hoops or long j-shaped pieces pierced through the bottom lip. "What is on the women's heads?" I ask Francis. Pulled up into a ponytail-type fountain with braids on top, their hair is caked with something brown.

"Mud and dung," he says. Some women have tomahawk-type cuts with long plaited braids beaded at the ends. The elder men wear a clump of hair at the crown of the head like a bun.

A man who must be a chief dons a feathered headdress. Warriors or hunters carry beautifully carved wood spears and elders carry u-shaped wood pieces that look like a brace for sitting anywhere they please.

We all mill around, watching each other like animals on opposite sides of the fence at the zoo. Wary, unfriendly looks mirror the inhospitable land. People stop to talk to each other. What is their purpose here?

Pale streaks line the dark arms and legs of many, as if they haven't washed. I survey the others. Most are dirty, actually. Elbows and knees resemble shriveled cabbages, whitened and chapped.

Max has a slow trail of gapers who follow him and catch up when he stops. A gangly "elder" wears boxer shorts under his goatskin and removes a small leather pouch from a shoulder bag. (The elder is no older than most of us, because elderhood begins at age twenty-nine; life expectancy is about fifty-something.) He extends his hand and opens his palm, little balls of golden dirt catching the sun.

We all crowd around. What are they—an hallucinogenic, an aphrodisiac? *Bangi* (marijuana)? Max asks. He picks one up, examines it closely, takes a smell and opens his mouth to take a bite. I jump. "Eeeiiii!" Francis starts. "What are you doing, mahn?" My first suspicion about Max was right.

The elder grabs Max's hand. "*Dahabu! Dahabu!*" he says, pointing to the hills.

Max's eyes narrow. "Gold?" The man nods. Max has another look. "Gold?"

The elder nods again. "*Dahabu.* Geld. Wun hunnerd pounds," he says.

"Bloody hell, a hundred pounds?" Max asks. The man nods. Sounds like his agent works on Wall Street. For all we know, these morsels are worth thousands. But that's just it. Who knows?

Jim and I decide to adopt the moving target philosophy. A young girl with smooth blue-black skin and big doe eyes scurries up to me and displays a fine leather vest filled with sewn handiwork and cowry shells—little marine snail shells used in African design and ritual. This looks like a Turkana ceremonial piece, and such a fine piece, I'd mount it on a wall rather than wear it.

"Sorry, I don't have pounds," I say. In an African nano-second, the international exchange is made. "Ten dollars," she says, holding up both ringed hands. As desperate as I suspect she is, she doesn't give me the pleading eyes and wringing hands. She's a proud one, this young Turkana, her eyes fixed on the vest as if holding her breath.

Ten dollars is a lot of money for an African; it's a lot of money for us in Africa. Our very plain local hotel rooms cost three dollars a night. Jim and I haven't spent ten dollars in weeks. On the other side of the Atlantic, I recall how many times I part with ten dollars in the course of a day. And this is a charity case if ever there was one. The only reason I waver is because I will lug it in my backpack for months.

Jim leans in with a furtive aside. "The real price is less than half that. Offer her five dollars and take four." Of course, he's right. But still, I know it took her weeks to make. I only wish the money could be shared around. I pull out my money concealed in a pocket hung around my neck under my blouse.

I slip her a five dollar bill and three ones. Of course, she doesn't expect that much. I receive my first unabashed Turkana smile, quite lovely. She takes both my hands to thank me, as the other women around us watch and smile.

I turn to see Katie standing with three women; she examines their necklaces closely. What a coup. How did she manage to insinuate herself in their fold? I ease my way over. The beads are handmade, porous and crudely hewn, though rich in color. One woman removes a number of strands from her neck and offers them to us, presumably to buy. We smile and shake our heads no. Now it's our turn. They all crowd around to examine our earrings, my silver cuff bracelets, our hair, my glasses. But mostly our eyes; Africans are fascinated by colored eyes. Their smells strike my nose, strong and musky, and then acrid—part the women themselves, part animal urine, Francis tells us, applied for good health.

They touch our hair and blouses, then our breasts. I can understand confusion about my gender, but Katie looks very feminine no matter what she wears. Both of us begin to squirm, feeling like picked-over fruit at the market.

Max rejoins us and the three of us walk towards the path that leads back to the police station. Another elder approaches Max, a true elder, bony and bowed with too little hair for a good plait, a young shy girl at his side. Why do people go straight for Max? Maybe it's because he's shorter and less daunting.

The elder also packs curious smells and jabbers on in Turkana, pointing to the girl. I catch the word "pounds."

"*Ohlala!* Only five pounds?" Max exclaims loudly, turning heads. (*Do the French really use "ohlala?"*)

"I don't get it. What is he selling?" I ask.

Max raises his eyebrows and fishes in his pocket. "The girl!" he says.

"The girl? Are you sure?" She averts her eyes and turns away when I look at her, thirteen years old at most.

The man's face lightens as he anticipates a sale. Max is scaring me. "Maxxx! What are you doing?"

He laughs and throws his head back. "No, sorry. I don't think so," he says to the elder. "I'm too young to give up my virginity." But the joke evades the elder who looks confused and angry, the veins flashing in his neck. For once, Max has stopped laughing. "No, no. No girl." He raises his arms as if in a holdup, his cheeks flushed scarlet as he musters a smile.

Our odiferous elder's gestures become sharper and more desperate as he changes his terms. He points to the young girl with one hand, then to me with the other and crosses fingers, breaking into a full rotten-toothed smile. I've been reduced to Max's chattel, his cow. "Oh no, I think he *likes* you," Max giggles. "Who would have thought?" The mere prospect sends a jolt down my back. Max smiles demurely. "And so? What to tell him?"

I stumble along the path back, my mind working faster than my feet. At home, our idea of desperation is being snowed in for a few days with no television or electricity. I wouldn't know how a desperate person thinks—the true pragmatism of poverty. That a child could be expendable. I'm guessing this child is the only thing this old man has left to barter.

Francis feels compelled to defend the elder's honor at the campfire that night. "No, no, eet tis not about the money. He wants a better life for the gurl than thees Gawd-forsaken place."

He smacks his palms together. "From the moment we are parents, life ees saying no.... eeet tis saying no, you cannot keep thees child. Why else are Ahfricans having six, seven, eight children?" he says, raising fingers on his hands. "The disease and the drought and the famine take them from us. They are our only security, and their children theirs. Who will tend the cows and gather thee firewood and look after thee parents in their old age?" He makes that curious tsking sound with his mouth. "No, I tell you, eeet tis not lightly that a mahn would give up hees child," he says, striking the air. "Not a'tall." He shakes his head.

As we drink our tea after dinner, Francis tells us about Sudan. "Thee only reason travelers like us are able to traverse thee country ees because of a verdy fragile hiatus," he continues. "Sudan gained eets independence from Egypt and Great Britain in '56. Since then, the Arab north has waged war on thee Christian-animist south. Finally, a peace agreement declared the south an autonomous area!" He throws his arms up. "But oil has since been discovered in thee south. Oops, we didn't mean eet. I have nooo doubt that thee north will recant their word and wage control again."

"Thee north would be happy if thee famine took care of thee problem for them. And everyone ees knowing about Eastern Equatoria's famines. Thee UN, thee World Health Organization, all of them. It has come for yahrs as surely as thee wind ees blowing. Where are they now? There is no regard for thee south," he says, flicking his hand as if shooing a fly.

Suddenly the meaning of the images I saw are clear. Why in the world didn't it dawn on me before? We are smack in the middle of the drought lands the policeman spoke of. That Francis speaks of now. It must have been the beautiful jewelry and colorful fabrics—the things we equate with wealth—that confused me. Finally, I thought to myself when we arrived here, finally, a tribe of some means in the bush.

But I realize that this is the way the Turkana dress every day. The tribal jewelry and fabrics we've seen for hundreds of miles coming south are as emblematic as they are beautiful. They define these people's place in the African world. Like a birthright, even the poorest Africans of the bush proudly wear the colors and symbols of their tribe each day.

I should have seen it. Why else is Kapoeta a desert in the wet season? Many seemed uncharacteristically cool and standoffish, almost surly. And dirty. Of course they were dirty; there is no water to bathe. They moved as if in slow motion, the elders resting at the sides of the paths, sitting on their heels. And vacant stalls stood bare like wooden skeletons—a market place with nothing left to sell. The people come here each day, clinging to the familiar. And I recall there were only a few children. Where were the children? Have they died? It is too extraordinary to consider. Is it really possible for the world to allow an entire town to slowly languish and starve?

Francis tells us more, by way of the driver who comes through here weekly. There is no more water in the wells of Kapoeta, he says. The water is not flowing until the Kenyan border. For weeks, the Turkana people have killed off their goats for the meat and drunk goat's milk or goat's blood for liquid. They will soon run out of goats. "Thee driver ees saying that Lodwar ees worse," Francis says. We are all silent, each indulging our fears in our own way.

Ben asks the obvious question on all our minds. "Do we have to pass through Lodwar?"

"Yes," Francis says. "Eeet tis the only road pahsing to Nairobi."

Sudan's problems are more complex than Francis says, Jim tells me. In addition to the tensions between north and south, annual drought and famine, and civil unrest pouring over from Uganda in the south—Libya's war with Chad destabilizes Sudan's western borders. Displaced people flood into Sudan from the south and west, our Francis being one of thousands.

In the predawn night, the driver shakes us to rise quickly. He wants to leave Kapoeta before sunrise. We pack while he revs the engine. No one speaks or looks back, as if we leave a hit-and-run accident.

The terrain remains inhospitable, desolate and rocky. Larger mountains rise up in the distance to the west. We reach the Kenyan border post in two hours, brush off our passports for the first time in weeks and unceremoniously drive through. As crazy as it sounds, I am sad to leave Sudan. And the prospect of Lodwar fills me with dread.

We roll into Lodwar in the early evening just before sunset and pull up to a bar, a *nightclub,* the driver calls it. Blaring regae music with an island feel greets us and business is brimming. A curious entrée to Lodwar. Ben orders beers around to celebrate our huge milestone: Kenya. Jim and I split a Tusker beer.

When we rise to leave, the beer goes straight to my head, feeling more like two beers since we haven't eaten all day. I am wary, waiting, when we walk out, as if someone will pounce. Ben and Katie and Jim and I sit on concrete pieces outside the bar to eat our only meal of the day. Jim and I share a tin of sardines between us and throw the empty container on the trash pile. And then the objects of my fear take breath and come to life. Barely.

Stick people approach us, Dali-like caricatures of women and children who walk uneasily. They make piteous faces with hand to mouth gestures, tapping their mouths like all the beggars in Africa do. The difference is they are not just without food, they are dying. Looking like survivors of the camps at Auchswitz, I can't imagine how they will live out the week without help.

Though they languish, they are polite. More than anything else, this rips me inside out. They don't push or grab our food from us. Don't people who are dying have the right to yell and make their needs known? Jim and I give them money. A child retrieves our discarded sardine tin from the trash pile and fingers out the remaining oil. The other children huddle close to watch us—two boys and a little girl, each less than ten years old.

Their heads seem too large for their shrunken bodies, their eyes sunken and too large for their heads. The younger boy, maybe six, with big brown eyes looks vacuously into my face. He has no eyelashes. His clothes hang on him like rags, dirty and torn. He wears a make-believe watch on his wrist, a green piece of cloth with a bottle cap face up and broken piece of glass inside.

I want to at least acknowledge their presence, their humanity, and turn to take the woman's hand in mine. But I give her hope, so she pleads all the more, her face contorted in pain. We can't do anything for these people and can't bear to watch them anymore. We are strange people, we *homo sapiens*. The four of us turn in towards each other, talking uneasily, as if they aren't there.

Those five remain indelibly marked like scarlet letters in my conscience, two women and three children. We couldn't save Lodwar, but we could have saved five. We should have taken them with us to Nairobi on the truck. We should have insisted they come with us and taken them to a hospital. I should have held those precious children in my arms and rocked them.

Ben, Katie and Max go to town to find lodging, excited to sleep in a bed again. "Hurry," the driver tells them, "the rooms fill up fast." Jim and I and Francis stay with the truck just outside town which will depart early in the morning. As hot as the Kenyan night is, I cannot keep warm.

These towns called Kapoeta and Lodwar live on the edge of the world. When we leave, we'll find that nothing in time and space connected them, that they never even existed. Because raucous reggae bars can't pack people in while others go to a barren market as they've always done, milling about, waiting, disappearing a little each day. And tourist hotels can't resume business as usual with little children wearing make-believe bottle cap watches outside, their time running out.

And people of means, all of us, can't possibly bear witness and do nothing. Such disparate worlds cannot exist, except perhaps in a vacuum. People cannot starve in a world of plenty.

We set out in the early morning darkness. After two hours or so, we wave goodbye to our driver and Francis who continue west. An ailing Land Rover picks us up. We finally limp into

Eliye Springs on the western shore of Lake Turkana in the early afternoon.

Elliye Springs is an oasis in the desert. A lovely German family takes us in and shares a beautiful meat and potatoes home-cooked dinner with us. The evening ends with a soak in a mineral spring under the stars.

An otherwise perfect reentry is tainted. Our acculturation back into the real world feels tenuous, too much too fast. Beds with sheets and hot water on demand seem extravagant. And the child with the play watch haunts me still.

The hotel owner gives us a ride to Nairobi in the morning. A colonial type, he speaks with a very gruff voice, which I assume is a cold. But no, he offers straight off, someone once tried to strangle him. Oh, OK. As we load the car, Turkana women who work at the hotel gather together and bid us farewell with tribal singing. Their voices are so beautiful and strong, it gives me chills.

To reward us for all our bad rides, the car is a new, cushy Range Rover, one of the most luxurious cars I've seen anywhere, much less rural Africa. But our host bores us with a litany of lion conquest stories on safari. I find myself rooting for the lions.

As we leave Lake Turkana, the scenery changes drastically. The mountains rise in height and overlook lush, expansive vistas of the valley floor below. The air has cooled, and the land becomes that rust-brown soil I love so much and that reminds me of Africa most.

As we near the city, the bright colors of the locals' *khangas* and clothes seem to dazzle against the rich earth tones. Roadside stands sell cabbage and woven baskets and fur skins. Many suburban homes are large and lavish with exotic gardens, set in walled compounds with Masai warriors and spears in full tribal regalia guarding the front.

We pass a great shantytown of cardboard and tin and plastic and moderately poor areas reminiscent of the US in the Fifties, then suddenly a modern area with skyscraper-type buildings, so unexpected. Francis told us to stay in the red light district, the only affordable area in the entire city. "You cahn try elsewhere," he said with a knowing glint. "But you weel see for yourself."

I wail to Jim: "I really loved that Francis. I loved all of them."

He laughs. "Mark my word. We'll be seeing all of them again, probably in the same hotel!"

The end blindsides me. The completion of an odyssey seems too special to share with this creepy man who has killed who knows how many lions in their prime. He drops us off on Tom Mboya Street, opens the back of the car to retrieve our backpacks and places them on the roadside. By the time Jim and I bend over to collect them, he's back in the car, waving from the window, croaking something in his strangled voice. "Same to you, buddy!" I whimper.

We stand on some corner in Nairobi looking as rough as the street people. We laugh at each other. I'd dreamt of kissing this Nairobi street. I miss all our friends who are scattered to the winds. "We never had a proper goodbye with any of them," I sigh.

The end has come too quickly and I feel like a waif. Poof, just like that, our sixty-five hundred mile, forty night trip that evades classification has disintegrated to the state of *being over*. Was it really only forty days? "Why, it's of biblical proportions! Did you ever think of that?" I ask Jim. "How can fewer than six weeks, a mere remnant of a human life, be so large?"

It was often terrible; I know I complained bitterly. I was a royal pain in the ass sometimes. And I'm mortally exhausted now. But the bush became our home.

"We deserved a better end. Not this damn crash landing," I say. Perhaps the end seems so far down because we soared more than we knew.

"So what were you expecting? A personal welcome from the Consulate?" Jim says, smiling, with eyebrows raised.

I shoot him a wary look. "I don't know what I expected. It just feels like a shoddy finish."

"But we aren't finished, remember? We have a very long way to go. We're going all the way to the tip of Africa yet, the Cape of Good Hope."

"I know, I know." I moan. "And please don't remind me just now."

Men smoking hookahs outside an Izmir, Turkey cay shop. 1980.

Ann with "friend" in Alanya on the southern coast of Turkey. 1980.

Jim and Abdul in Daphne, Turkey, once a wealthy Roman suburb of Antakya. 1980.

Jim with backpack entering the valley of Petra, Jordan, the Treasury building facade just visible. 1980.

An invitation to coffee with artisans in Aswan, Egypt. 1980.

Tomb of Sheikh Hamed El Nil, a prophet of Mohammed, where devotees chant and whirl each evening; Omdurman, Khartoum, Sudan. 1980.

The interminable four-day train ride from Khartoum to Wau, Sudan; the vendors who provide our daily sustenance. 1980.

The people of Wau, southern Sudan. 1980.

A rousing day at the youth hostel in Wau. 1980.

Jan and I draw a crowd of kids outside our window at the train station in
Sena, Mozambique. 1981.

The day of no rides outside Francistown, Botswana. 1981.

Jim and Romeo at the famous Swayambhunath Temple outside
Kathmandu, Nepal. 1985.

The bathing ghats of Varanasi, India at sunrise on the Ganges River, the former Maharajas' palaces above. 1985.

The weekly market in Mae Hong Son, a mountainous northern highland of Thailand bordering Burma where various hill tribes gather. 1985.

The official wedding photo in Bangkok. 1985.

A shop in Hoi An, Vietnam, with a *yin yang* sign over the door. 1993.

Pros, Ra and Bono, Kompong Som (Sihanoukville), southern Cambodia.
2001.

The first day of school for the second round of students, in front of Psar
Leu Primary School, Sihanoukville, Cambodia. 2002.

Women wiling the day making offerings in Ubud, Bali, Indonesia. 2004.

The Kajeng Kliwon festival at a community temple, Ubud, Bali. 2004.

KENYA: THE SIRENS OF SERENGETI

Don't go to sleep this night, one night is worth a hundred thousand souls.

Rumi

Three times in my life I fully expected to die: Africa holds the first two hallowed places, a rendezvous with a lion in Kenya, the first.

After five weeks in Sudan, the prospect of a long hot shower and a real bed with a mattress loom large on the horizon. More than anything else, though, dreams of our first safari got us through the last leg of the punishing trip across Sudan. If you do nothing else in Africa, you must go on safari.

The city of Nairobi looks like heaven on earth to me. As Francis suggested, we stay in the red light district. Most places are full; out of exhaustion, we finally stay at the notorious Iqbal Hotel, a far cry from heaven on earth. Our hot showers will have to wait since the electricity comes on at eleven at night, "as a rule," and an electric pump delivers the water upstairs. Delayed pleasure is all the sweeter, we tell ourselves.

We spend our first full day waiting in line at the public hospital where a doctor confirms that I have dysentery. A wave of love and guilt fills me. I feel a great debt to my body and vow to really take care of it now.

We baby ourselves and tend to everything that ails us. We sleep late and read indigenous African literature bought at the sidewalk sales. We eat exquisite food each night at the local Sikh temple. Gaining weight is actually a lovely quandary. We sort through our memories that linger like a dream.

Our maiden outing into the depths of Nairobi takes us straight to the safari shops. The prices shock us, so we beat the streets for days in search of a reasonable package. Photography safaris (as opposed to hunting safaris) range from hundreds of dollars to thousands for a few days —the equivalent of months of travel for us. After nineteen months on the road, the highest priority has been making the money last. In our two-person economy, money means more travel, more countries, more sights. Is a safari really worth it? we ask ourselves. Yes, of course; leaving Africa without a safari isn't an option.

Other travelers at the Iqbal Hotel in Nairobi recommend a German man named Hans who runs a safari business, a good safari for the price, they say. The eight hundred Kenyan shilling package (over one hundred dollars each) includes four nights and five days, all food and Reserve entrance fees. We sign up with Hans and will set out with a safari leaving the next day.

Instead of a couple of Landrovers, as we'd expected, a large truck collects us at our hotel—probably a Kenyan Army surplus truck, Jim says. Big is good, I decide, just in case of charging rhinos. We're the last stop; everybody's here now, they say. I look around and my heart sinks. We are six guys and me, a gender gap that's growing old. There's Brian and Steve, two lily-white Brits from England; Atay, a short, swarthy Israeli; our friend Peter from Australia; Jim, me and Hans, the guide-driver-cook-chief bottle washer. We're all pretty close to the same age: late twenties to mid-thirties.

Thanks to *Born Free, Uhuru and* other sundry African novels chocked full of valuable information about the bush, I'm ready. You never know when these pithy morsels might come in handy—like look up for sleeping leopards when you walk under a tree, run downhill when pursued by an elephant, run uphill from a buffalo (or just run like mad if there are no hills). Never run from a cat or look him in the eyes. And freeze if a rhino charges you; he's so nearsighted, chances are he'll miss you completely.

Hans looks very much the African *bwana* with his fair brown hair touched with sun, deep tan and safari shirt. He shakes hands with each of us and flashes me a winning smile with a furtive glance. This might irk me on another day, but not today. Peter jumps in front with Hans, and all other fares climb aboard and fill the parallel seats with gear. The men look almost detached, while I can't stop smiling like a fool. An involuntary shudder runs through me. This is definitely going to be the *real thing*.

Our old Mercedes truck is perfect for a safari. Open in the back, convex steel bars run across the top and sides. Canvas covers the top bars, and canvas flaps on the sides roll up and tie for animal viewing. The engine lugs as we leave the city. Reminiscent of many hitches we've had on the road, the ride is hard and stiff, taking the ruts with brain-rattling bangs. As we pick up speed, the dust compromises viewing. We push for hours, silent, taking it all in, drinking out of army surplus canteens. The gritty, dusty discomfort only lends authenticity for me.

To the north, we enter the great Rift Valley, the three thousand mile fissure in the earth's surface that we saw in Jordan too. My heart bumps up a beat as we round a bend, our first panoramic view below.

The land rolls out in a carpet of glorious beiges and pinks with acacia and cactus trees that hug the land like moss from this high. Riverbeds etch deep windy cracks in the earth. Large statuesque clouds have rolled in for days, heralding the short rainy season of November. There are no clouds on earth quite like wet season skies in Africa. We are fortunate to be here now, Hans tells us through a sliding window to the front, as opposed to the dog days of the dry season when the land is a desert.

In the course of the day, the plains and hills change as much as the weather, no doubt the reason why the landscape varies so widely too. As if separated by a line, fertile green areas share the same plain with barren desert. Lake Navaisha, the beautiful lake sitting below the extinct volcano of Mt. Longonot, is where we'll spend the night.

Pumped and ready for anything the first day out, everyone looks a little downcast when we stop to make camp at Navaisha's turquoise freshwater lake surrounded by dense papyrus trees. Hans points out storks and ibis and eagles on the lake. Navaisha is known for its birdlife and hippo visits to the lake, though we see only impala and donkeys. Lovely; but too tame for the guys, I suspect. When we settle down for dinner, Brian the Brit asks the question on everyone's mind. "Will we see more animals tomorrow?"

"Ya, of course," Hans says. "Today we must travel to get here. You will see de animals tomorrow, at de Masai Mara."

We enter Masai Mara, the Kenyan side of the great Serengeti plain in Tanzania, the next afternoon. We know we're here when we sight our first herd. Hundreds of wildebeest with long, thin Ho Chi Min-type goatees cover the landscape, breaking into a run. The sound of them alone inspires awe. Like a great epic movie, they stampede the plain and fill the horizon, jumping and kicking up dust.

Further along, we encounter a small herd of elephants with two young ones. The herd's caretaker, the matriarch with medium-sized tusks, turns to face us. When the truck approaches, she lifts her tusks like brandished weapons and trumpets loudly by way of warning. To show she means business, she charges, then stops, charges then stops, in a cloud of dust. Her ears flop forward. "If we go too close," Hans says, "she will charge de vehicle." To me, we are too close now. All of us are *extremely* attentive.

As we circle, she moves with us, facing us head on and backing up slowly so the others in the herd can move off. She keeps an eye on them, as she does us, turning to join the herd only when they're out of harm's way. She sounds a last small trumpet as if to say "and don't come back!" It's enough to make you cry. What an impressive creature the matriarch is. We all turn and look at each other, remembering to breathe.

Buffalo, gazelles, antelope and zebra are in good supply throughout the day and later we see a lone cheetah, a highlight for us all. Hans pulls off the road and down into a tree grove, cutting the motor to watch giraffes feeding high among the treetops. The cool reprieve of the valley is welcoming. "Look there, a baby," Peter says, pointing, as we turn to see a fuzzy-looking giraffe about six feet tall to our right.

We all dote on the baby. A movement to the left catches my eye: an adult giraffe who stops feeding to look down. She emits an odd, distressed sound, and I realize we are sitting squarely between her and her baby.

Hans realizes it too and starts the motor just as the mother's alarm rises, poised to charge and kick. The truck jerks backward, whipping all of us with it. The mother follows us, but stops, more concerned about joining her baby. Shaken, we watch from a distance as the two reunite.

"A giraffe can break de lion's skull with one kick," Hans says. "Remind me to show you a picture of de last truck I had."

Oh how funny, a picture of a demolished truck from another safari. Does he need to share this with the clients? And then it hits me for the first time. This is really dangerous, even under the best of conditions. In a pinch, our *bwana*-guide could save us from really very little. People have no doubt been mortally wounded or died on these things. I wonder how many.

We were so tired of researching safari packages, we neglected to ask some basic questions. Our information about Hans was actually hearsay. "I forget, how long was it that our friends said Hans has been in business?" I quietly ask Jim.

"A few years. It's a relatively new business."

"Hmmm," I say. We had definitely deferred to everyone's glowing reports. When you think of it though: exactly what questions do you ask when taking a safari?

Invigorated by the elephant and giraffe standoffs, the guys are very keen to see the big boys—the lions and rhinos. OK, I am too. Our safari won't seem complete without a lion, at the least. But Hans announces we must leave to set up camp before sunset. We are all nonplussed; it's only four o'clock and we're ready for more.

The first alarm sounds in my head when we arrive at "camp." Our camp is the wild African plain, not a camp at all, an open stretch of dry, scratchy land that sits below a slight rise with a few acacia trees. A riverbed runs alongside. Silly me, I assumed we would camp at a campsite. Surely the British *bwanas* of old, hunting rhino and lion, afforded themselves more protection than this.

Hans and Peter unload our accommodation for our remaining three nights: dark green canvas tents for two with claustrophobically squat interiors. Probably army surplus again. The tent is so small, sleeping bag mats just barely fit on the floor. The tent Jim and I brought from home for camping seems downright airy and luxurious in comparison.

But forget the tents; the ground underneath our tents concerns me most. Running perpendicular to the riverbed is a cleared trail. Jim concedes that it looks like a trail and, knowing me well, adds, "I really think Hans knows what he's doing or he wouldn't have lasted in this business." The others don't seem to take notice or care either.

It's been a long day. I work on a slow boil, trying to calm myself, contemplating how best not to sound like the hysterical female and make everyone sorry I came.

I saunter over to Hans as he wrestles with tents and pegs and mats. He turns to greet me, his gnarled brow replaced with a dashing *bwana* smile. I'm not flattered; and any inclination to be flattered is squelched by the realization that I am the only two-legged female in quite a distance.

"Hans, I was curious about why the land is disturbed here. It seems to run all the way across that river bed." Brian the Brit shoots me a look. Hans' *bwana* smile evaporates. He turns to hammer a tent peg. "Could this be an animal trail?" I continue.

"No, no," he says quickly, shaking his head. "De river is dry, de animals is not comin' here." He brushes past me and returns to the truck. Matter closed.

I walk over to the riverbed for a closer look. A healthy thread of water comes up and widens at a bend further below, certainly enough water to drink. I follow Hans to the truck. I'm pretty good at getting up my nerve when I'm afraid for my life.

"There *is* some water flowing there, honest, Hans. Have a look for yourself." My voice rises and wavers. "I think the animals must use this trail because they know there's water here." I pause for air. "I'm just afraid we're pitching our tents smack on top of an animal crossing," I say with remarkable calm.

As if not hearing, Hans hammers pegs in the ground with a vengeance. It's not like I don't know this hard-headed Teutonic temperament; my family is German on both sides, after all. But isn't my concern precisely the kind of thing that men ordinarily notice?

I know I am skating on thin ice now. "I mean if there's any doubt, why would we camp here?" I ask the sky.

"Because der is no doubt. De tents are safe," he finally says under his breath, with remarkable calm too. At least he isn't a hothead; I appreciate that. "Animals see de tents as structures, like de house," he says, a singsong tone in his voice. I want to believe him. I want so much to believe he knows what he's doing.

The four tents are fully pitched now, their measly little peaks looking like a Cub Scout meet on the great Serengeti plains. A charging elephant would surely take them for silly looking plants. But then I can't presume to know elephants.

To allay my fears, Hans reaches into his truck, pulls out a rifle and flashes a charming smile meant to completely disarm me. The only turn-on in a safari guide right now would be competence, not tanned good looks. And certainly not a gun. Am I now meant to prod him to tell me more? (*Have you ever used that thing? Tell me about some of your narrow escapes*). At a loss for words, my face flushes profusely. I feign a smile instead.

In an hour, Hans rustles up a lavish gourmet dinner for seven with two pans over a campfire. Now that's impressive; I couldn't possibly do that. All is well with the world as we sip wine and eat our grilled chicken sautéed in lemongrass. The buzz from the wine is very welcome, making me forget my troubles for awhile. That Hans has proven to be a cook extraordinaire consoles me somewhat.

As night closes in, the animals do too. We sip tea as the fire light reflects pairs of little green and gold eyes around us. Buffalo surround us, easily recognized by their deep grunt-type peals, followed by heavy, short, loud huffs that are hard to ignore. And some are uncomfortably close. Hans points out other animals.

"Look, dere's de varthog. See de tusks? I think dat's de hyena dere." Hyenas scare me more than anything I can think of. Ah, it's going to be a long three nights in the Reserve.

And then about thirty feet away, "Look, look, come in close." Hans whispers as everyone crowds around. "Can you see dare? Dat's de lion."

Brian comes through for me again, always asking the questions I'm thinking. "Aren't we attracting the animals with the fire?" He sounds whiny but I love him for it.

"Animals like de fire," Hans says, "but when de fire dies, dey go away."

The second alarm sounds in my head when Hans bids us good night and jumps up into the very high, heavy safari truck to sleep. That beats all. I'm hot all over again. "What does it really matter where Hans sleeps anyway?" Jim says. I watch stupefied as Hans ties himself securely in the truck.

"What does it really *matter*?" I wail. "It *matters* because if the tents are so damn safe sitting on top of an animal crossing, why doesn't he *sleep* in one?"

Jim shrugs: "Give him a break. He probably does this so much, he has to have some comforts, you know."

"OK, OK maybe," I concede. "Me, personally, it would never occur to me to do anything but camp like everybody else. It's terrible PR. How can he have any business at all doing this?"

It's obviously everybody for herself out here. The men ready themselves for bed, seemingly unfazed by Hans, confirming my suspicion that I am probably an hysterical female. And very alone. Maybe Jim's right, maybe Hans deserves some comfort on the job. He couldn't succeed this long if he didn't know what he was doing. And everyone has survived so far. Right?

The loud huffs of the buffaloes draw closer as the fire dies. The African buffalo is not related to its Asian counterpart, Hans tells us. Unlike the Asian water buffalo, it has never been domesticated because it is so dangerous to humans.

Jim sleeps like a man secure in his own bed at home, not mere steps away from one-thousand-pound buffaloes. It isn't normal. Doesn't anyone else find this extremely dangerous? My only hope is that nothing jars the buffalo tonight. I lay there for hours hearing every sound, every shift in the dry grass, wondering how anyone can sleep under these conditions. Am I the only one awake?

The buffalo move off, though not to be replaced by quiet. An odd cacophony sounds in the distance; I sit up to listen. The grunts and huffs of the buffalo, I realize, have muted for hours the background theatrics on the plains. A piercing cry sounds—heart rending and heaving and piteous—protracted appeals that would move the Marquis de Sade. They seem to go on for an eternity. Hyenas, I am guessing. They bring down larger animals, moving in packs and killing their prey slowly by tearing them apart. Horrible creatures. I cover my ears and have a good bawl, wiping my nose on my T-shirt. I just want to get out of here.

Stereophonic snores pirouette across the campground: first Jim, then somebody else. The higher primates sleep soundly with no worries of whether they'll eat tomorrow morning, while some wretched creature out there is already breakfast. Of course, it's no surprise, it's the way things have played out in Masai Mara every night, night after night, since the beginning of time. The carnage never stops, the animals must kill to live, and are themselves killed. It happens each night in our own back yards at home. Nature is inherently violent. We always knew that; we just didn't have to watch and listen.

I cannot see my watch in the dark, but it has to be at least two-thirty. I ponder how far I've come in a few hours— precipitously downward that is—as anyone at their sleep-deprived worst at night in the middle of the African plains might understand. I do manage to enjoy snatches of calm. You could say, even bliss.

And then a welcomed gift, a circuitous, serendipitous thought arrives. For better or worse, I'm in the moment. You could say the senses have never worked better. The night mysteriously conveys every sound and connects all of us on the great Serengeti plain. I'm glad I'm awake. No, actually, I conclude, it's important to be awake. I'm as alive as human beings can be, and I'm experiencing Africa fully. Too bad for the guys; they're missing it. Why would anyone come this far and pay for an adventure without experiencing all of it, wakeful night included?

Jim's snores suddenly give way to loud sucking gasps. Do the animals on the plain stop short and lift their heads? Will they come in search of a wounded animal? I poke Jim to roll over. Sublime quiet, quiet as we haven't enjoyed all night, follows.

The whole drama has set on my bladder like a rock for hours; I can't put off a trip outside another minute. I curse my body, unzip the tent and peer out. Seeing no buffalo about, I take a step. The air feels fresh and damp. The night is sumptuous and buoys me up. The moon sits high in the sky and shines brilliantly, as if a white transparent veil covers us. A fine vapor halo, tinged with mother-of-pearl hues, ripples with the moving clouds below. Cloud tufts float by like helium balloons.

The landscape looks eerily frozen, and innocuous now. The animals have moved off; all the plains seem to sleep. I breathe deeply for the first time in hours. The night nurtures me, works in and lifts my sense of dread. I laugh at my silliness and venture out to take a leak. Convinced the danger has passed, that the night holds only asylum, I walk a bit farther towards the smoldering campfire.

When I get back inside, a weighty fatigue consumes me. I know I can sleep now. Jim stirs as I zip up the tent. I tell him how beautiful the night is, how there's a colorful vapor ring around the moon. I turn and lie back down when a roar fills all consciousness, all matter, all being—a close angry roar that blasts through us like a bolt of lightning. Unmistakably a lion.

I can't move. My heart threatens to take leave of my chest; my throat and chest tighten like a vice—like the time I got the wind knocked out of me. The diaphragm actually locks up when you're really frightened, someone once told me. All I can think of is to pull my one-inch mat over my body for protection, to put anything between me and the lion. But I don't want to budge. Jim and I wring the life out of each other's hands. "Breathe deeply and slowly," Jim whispers. Breathing is indeed on manual pilot, no longer involuntary. How can he be so calm?

It must be the Eagle Scout training. Through the fog, I marvel at Jim's collectedness. The lioness hunts at night; it must be a lioness. And the buffalo probably moved off because of her. I imagine her sniffing the wind, getting closer to the tent. I press my hands to my chest to contain my heart, then cradle my head in case she jumps on us. Hans' voice plays in my head: "No, de animals think de tent is de structure like de house."

Did she see me the first moment I went outside? Did she watch as I pulled my pants down? How close was she? Did my own urine save us? If there's one thing animals respect, it's markings. Oh God, what a way to go. I'm only grateful she didn't attack me with my pants down.

That wasn't your ordinary MGM lion roaw-roaw. She was outraged, as if she came smack up against my scent. I definitely surprised her, as if she were saying *HEY!!! WHAT THE HELL ARE YOU DOING HERE?* Is she gone now? Or is she still only feet away? How can we know? We lay rigid many minutes more, living a lifetime in seconds.

Jim's grasp loosens and he starts to snore again, leaving me alone to suffer. I can't believe this.

My breath comes more naturally in an hour. The lioness has to have moved off by now. The dark walls of our little tent seem to lighten and rise with the first light of dawn. A few lone birds sing in the new day. Maybe now I can sleep.

I sleep for maybe two hours. Everyone but the two Brits pitched closest to us come to breakfast, refreshed and chipper. I must look like I'm nursing a hangover. The Brits finally surface. Kindred spirits that they are, they look like mirror images of myself. They, too, heard the lion and were awake *all* night.

Brian and Steve's credibility with our more masculine members has been in question from the start. It's likely they are gay. Donning frumpy safari hats with chin straps, dark argyle socks folded over and long Bermuda shorts, their white, transparent skin, seemingly untouched by the sun, all evoke—let's be honest—unmanly uncoolness. The first day out, they bored us silly with minutia about their expensive electronic devices guaranteed to ward off female, malaria-carrying mosquitoes. Both of them are just too effusive about the mosquitoes, the ants, the hardness of the sleeping bag mats. I know the others find them poor male specimens for a safari. It's as if our photography safari has become a *bwana* hunt without the guns.

That Brian and Steve surfaced from their tent reduced and shaken like a couple of women sealed it. I want to kiss them; I am unspeakably grateful they are here.

The lion roar comes down to the word of me, Jim and the Brits, because no one else confesses to hearing it. My credibility doesn't seem to rank any higher than the Brits'. Jim admits he heard it, but doesn't defend our honor or regard it as a fight worth defending. But the four of us agree the lion was quite close, maybe ten feet away at most. That no one else heard the-roar-to-end-all-roars defies sensibility.

Hans and Atay, but mostly Hans, can't let go of ridiculing us unmercifully through breakfast (fruit pancakes on the grill and Arabic coffee). We can't even tell the difference between a buffalo and a lion, they laugh. For some curious reason, I feel compelled to prove I know the difference by mimicking the lion roar, as compared to the buffalo huff. This amuses the naysayers all the more.

Jim has a completely different take on all this. Later he tells me: "The whole lion thing wasn't about the lion at all. It was about money. Come on, Hans heard the lion; everybody had to hear the lion. He was afraid clients would be scared and bail on him before he'd been paid. Didn't you notice how he made a beeline straight to the resort hotel that morning, so we could all cash our travelers checks and pay him?"

"Hmmm," I say. "Good point."

The third night out, convinced one can't live on adrenaline alone, I ask Hans if I can sleep in the truck, if only across the driver-passenger seats. "Fine with me," he says, "but it's OK to sleep in the back if you want."

"Is there room for Jim too?"

"Sure, if he wants."

I am bursting to tell Jim our good news. But Jim is unmoved, assuring me he doesn't need a place to sleep. In a fit of complete amnesia, this person who wrung my hands the night before says he'll be fine in the tent. Somehow I always thought survival was instinctive. How can machismo possibly be stronger than the will to live? And, more so, how has this mental affliction taken up residence in my Jim?

Inside the truck that night, I watch as Hans ties up the canvas flaps securely. "Why are you doing that?" I ask.

"Oh, dey monkeys, dey make dey mess of everything if you don't."

He also keeps a kerosene light burning all night. Until I slip off to sleep, I enjoy every weird sound in the night.

Before daybreak, a vague movement awakens me. The truck rocks from side to side as Hans sleeps. I untie a canvas flap and look down to see an enormous buffalo scratching its back against the truck. He must be four or more feet wide. If I hung over and stretched down, I could touch him. In the moonlight, I see about ten others encircling the tents and bellowing. What if this big guy tried to scratch his back on Jim's tent? It isn't normal, the blithe trust of these guys.

The next morning, as Hans shaves in the truck mirror, I ask if he heard any buffalo last night. "No, why?"

"It doesn't matter. I just wondered," I say, smiling. I really want to sleep in the truck again tonight.

He turns to face me, his neck dotted with red toilet paper blots, his face white and foamy. "You know, you really should get some bush experience and camp out in de wild for a month or more."

MOZAMBIQUE: THE TRAIN TO NO MAN'S LAND

*The man who has seen the rising moon break out of the clouds
at midnight has been present like an archangel at the creation of
light and of the world.*

Ralph Waldo Emerson

Our train enters the station at Sena, Mozambique, half
an hour late. Jim and I and Jan, our Dutch companion
for the last few days, hop off before the train stops and break
into a full run with backpacks bobbing. We fear we've missed
our connection to Malawi. Since there are only two tracks, the
train standing next to us must be the train to Blantyre.

It's after eleven at night. For the love of some sleep, we
scramble aboard the train and round a blind corner. Jan almost
mows down a small woman who gasps and recoils in horror.
Scaring people takes some getting used to. In the bush, Africans
rarely encounter *brancos* (white people) so they're afraid of us,
especially in the dead of night.

Jan and I scare them most. In the weak overhead light,
our tanned skin and light clothes render us more ghoulish,

more white-haired, more white-teethed than by day. Like apparitions in the night. Jan looks ghoulish to *me*, his white-blonde eyebrows catching the light. If we forget ourselves and laugh aloud, open mouthed, children cling to their mothers as if we might eat them.

The conductor saunters down the aisle collecting tickets. "Is this the train to Blantyre?" Jan asks.

"Yes, thees train goes to thee border, thee *frontiera*, thee border," he says. His finger loops three times in the air. "And then Blantyre."

We work our way back through the cars, smiling, saying hello in the Sena language, careful not to show too many teeth. As we pass, the adults watch surreptitiously without staring. The children turn their heads and gape.

We must be charmed. We find space enough to lie down in the last car of the train. I am ecstatic. Space on anything that moves in Africa is dear, even benches made of hard wooden slats. After eating dust for eight hours on the last train, we're sure to sleep well tonight. With a victory yelp, I claim my spot and hunker down for the night. A chubby-faced infant in front of us holds his mother's blouse in a vice grip, but dares to peer over her shoulder to watch. If the mother moves closer, he shrinks. If she moves away, he cranes to keep us in his view. It's nice to see fat on a baby; excess anything is rare in Africa.

The morning light brings food hawkers knocking at the window, startling me from sleep. I look out to see that the train hasn't budged. We still face the derelict Sena station canteen, though the people who huddled in small groups, African-style on their haunches, have gone. The same hawkers knock at our window selling the same stale food, their faces more desperate and pleading. Trains moving eastward have come and gone.

Four hours have passed. Jim and I and Jan are remarkably calm, taking our cues from the masters—the men, women and children who have shown us the art of patience these many months traveling on public transport. We watch, transfixed—

this patience that surpasses all understanding and spills over into everything Africans do. It's a patience we've never known; something more akin to surrender.

Take the people in our car. Devoid of anticipation or concern, their faces tell us that waiting is a way of life. All things under the great African sky unfold precisely as they're meant to. The children sit quietly without a peep these many hours. Four little boys across the aisle who never seem to speak keep a watchful eye on us. An old man with a hand-carved cane peers out the window as if this is the best thing he will do all week. He turns now and meets my gaze, nodding and smiling slightly, the whites of his eyes speckled with age. Everything is about the process in Africa, not the getting there. So why rush? The African people are veritable shaman without knowing it.

The chubby-faced, runny-nosed baby in front of us blinks intelligently at these strange *brancos*. I lean forward to see that he's actually a little girl wearing a blue jersey on top and buck-naked with fat dimpled cheeks on the bottom. Her eyes are deep pools of black glued to our every movement. She pads across her mother's stomach and clutches her neck for protection. Try as we may, there's no eliciting a smile.

We find a train employee who speaks some English and ask about our departure. "Yes, the train will move soon," he tells us. "Just a delay." No one else seems to take notice or care.

"But when will we move?" I ask.

"Shortly."

It's all the same, asking or not asking, because misinformation is endemic in Africa. It's more important to try to help than to provide correct information, even if you're an official wearing a uniform. Granted, it makes you feel better if the news is good. And, for a fleeting moment, we do feel better.

Another two hours pass, the temperature climbs, and it's now after noon. I spring to my feet. "That's it. I'm done!" Leaving patience to the Africans, I climb over my sleeping companions. I step down from the car and walk towards the main station. Few people mill about; everyone clings to the shady spots instead. I can almost see the engine which means we're a very small train only five cars long.

I reach the front of the train and stare uncomprehendingly at the place where the engine should be. There is no engine. We are a train of cars with no engine in sight—not on the next track, not anywhere. I can't quite take it in. For more than twelve hours, like a bunch of dunces, scores of us have sat on a train with no damn engine.

Depending upon who you talk to, the border to Malawi is forty, sixty, a hundred kilometers away. And no one is saying the train will leave soon anymore, not even the conductor. We're pretty confident it won't. Our threesome votes in favor of walking. It's a risk; the train might pass us by, but there's a lot to be said for getting out of here and just moving.

A year of traveling overland in Africa has converted Jim and me into born-again optimists. Not that it came easily. When Africa conspired against us, we complained a lot and shook our fists at the heavens. Then we saw the folly of our ways, being that it happened almost every day. What was the sense of being frustrated? Africa would eat us alive if we didn't make a swift attitude adjustment.

We learned to become philosophers instead and fielded the curveballs which often masqueraded as serendipitous adventures. We've never been disappointed so far, though it's definitely an acquired taste.

But our present venture proves a bit more challenging. We lack correct information concerning the distance between the borders of Mozambique and Malawi. This buffer of land is not under the sovereignty of either country—hence "no man's land"—called *frontiera* in Portuguese, the former colonial power. We don't know whether local transport can take us or if we can walk it. More worrisome: since we thought we'd leave Mozambique last night, we have no food, water or local currency.

We walk along a wide path bordered with paprika-colored soil and green shade trees. Streams of women in colorful *khangas* pass us. The sun is treacherous and bakes our heads. A woman carrying a large basket of cherry tomatoes on her head stops to make a sale. "Sorry," Jim shrugs, "no *meticals*."

Without a thought, she donates a bag of tomatoes to the cause, to become our lunch, dinner and breakfast.

The people who surround us on the path are local Africans connected to a tribe and moving to a village. We meet a Mozambican man named Vasco who comes from Maputo, he says, and travels to Malawi too. He shares his water with us.

He puffs up, telling us his father named him after Vasco de Gama, the Portuguese explorer who came to Mozambique in the fifteenth century. Vasco's effusive manner and fluid movements are very Latino, not African. Dark-skinned with Caucasian features and curly, short-cropped hair, his demeanor always bears a large, winning smile. He laughs easily too. I'm always inspired by people who can only muster ten English words but chatter on with complete abandon. The four of us reach the town of Don Anno, where a local convinces us to push on to the last village before the border. "He say 'OK, walking all the way,'" Vasco says.

The sun sets as we arrive. The earth is lush and fertile here, dotted with well-built huts, some quite large with windows, all anomalous sights in the bush. There are even dovecotes— lovely little houses built on stilts for doves. The last train to Sena carried us through impoverished drought-torn areas, so we're heartened to leave Mozambique on a prosperous note.

The custom is to enter an African village by way of its chief. We locate the large hut of the chief, who surfaces dressed in a colorful tribal *khanga*. Affluent by African standards, he welcomes us warmly, formally, running back to the hut to produce three Western-style wood chairs. Vasco doesn't rate one. The chairs look foreign even to us. People congregate to see the show. We must cut a ludicrous sight, three *brancos* sitting like stiffs on straight *branco* chairs on the hard-baked earth, surrounded by an entire village.

The chief and elders confer in Sena—the chief and Vasco, in Portuguese, talking on and on in animated tones about our fate. Or perhaps the weather. Then all is quiet, as if a pronouncement comes. A full moon rises on the horizon, huge and portentous.

The chief speaks through Vasco: "Sleeping, OK (pointing to a hut). No walking, Mama (who is me). *Frontiera*, too long. Train coming. Maybe tonight coming. We wake you."

So we still don't know when the train comes. The chief delivers us to our home for the night, a small hut with bags of ground maize stacked on a concrete floor. A corner has been cleared. We prepare tea on our little propane stove, save some cherry tomatoes for breakfast, and sleep soundly in our sleeping bags.

At 11:30 pm, the police wake us to make a full document check. At 5:15 am, Vasco wakes us again and addresses Jim and Jan. "*Amigoes*. I go *frontiera*."

"No, wait," Jan says. "We go too. How long to *frontiera*?" Jan points to his watch. "What *time frontiera*?"

Vasco points to the twelve, then shrugs; maybe eleven.

"So lunch time *frontiera*?" Jan asks.

"No, no, *amigo*," Vasco smiles. "Night time, *frontiera*."

Ohhh, this is not good news and, as usual, I am outnumbered in the decision-making process. A nineteen-hour trek with a heavy backpack and no food? Have cherry tomatoes gone to their heads?

"But the train. Doesn't the train come later?" I ask.

Vasco shrugs. Maybe, maybe not.

We all set off in the predawn night. A single thought consoles me: what good is a chief if he doesn't know his own land? I'm putting my money on the chief. The train has to come soon, as he said. We follow a path which forks after a short distance. People stir behind the trees. A woman cooking on a small fire waves her hand toward the right, nodding emphatically. This is the way, she is telling us. But how does she know where we go?

"*Frontiera?*" Vasco asks. She nods, as if the hour is too early to speak. The path is well worn, which consoles me.

The moon sits high in the sky and a heavy fog settles over the savanna like a blanket, a resplendent but eerie Miltonian setting. I am not yet awake, but this luscious, other-worldly landscape jolts me to life. Thousands of star pricks flicker. The moonlight illuminates a few puffs of cloud floating by and a carpet of fog below. Am I still dreaming? I think not; even my dreams aren't this good. I feel so alive, almost giddy.

Like annoying children, the guys steal my reverie. Moving at a military clip, they're way ahead. I can barely see them. Do they even see anything around them? Are we on a drill here? Can we possibly enjoy this for a few minutes? I wish they would lose me. As I descend the wet grassy bank, their figures enter the savanna floor below. The mist envelopes them like swimmers wading in deep water, their shoulders and heads awash with moonlight.

The moment begs to be captured on film; this cannot be left to memory. I cup my hands to my mouth. "Guys! Waitttttt! I have to get a photo."

They stop and turn. I can just imagine Jim's face, scrunched up in a dubious glare. I remove my backpack and unzip the top. "Just let me get this real fast. Come on, it won't take long."

And then the unthinkable.

A train whistle sounds in the distance. Panic undulates through me. We hadn't even considered the train yet. The guys take off. I throw my backpack across one shoulder, running towards the whistle as if a lion chases me. My pack flops wildly on my back. I push myself beyond my strength, fearing that I will pitch forward flat on my face. The whistle sounds again, clearer now, a glorious peal in the night. The slow *chuggachugga* of a steam engine follows. We have no idea where to go, where the tracks lay.

The *chuggachug-chuggachug* is clearer still, resonant, as the train comes up over a rise. A brilliant conical headlight pierces the sky, then levels down and shoots across the plain in front of us. The track can't be far. We push ourselves some more and reach the beam of the headlight, yelling and jumping and waving like crazy people. Surely the engineer sees us now. But how will we get on? There's no station, no stop. What were we thinking? We'll stand here and watch it pass us by.

A white shirted arm waves from the engine window. The engine chugs and heaves, gasping as the train slows, and slows, and slows some more. Is it really stopping for us? The engine car passes as we strain to reach the first car. The guys scale the steps easily. But I can't manage. I run as fast as I can but lose ground, too weak and too spent.

"Ohhhhhhh," I cry out in frustration in a little girl's voice and drop back to meet the next set of steps. And then I see them, just barely in the night. Phantom black hands reach down and grab me. Strong taunt arms lift me easily into the air to the first step. I am winded and bruised and crying, but deliriously happy.

Passengers wave and cheer from the windows. *Ayyyyyyy.*

The four of us move through the train to car number five, veritable heroes. Our car mates from Sena giggle and greet us with *ayyyyysss*. Our empty seats are there. Everyone is there, just as we'd left them.

My chest still heaving, we sit in silence, too tired to speak. From the east, the first rays of the new day burst into the car, bathing everything in opaque pink. The light blinds us; there is nothing to do but relent and close our eyes.

When I close my eyes even now, I can see those people, stretched from early morning to early morning along a train track, as crystalline as that day. The little boys, the chubby baby girl and her mother, the old man with the cane: all their faces luminescent. It's the surrender, that lovely sense of surrender that is quintessentially African that illuminates them still.

SOUTHERN AND EASTERN AFRICA: THE GOD OF UNKNOWING

O wild and wondrous midnight, there is a might in thee, to make the charmed body, almost like spirit be, and give it some faint glimpses, of immortality.

James Russell Lowell

Africa won't be rushed. For six hours, in the middle of July in the dry season, Jim and I have languished in the sun outside of Francistown, far eastern Botswana, trying to hitch a ride to Zimbabwe. Much of Botswana's year is dry actually, lending most to its low rainfall. *Pula*, the Setswana word for currency, doubles as the word for rain—no doubt, because both are held dear.

The pancake-flat, desolate terrain mirrors our own spirits. And now our drinking water has run out. At least the afternoon air has cooled.

We jump as a car rounds the bend, the fifth vehicle today. Isn't this the way things go? Just when you think you're defeated, a ride comes. He asks where we go. No, sorry, he says, he doesn't go north. I've had it, and move off the road, plopping down on the ground under a lone tree.

From the road, Jim points to my leg. "Watch yourself there. You're sitting next to a trail of ants." He's right; a long, serpentine black line crawls under my leg. Like band members in a parade, each carries a dried piece of grass taller than himself down a hole. They move with good humor, stopping and deferring to other ants crossing their path. How civilized.

I watch some more, then join in their work, breaking off little pieces of grass and handing them to the first ant out the hole. They're very clever and adjust to the change quickly, taking my grass back down, retrieving them faster than I can deliver. "Come here, hurry! You won't believe this!" I yell to Jim.

He sprawls out on the ground too, and we all build an underground ant nest, or whatever it is we build, for a solid hour. Nothing is happening on the road. "Do you think the ants will knock off early today and take a rest?"

"From what I know about ants, it's doubtful," he says. "They have a formidable work ethic."

I'm grateful to them for redeeming this pitiful day. They're hard at work as we leave, their miniscule piece of the world cast in shadow.

The sunset paints mauve-purples across the plains. The inevitable has come—the dreaded return to town. Jim does it first; he picks up his bag. It's not like this is the first time we never got a ride. But to wile away the time today, from shade tree to shade tree, we walked and hitched about five or six kilometers out of Francistown. Five or six kilometers to walk back now.

We take turns lifting up each other's packs on our backs. The last light of day is thin, weak. Long shadows stretch across the road. I hadn't realized it was so late. "Oh, great, and we've waited too long to start back," I say. "Now we're lion bait."

A fellow traveler from Switzerland told us an all-too-similar story. Stuck in the bush with no ride at the end of the day, he pitched his tent on the spot and spent the night—something we've done various times before hearing this story. He awoke in the morning to find a huge male lion lying on the other side of the road—napping with one eye and watching him with the other. As nonchalantly as possible, writing notes to family in case they found his body, he watched the lion from just inside his tent. "I couldn't possibly move. I was glued to that spot for hours," he said. "Finally, the lion yawned, got up and took off, apparently too bored to eat me."

I doubt Jim is worried about lions as we walk back to town. As tired as I feel, that story puts a lift in my step.

I retrieve our map of Africa and count finger-inches from Botswana to Nairobi, our final destination before flying home: about three thousand overland kilometers and five countries of roadless terrain. The enormity of it dizzies me. We've been traveling for twenty-eight months since leaving the US, our two-person expedition winding down fast. The trip south from Egypt to Kenya, though tough beyond reckoning, sealed our love for this continent. Rested up and fit again, the trip through Tanzania, Zambia, Zimbabwe, Botswana and South Africa, another three and a half months, seemed charmed in comparison, though painstakingly slow.

But Africa takes more than I can give, as it does to its own; it doesn't discriminate. I've been running on two cylinders for months and my hair is falling out. The doctors, the clinics, the public hospitals tell me I'm parasite free and give me a vitamin B shot. I seem to be the only one who knows I've still got the little buggers.

"You are weak," one doctor told me. "You have to rest." Sure, rest; that will happen only when I go home. Though we hadn't anticipated depleted bodies, we did plan for depleted funds, securing a small nest egg to cover our flights home. But the money meant to bring us home swiftly by air from southern

Africa sits frozen in our accounts, following a savings and loan crisis in Maryland.

The cars moving on the pocked trails they call roads provide our only way out of here. The mere prospect of more travel days like today—in fits and starts, the interminable waiting, the lack of water, the sunburn—renders me completely inert if I ponder it too long.

The continent first loosened its hold when we reached Capetown, South Africa, an oasis in the desert. The walk out to the Cape of Good Hope, the southernmost tip of Africa, marked more than a symbolic milestone in our journey. We'd filled countless journals and traversed a continent. "I don't know if I can do this anymore," I said to Jim, who could have probably continued for another two years.

All is well again when the next day brings a comfortable ride in a Landrover that takes us from Francistown to Salisbury, Zimbabwe—a very full day, about five hundred fifty kilometers. A bonanza. We stay with the sister and brother-in-law of Henry the Brit of overland Sudan to Kenya fame—our second stay there. We visited them, and Henry, on the southward trip to South Africa. This time we've missed Henry, who has returned to England. He's finally had enough.

The next morning in Salisbury, we run to the main post office to check for mail. Much like the light of distant stars, by the time our letters reach us, the news is old, or has long died. *Post restaunte*, the international, general delivery system found at capital city post offices, is a repository of unrequited letters. Many find their mark, but too many "postage due" letters, torn letters, misfiled and misread letters do not. For each three letters we receive, we miss about one. (*Can't find your letter under the Vs? Here are a few hundred more to look through.*) The good wishes and love from home, including critical news, often miss their mark.

We last received mail from home via *post restaunte* about a month ago. After that, travel in the bush brought communication to a halt. The bush demands your undivided attention, and the austere conditions create a disconnect. Where our friends and family think of us as enjoying a lovely extended vacation, our days feel more like survival. Granted, we chose to take on this rocky ride. But it doesn't make for good postcard chitchat many days.

The minutia of life at home seems light years away, our letters and calls weak radio signals between two universes. The first six months away from home, I was seized with bouts of homesickness. In the bush, family and friends seem as if from a different dimension in time, another incarnation.

We try to reconcile the yawning disparity between life here and life in the US. Our former selves wax superficial. In Africa, villagers carry their water for miles and live without basic necessities; poverty is endemic, starvation seasonal. My sister writes that she and her husband are learning to dance on roller skates. With enough time in Africa, life in the US, life almost anywhere, and everything held dear before become indefensible.

So home consumes little space in the vacuum that is Africa. We relegate it instead to an obscure closet of the memory, like a beloved, though extravagant grandmother since departed. We don't tend to worry about home either. The presumption is that everyone at home has to be fine, compared to here.

So we never expect bad news from the world of standing still. It blindsides us when it comes crashing into our new strange world. Even the light of a distant star must reach earth eventually.

Since I know I am missing mail, and what little I have proves uninformative, I call home. Calling home can be very dear in cost, the equivalent of months in the bush.

I learn that my father has had another heart attack, two weeks before. My mother's replies to my questions seem scripted, cautious, my father no doubt listening close by. Unconvincing assurances aren't even forthcoming. There was more damage this time, she lowers her voice. "But what happened to that wonderful cardiac exercise program he was in?" I ask. "Wasn't he doing so well in that?"

"Yes, but he quit that," she says. "Sometimes he had heart palpitations that scared him." Her voice is tentative, strained, perhaps just with me, perhaps with life.

It takes a long time to get my father on the phone. His voice rattles in his throat, labored. He assures me he's OK, belying everything I hear. The conversation tires him. I tell him we're working our way northward to come home as soon as possible. He says he's proud of me.

We pass through Mozambique and Malawi, moving as swiftly as Africa allows us. Seasoned veterans of the bush now, we sniff out the places where trucks pass through town— behind the barber shop or the local auto garage in town. But rides are few.

And I am no longer present in this trip.

We left Malawi this morning by way of the far northern tip, on September 19th, a date indelibly branded in my psyche. We waited to be checked in at a Zambian border post, though we weren't officially in Zambia until they affixed the entry stamps to our passports. We stood on solid earth, apparently non-earth, no-man's-land between the two countries—not Malawi, not Zambia—which is to say, limbo, a place that is no place. And which perfectly reflects my state of mind now. Does one hear a tree that falls in limbo?

It was the message. Of course that was it—how disoriented that terrible message left me—and then this place *non grata* where we find ourselves, the screaming locusts, and the heat in that tin box that sucks the life from you and makes you question what's real.

As certain as I can be of anything, we were stamped out of the building and officially stand on Zambian soil waiting for a bus to take us to the border town. The time in between is less clear. The time since we entered the building and walked out again. The time after that official called me into his office. I sit under this great baobab tree now, so I must have walked here. Such an exquisite tree; its great arms nurture me. And Jim next to me.

If only Berthold would just go away. Over and over again, he won't stop saying it, what happened; he confirms it. As do the words that I write now, The Truth, as true as anything can be in the middle of the bush, waiting these many hours for the illusive bus that never comes.

Berthold is a slightly older, gay guy who we met in Monkey Bay, Malawi, to the south. He is German. Our first encounter was memorable. As Jim and I sat in a small canteen-type place, a crazy German across from us asked the waiter: "Can you bring me a cold beer? It has to be really cold, with ice." We looked incredulously at each other. Ice is virtually non-existent in Africa, except perhaps in posh hotels in the cities. How could this guy have penetrated the continent this far without knowing this?

When his lukewarm can arrived, he rolled his eyes. "Uh! Jesus Christ, can you believe it? It's not even cold." And upbraided the continent for its backwardness.

These were his first words to us. In lowered tones, he asked us to call him Eric, not Berthold, the second tip-off he was certifiable. "I want people to think I'm Swedish, not German," he said. I couldn't help but smile. (*Because of the war? Because Africans love Swedes? As if they might not detect his thick German accent. Or really care that he's German.*)

"Why do you want to be called Eric?" I asked. "Because of World War II?"

"Yeah, yeah," he said, nodding. "You never know."

We parted ways before the Malawi border because Berthold couldn't join us on the truck. He had to be true to his yet-to-be-written book entitled *Hitching Around the World* about traversing each continent from tip to tip. With five more countries to go in Africa, he forbade himself the use of any paid transport, which would be cheating. The book came as a surprise, since we'd traveled with him for more than two weeks with no mention of it. "So where are all your notes for your book?" I asked.

He tapped his head and smiled cleverly. "Dare all in here."

Jim and I looked at each other. At least he had his title.

The truck ride is very rough, through the mountains of the Mafinga Hills, finally depositing us at Chitipa, a lazy border town. We check-out at the Malawi checkpoint and make the slow walk—eight and a half kilometers—across no-man's-land to the Zambian border post. We're higher here and still in Malawi's dry season. The nights have been cool by African standards, the days pleasant with less humidity.

After a long wait on the Zambian side, a corrugated tin building opens for business and fills to brimming. Jim and I stifle in a mix of sweat and dust for another hour, waiting to be stamped into Zambia.

We finally manage to get a seat. The lack of oxygen makes us sleepy; we nod off hugging our backpacks.

I open my eyes to see a uniformed official come from the exterior door, walk past us and return about ten minutes later. Jim and I move our feet for him to pass, but he stops instead and stands directly in front of me. We're the only *mzungus* in the place.

"Would you come weeth me, please, Mees?" he says.

I sit up straight. But why? What in the world would someone here want with me? "Do you mean me?" I point to myself. The mistake will surface soon.

"Yes, Mees."

Traveling these many months in Africa, we've heard stories about some of the ploys—big fishes in little ponds who like to wield their power and make Westerners squirm. They are willing to overlook a problem of their own invention in exchange for padding their meager incomes. (*Oh, I see you don't have a yellow fever stamp, or, didn't you know the new rule about visas?*) For us, these incidents have been rare, directed at Jim only once. Across the continent, African men have never given me a moment's pause—not one, not even the glimmer of an inappropriate touch or sexual overtone.

I have no cause for alarm, I tell myself. "Well, can my friend come with me?" I ask. Jim stands.

"No, Mees….. you only, please."

Now I am getting alarmed. "I just don't understand. Where are we going?"

"In the office here only, Mees," he says. He does not smile and guides the way with his hand. "Thees way, please."

I follow him to a stale-smelling office lighted by natural light from an open window. The light is diffused, the room eerily empty. A single desk with a few papers on top sits to the side, almost like props on a stage—not a real office where business is conducted. Papers stand in tall irregular piles in the corner, lots of piles. The rest of the room is completely open, collecting dust.

Two other uniformed officials greet me. One sits at the desk, the other stands. But they both leave. Everyone acts starched and officious. A dusty haze hangs in the pale light like smoke, adding to the unreal, Kafkaesque feel.

The man who summoned me retrieves another chair from against the wall for me, while he sits at the desk. I realize his uniform is different; he wears the bermudaed pants the Malawian officials wore. His uniform is dark with a line of perspiration across the back. He faces me straight on. As he talks, I know this face—he's the one who checked us through at the Malawi border. His countenance has altogether changed. His youthful, kind smile put me at ease before. I wondered how long he'd had this job, what it paid, if he went home to a wife and kids yet.

His eyes are steely now, his jaw clenched. And why is he here on the Zambian side? A bead of perspiration runs down his face and catches the light. He wipes his brow with a spanking white handkerchief and collects his resolve. With hands clenched on the desk, he clears his throat and rocks forward, staring vaguely behind me. Then blurts it out. "Mees, I am verdy sorry to tell you your mahther has died."

The words sound like a strange tongue, as if he speaks a foreign language that I glean without comprehending. How can a stranger in the bush of Africa, in a tin hut in limbo, no less, a place that doesn't exist, elicit my mother? Is he a shaman or something? How can he speak of someone precious to me another universe away?

"I am verdy sorry, Mees." He wipes his brow. "Eeet must be verdy difficult for you." His words strike me again, said as if they're true—as if he knows me, knows something extraordinary about my mother.

I finally find my voice. "How do you know this? How do you even know who I am?"

"Thee Amedican embassy has told us."

"But how?"

"By wire, Mees."

"Do you have the paper that says my mother died?"

"No," he shakes his head; he has no paper with him. It's back in Malawi.

An inert malaise holds me fast. I can't say how long I sit there mute. If anyone has died, it has to be my father, not my mother. "Is it possible they got it wrong? That someone got it wrong, that it was my father who died?"

"I'm sorry, Mees, eet tees your mahther." He looks down and fingers the papers. "I know eet tees verdy difficult."

He waits patiently. The door opens a crack and a head peers in. I realize I'm holding up this man, the others, their office. "Thank you very much," I say. I manage to rise to rejoin Jim and move like an apparition, not present in my body— skimming the ground, finding the space next to him, rehashing the whole bizarre pronouncement to him. In a mutual haze, we both sit comatose.

Africa has been the only place where we've ever called upon the American Embassy for help. They proved unhelpful even for the smallest things, so we'd stopped asking. Yet, in an act of unprecedented organization, this man asks me to believe that the American Embassy tracked me down in the middle of nowhere? And that my perfectly healthy mother has died?

But he delivered the message to you, I keep telling myself. Jim pieces it together, why this Malawian official is here in Zambia. My family knew we traveled north. I always told them our itinerary, the countries we'd traverse. The American Embassy wired every border post from Zimbabwe north. They must have a network for such emergencies. At the last border post, I slipped past without notice. After I'd left, our young officer realized I was the subject of the Embassy's wire. So he followed; five miles behind us in the bush he followed. To dismiss the whole matter would have been much easier. To his credit, he did not, and must now walk back for his trouble.

Everything is cast in a different light. I realize his stiff overtures were no more than attempts to lend sympathy to a female foreigner, and, very likely, a first in his career. Everything he did confirmed his unease—his hunched shoulders, his arms hugging his body as he rocked, his head bent forward unnaturally as if by a weight. His eyes flashing with the gravity of his news, meeting mine only once. They had not been insignificant moments for him either. Perhaps he'd lost his own mother, or pondered losing his mother those many minutes walking from Malawi.

As if propelled, I stumble over my pack and make my way back to the office. I need to see him again, to thank him. The other official tells me he's left for Malawi. At the only door to the building, more transient travelers block the way as I push my way past. The midday heat outside feels almost refreshing compared to inside. Locusts turn up their sirens and the air shimmers.

I shade my brow with my hand. In the distance, walking in the high bleached grass, I can make out a lone figure: the speck of a man in bermudaed uniform. His head must be down; I cannot discern his head. I squint hard against the light. The heat waves rising from the earth slowly consume him, scarcely a line, a soft gray hue. And gone.

Jim and I agree. My messenger's goodwill lends credence to possibility. I'm willing to concede that this message is linked to me. A surreal event in the bush can be possible only if something extraordinary precipitated it. The correctness of the message is what's in question. That it came across the world at all suggests something has happened. Healthy mothers die prematurely all the time. But it's still unlikely my mother has died; it has to be my father.

Berthold arrives by foot just as Jim and I sit under the baobab tree. He takes my news very hard, as if he's known me all my life or known my mother. As if we're related. To hear him, one would think my message was his. He delivers a stream of consciousness monologue for all to hear. "Oh Jesus Christ, I can't believe this is happening," he says. It's just a matter of time that this will happen to him, to his eighty year old mother. Just like me, he'll get this message someday. No, worse yet: he won't get a message, his mother will be dead and buried for weeks before he'll find out.

What can he do? he goes on. If he returns to Germany, he'll languish there. And she could live to be ninety-something. It's not like he's that young himself. Is he supposed to stop traveling and stay home all the time, waiting for her to go? On and on and on, like this.

The Africans sit back and watch, like good theater, scarcely blinking, following every movement of this odd *mzungu* with so much flesh on his body. Berthold draws me out of myself, because I end up consoling him instead. With intermittent quiet, I settle back into my own crazed thoughts. But he pipes up again. "I don't understand you. How can you be taking this so well? What do you really think happened? Do you think it was your mother, or your father? What are you going to do now?" And then, "Uh! Jesus Christ, I just can't believe this is happening. Jesus Christ. Jesus Christ."

The lives of three parents hang in the parched afternoon. Like a Greek chorus, Berthold fills the air with soliloquies from the time the sun sits high in the sky until it sinks to the earth. Even the Africans have tired of him.

For hours, I hug my legs, no doubt looking ravaged, red-eyed, weeping quietly for my father, then my mother, as Jim consoles me. I look up to see African faces mirroring my grief, watching me with long, sad eyes. Their love consoles me; is all I need. Berthold has finally shut up, and I now anticipate the bus which everyone says is ten hours late.

At eight o'clock, the bus arrives. The three of us travel directly north towards Tanzania to the Zambian border town of Nakonde. Nakonde isn't far, but it takes another six and a half hours to get there due to two flat tires on the way. We arrive at two thirty in the morning. We'll cross the check point to Tanzania the next morning.

Jim and I bounce from one side of the street to the other in search of a double room. Nakonde is a slimy little place; no one sleeps, it seems. The bars hop, the contraband flows, the hookers vine themselves to every door. An Indian guesthouse owner takes pity on us and puts us up in a tiny back room with a single bed used for storage. There is no international phone service in town, he tells us. We must go to the main hotel in Mbeya, the largest town in southern Tanzania.

Jim sleeps and I fall asleep for a few hours; with a single blink, I am awake again, eerily clear. I feel very content. Has my body put my mind on a slow adrenaline drip? I watch the crescent moon and stars move across the sky. The longer I distance myself from the message, the more surreal my thinking becomes. The specter grows again that all of this could be a bizarre mistake. Then the specter shrinks, rendering all of it gravely true.

I picture my parents' bedroom and the little squeaky double bed they've huddled in together since the day they married. Is it just another night? Do they kiss goodnight, turn off the lights and lie there? Or does one lie alone, numb and shaken with loss?

I ponder the practical solution, the death of my father. Independent to a fault, he never seemed to need anyone. The truth is, he's actually very vulnerable. His first heart attack raised his need for us. I haven't really known my father these many years. No one has. Maybe it's the German stoicism, but he has never let anyone in. His convalescence period brought the two of us closer. He wanted so much for Jim and me to live our dream of traveling the world. It would realize a dream for him too, he said. When I left him in good health—better than ever, it seemed—we knew we'd pick up our lives where we left off.

If my father lived now, he could make up for lost time with his three children. For the first time, I embrace his death and cry bitter, sad tears. Because I fear I won't get to know him better. I cry some more for the immutable end of this heady ride that took on a life of its own—this extraordinary odyssey that I've loved more than anything I've done in my life.

We whisk through the crowded Tanzanian border post with our special papers and take another bus to Mbeya, arriving in the afternoon. We aren't so far from Kenya now. With all my being, I wish there is some way we can get back to Kenya faster.

There is no room at the Mbeya Hotel, so we look around and settle on another substandard room out of desperation. As soon as we're checked in, we head back to the hotel to make an international call. We must wait as other people call. Part of me wants to yell, *Excuse me, I have an emergency here!* Part of me never wants to call; to simply wake up and say that was such a vivid, terrible dream.

When a phone is free, the operator makes various attempts to get through for me. So another person takes a turn. We try again; the call cannot be completed. "It's OK," I say to the operator. "Thank you. I'll try again tomorrow."

We go to eat, and I eat heartily for the first time in two days. There is sanctuary in not knowing. Both my parents are alive in this hallowed place.

Though I still can't fathom it, I consider the death of my mother. I've always been closer to her; her loss would be devastating. And my father couldn't live without her support now or cope with a sedentary lifestyle alone. He would languish, a slow, unsatisfactory kind of end without her. It would be better if he preceded her. I can't cry for my mother's death because I can't embrace it. I sleep fitfully that night; I know the next day will bring the real message.

In the morning, we find the phone room empty. This is it. Jim and I park ourselves in front of the clerk and wait while he calls the US again. I'm ready, I tell myself. It's the middle of the night in the US and the call doesn't go through two times, the clerk tells me. The adrenaline drip has stopped. I'm a mess, standing and stretching and pacing. He tries again. "Thanks for your help, again," I say. "We'll come back later." I can't face the prospect of living like this for another day.

Jim and I go to breakfast. I pick at my eggs, the only food I really enjoy in Africa. We return to the hotel in the early afternoon—early morning in the US. The clerk smiles warmly when he sees us again. He must sense this is a terrible time for me. I can't even imagine how he sees me.

I watch his face as he places the call, looks down, listens carefully with wide bird-eyes focused on the counter. "Yes... yes," he says, and looks over to me, nodding the okay. I stand there, not knowing what to do. He points to the phone in the booth, impatiently, repeatedly, like a commandant who screams, *Pick up the phone! This is it! You must know the truth!*

My body feels thick and heavy. I retrieve the receiver. The call pauses and goes through. *Click-click-click.* A phone rings once, twice. The rings sound like the phone rings of my childhood. My mother always answers by the third ring; four rings are rare. I can see it ringing, the ancient lemon-yellow phone that hangs on the yellow tile kitchen wall. There's a fourth ring; this can't be my house. He's misdialed the number; this is a mistake. All of it's a mistake.

Then nothing, it stops ringing. White noise. Someone fumbles with the cord. I can see her, my mother untangling the stretched cord like she does, so practical, my father looking up to hear who's calling so early. I interrupted them. They were having breakfast and Uh, here's the phone ringing already. My mother chews quickly and swallows with a little nod of the head, like she does, before answering.

My skin tingles, the air pulses, and the breadth between heaven and earth narrows. A throat clears; my mother clears her throat. In a slow, subdued voice—a lonely, broken voice says, "Helloooo?"

Try as I may, I can't remember the face of my messenger who walked so far that day, the young officer who remains an inextricable part of my destiny. I strain to see his features. It haunts me that his face evades me. If I could just see him once more, if only an errant image would come. Even without that image, I still feel his gentle presence and unease.

I've tried in vain to pinpoint just where I was in Africa and what I was doing when my father died. For some reason, I need to know this. Surely he wouldn't part without some small sign, something I could point to that happened the precise moment he passed. With microscopic scrutiny, I surveyed the possible clues. My writings would tell me where I was. If I had that journal, which was shipped in a box that never made it home from Africa.

My father died the first of September, eighteen days before the message in the bush, twenty days before I called home. We traveled in Malawi at the time. And I know he died in the afternoon, Malawi's evening. Just about the time Jim and I would sit outside. Those Malawi nights seemed somehow sacred. We listened to the tribal drums under the candles of night. The moon encircled our bodies and cast us in its shadow. The drums filled us up, like ancient, enrapt songs emanating from the African soil. We never tired of the drums.

I like to think that's when he died. That my father's last breath was the voice of an African drum.

NEPAL: PRAYERS ON THE WIND

O wild and wondrous midnight, there is a might in thee, to make the charmed body, almost like spirit be, and give it some faint glimpses, of immortality.

James Russell Lowell

Jim, Romeo and I clink our drinks together—our beers, Romeo's coke —and turn to face the river. A long wooden counter on the second floor of the Foreign Correspondents Club opens up to the outdoors like a picture window overlooking the Tonle Sap river in Phnom Penh.

Known as the FCC, the club's watering hole and restaurant bustled with foreign correspondents during the Vietnam War. Sydney Schanberg, an American journalist, and Dith Pran, a Cambodian journalist, sat here pondering their fate after the fall of Phnom Penh to the Khmer Rouge. Nine years later, *The Killing Fields* book and movie told their story and put Cambodia on the map. The tourist map anyway.

Tourists flock here like groupies today and pay too much for the trendy Western food in exchange for some vague, ineffable linger of a defining moment in history. At least that's why Jim and I came. It sounds like the others came for the Angkor beer. The spirit of Dith Pran seems lost on happy hour. A fleeting sadness and sense of irony mingle with my beer. This place should be a shrine, not a damn bar.

Romeo shifts in his seat and looks bored. How could Jim and I have forgotten he doesn't drink? It's April, 2001, and our visit to Phnom Penh marks the first time the three of us have been together since we met in Kenya sixteen years ago. Jim and I fly home tomorrow, so this serves as our farewell outing. We all hang on the sunset like it's our last. Perhaps the prices are fair exchange for the view, I decide.

Once again, Jim broaches the subject of Romeo getting an email address; how easily he could do it with the help of someone at the Internet café. We sit smiling, awaiting his response. "Soooo, what do you think?" I say.

Romeo's large doe-like eyes reflect nothing, not quite with us, not quite among the living. Romeo and technology are a futile cause anyway. "Don't worry, it doesn't really matter if you get an email address," I say. "We'll always be in touch, you know we will. If we could find you in Nepal, we can find you anywhere."

Romeo lifts his eyebrows, Kenyan-style, smiling politely, unconvincingly, in agreement. "You know what I mean, when we met up in Nepal?"

"Oh, yeah, I know," he says quietly. He still doesn't consider the incident in Nepal of any significance.

"Well, that whole thing still raises the hair off my arms," I say. "Did I ever tell you I consulted a psychic about it? I felt there had to be something else going on that we weren't aware of. How could it have happened otherwise? There's no logical explanation. Anyway, I was curious what a psychic would say." Since he's a staunch Catholic, Romeo may have a problem with this. But he also believes in miracles. His own recovery was a miracle, he once told me.

He turns his head slightly, fidgets and blushes. Jim is looking ill too—all the signals that I should recant this story as soon as possible. But it's too late. The beer has gone to my head and they're both being annoyingly stiff.

I inhale and continue. "She *said* the reason this happened is we're all related, there was a past connection in another life. I'm not sure what I think of that either but it's interesting to ponder, isn't it?" Romeo raises his eyebrows and nods again, half-heartedly; maybe even less than half-heartedly.

Ending this story doesn't seem like a bad idea now. We all take another drink and look out to see the edge of the sun slip behind the river. And no one misses the most interesting part of my story.

The story actually began in Nairobi, Kenya, in 1980, when we first met Romeo at the notorious Iqbal Hotel in the red light district. Since Jim and I traveled to different parts of Kenya over a couple of months, we found ourselves staying in Nairobi frequently. Due to a housing crisis, an influx of refugees from Uganda and political instability in Kenya, a dive in Nairobi cost twice as much as lodging any place else in Kenya. We were hell bent on not spending too much money for a bed. And going for the memorable places counts for a lot in matters of travel, and for this, the Iqbal shone.

Most of our friends from the Sudan trip ended up there too. A lot of the people who stayed at the Iqbal were budget travelers. The rest were tenants, transient down-on-their-luck types who lived in dormitory rooms. We always thought of Romeo as an exception.

The Iqbal had probably been unapologetically substandard throughout its history. No romantic colonial ghosts lurked there; no hints of fine architecture. The staff went through the right motions every day, gliding large wet mops across the floor.

But when they finished, the nondescript tile pattern remained the same opaque gray.

To be fair, there was one redeeming feature of the Iqbal—the large restaurant that spanned the entire first floor. One can only imagine what mysteries the full menu held, but we ordered only three things the entire time we lived there: *chai*, *mandazi*-donuts and *makati miai*, a curious pan-fried egg and dough mixture—Romeo's entire sustenance.

Even people who stayed in starred hotels would hang out in the restaurant. The strong sweet *chai* (colonial-African *chai* cooked with condensed milk) could make you forget how seedy the place was. Since Romeo was an Iqbal fixture, we got to know him over many a cup of *chai*. Any time we were coming or going, we could count on finding him ensconced in his chair in one particular spot.

Romeo hails from three continents, an international mishmash of lineages. He's a citizen of Kenya, having grown up there. But, unlike Kenyans, his skin is not black but tawny-colored, his features fine and Caucasian. His father hails from Goa, India, and is of Portuguese descent—hence the name Romeo. His mother hailed from Somalia. Because Romeo attended British schools in colonial Kenya, he speaks in quick trills typical of East Indians.

Romeo's most striking feature in those days was his shoulder-length hair—a wild Rastafarian mop. Bob Marley and his politics had nothing to do with it. Romeo's style was mostly about knitting all his hair together and forgetting it. To follow behind him on the street, you might wonder how that slip of a body could support such a prodigious head. His frail, concave frame looked like it might blow away with the next puff of air. Standing next to him always made me feel like a great mythical Amazon.

To mix things up and avoid consistency at all costs, Romeo portrayed a different person from the neck down. He favored tailor-cut pants and shirts, always long-sleeved shirts, with a nice leather belt and shoes. Clean, ironed clothes and fine cigarettes were considered basic necessities. How he pulled off this neat appearance with all his worldly possessions jammed in balls under a single bed baffled me. He reminded me of the shanty-town office workers who miraculously emerge each morning out of their cardboard houses looking like professionals dressed for work. A mutual friend who knew Romeo for years once told us he held a civil service job with the Kenyan government before he "fell apart." Romeo never shared details of his past with us.

All physical trappings aside, the single feature that stayed with me most, that haunted me, was his eyes. They reminded me of a picture of Jesus on the Sunday school wall of my youth—kind, gentle eyes that drew you into deep reflective pools of suffering. *(Now if Jesus came back on earth today,* my Sunday school teacher would ask, *who would he hang out with?)* What I appreciated most about Romeo, and Jesus, was they both deplored classism and gravitated towards inherently flawed people.

At the time of our first meeting, Romeo neared the age of fifty. His health was less than borderline. Against all odds, he has endured, a testament to the fact that low body weight contributes to longevity. He completely neglected his body, snacking on nothing more than *chais* and greasy *mandazis* between chain-smoking and fits of coughing. A fancy, expensive Kenyan cigarette was his brand, though he lowered his standards when bumming from others.

He did eat heartily at Sikh temples where they served free food to poor people and travelers each week, all part of the religion. God bless those Sikhs. Since Jim and I qualified too, we enjoyed some of the most memorable meals we'd ever eaten. Romeo knew all the Sikh temples in Nairobi and their meal schedules.

Romeo confided to us that he'd been an alcoholic years before, now reformed. Rosie, the love of his life, was the major loss of that era. They had never married but had two children together, twins, who died at a young age—that other friend told us. Our friend never knew how the children died, presumably a tragic accident since they died together. And he knew Romeo blamed himself for their deaths.

Years after the breakup, he continued to visit Rosie. "I'm going to Eldoret for a few days," he'd tell us, and we knew it was to visit Rosie. He'd return each time downcast and diminished. We would coax him to the restaurant from his room.

"Why do you do this to yourself?" I'd wail. He'd shake his head; he couldn't say. It wasn't a matter of choice, I think. Rosie remained his only semblance of family or history, his last earthly connection. And with time, Jim and me.

Romeo's hard-knocks wrought a deeply spiritual, gentle person who made a valiant effort to seem okay. In fleeting moments, he'd forget his problems and actually let go. Stories in the newspaper about some injustice or hypocrisy got him hopping mad. Hypocrisy made him most spunky. With arms waving, he'd get on his soapbox and say the kinds of things that would get some people in Kenya killed. But of course anybody who knew anybody didn't hang out at the Iqbal.

I marveled at how Romeo just kept going, getting out of a dirty bed every morning, living hand-to-mouth day after day with no real hope for the future. Then I realized that millions of people actually live like this. The need to survive protected Romeo, creating a blind that opened only on the moment. The future doesn't really exist for the Romeos of the world like it does for us.

More than once, Romeo teetered on the brink of getting ahead, accumulating some money from his business of buying and selling travelers' paraphernalia. The problem was, he was fiercely proud for a poor person and generous to his own detriment. Snatching up our *chai* bills and trying to balance each kindness paid to him made it harder to get ahead.

And then the streets of Nairobi were riddled with snakes that can hear a little loose change in the pocket. The stakes were always high, their pleas never modest—medication for a feverish, dying child, eviction on the street, deportment by the government—all things Romeo understood well.

Convinced he'd been unspeakably stupid and ripped off, Romeo would retreat into a black, self-flagellating pity-party in his room. "Maybe some of those hard luck stories were true!" Jim said to Romeo. He was unmoved.

We knew these stories on the street well; they were very convincing. We gave to some. But we could afford to part with some money. In the end, it didn't matter whether all the characters who drained Romeo's meager savings were lying or telling the truth to eat.

We persevered. "Look at it this way," I said. "People with plenty to eat simply don't spend their days scamming people on the street. What concerns me is that you may be a lot less persuasive than they were when you run out of money."

When the time came to leave Kenya and Romeo behind in 1981, I was almost relieved to say goodbye. I can only see it now. Africa gets in your blood unlike any place on earth. Though it gives so much, it takes more than you can know. Only when I left did I feel the weight lift. Looking out from the window, I soared with the big whippy African clouds hugging the plane.

For the next three years through the beginning of 1984, Jim and I kept in touch with Romeo by mail. His next-to-last letter announced a plan to travel to India to claim his deceased father's inheritance. Jim and I were ecstatic. No one was more deserving of a little nest egg. But where would Romeo get enough money to pay for the expensive trip to India? we wondered.

A month later, we received a new letter sent from Goa on the west coast of India. Romeo had arrived at the ancestral home of his father. The letter read like the plot of a bad Hindi movie. His aunts and uncles stole his inheritance, contested the will before he arrived, and took everything—his father's land, the family possessions, all the things that were rightfully his. Why they summoned him to come home remained a mystery to us. To give him the bad news?

We wrote back to the post office box on his letter and encouraged him to get legal counsel. One of the positive legacies of British colonial rule was the rule of law. India abounds with excellent solicitors. But even as we penned our advice, we knew Romeo lacked the financial or emotional wherewithal to pursue legal counsel. Life had already taken too much from him. An answer to our letter never came.

Jim and I knew we would soon travel to Asia, and the trip was to include India. But how could we meet Romeo or help him if we didn't know where he was? I sent another letter telling him we would come; again, there was no response.

The first leg of our trip in October, 1984, took us to Europe, followed by Greece, Bangladesh, Nepal (and India thereafter). I thought of Romeo so often, wondered how his drama played out and where he was now. When we reached Asia in late January, 1985, the irony of being so close never evaded me. I began to question whether we would ever see or hear from him again.

Even if Romeo had remained in the home of his birth, we opted to skip Goa to the west and Kashmir to the north. Tensions with Pakistan were escalating and tourists were discouraged from coming. Most likely Romeo had returned to Africa anyway. The least the wicked aunties and uncles could do was ensure his flight home.

When we reached Nepal, it was as if I fell in love, as if the Himalayas left room for nothing else and displaced all thoughts of Romeo.

We arrived in Kathmandu in February. The bus from Bangladesh dropped us off just as the morning sun illuminated the sky. Nothing can prepare you for Kathmandu, the city-valley at the foothills of the Himalayas.

We strained our necks to find the ridge tops. The mountains were higher than mountains are meant to be. Snow-capped peaks jutted through clouds at the top. "And this isn't even the highest Himalayan range," Jim said.

The morning air was crisp, soothing; the sky was a deep limpid blue. Something palpable moved on the wind, something as tangible as a thunderstorm brewing. I cocked my head to take it in better. "I don't know, it just doesn't feel like the earth where we live," I said to Jim rather inanely.

"Well it isn't, you know," he said. "We're about forty-five hundred feet higher than our house in Baltimore."

"No, it's not the altitude," I said, "it's something else."

"Maybe it's the lack of oxygen." Jim said, smiling. I frowned.

In Nepal, Buddhism is basically an airborne religion. From each little house, shrine and temple, prayers ascend on black puffs of smoke, swirling and lifting on gusts of mountain air from little forests of incense sticks below. Prayer flags, homemade pieces of cloth sewn together, bear hand-written Sanskrit prayers that *flap-flap-flap* their requests on the wind from balconies and rooftops. In the temples, supplicants rattle and spin huge prayer wheels that drone their prayers up to heaven. Rooftop bells of every size *ting-ting-ting* their notes across the valleys.

Few places on earth evoke more love and devotion. How could a god in his heaven not be pleased? I hugged my arms, looking up. Whatever it was, it was ubiquitous, the kind of energy you feel in a church or temple. "Honestly, you can almost touch it," I marveled.

So many things lent to the feeling—the imposing mountains, the prayers on the wind, the simple devotion of countless people lifted up. The connection between heaven and earth seemed somehow sharper there, as if Kathmandu stood at a fine meridian. "Do you think it's what people call the divine?" I asked aloud. "And is it any accident that a buddha was spawned in this land?"

Later that day, we found Kathmandu's man-made attractions no less transcendent. The first sight of Durbar Square took my breath. We rounded a bend and met the old royal palace, Hanuman Dhoka, one of the various palaces where the Malla and Shah kings of Nepal made their homes since the eleventh century. Palace and temple styles were most commonly Hindu architecture built of soft pink and peach-colored bricks with dark intricately-carved wooden windows that rose up into Chinese pagoda-type tiered roofs.

Like the surrounding Himalayas, the architects of the buildings hugging the center of Durbar Square went for the sky. At every turn, we found temples, Buddhist *stupas,* shrines, civic monuments—all set snuggly within a three-square block area. Bright pastel-painted deities, golden deities and demons with warning grimaces stood guard outside, lending a storybook quality. To complete the fable, a young goddess in residence with round blush-powder cheeks peered from her window in the Temple of the Living Goddess—the stuff that little girls' dreams are made of. Where else on earth do kings and queens and goddesses still hold court?

But the mundane pressed in too. Tourists and locals, rickshaws and bicycles, monks in saffron robes, cows and goats all vied for space and milled around the textile peddlers who spread their colorful handmade wares at the base of the temples. Beggars descended upon us—old, young, blind and crippled— jostling for an audience. A mother carried a sick child in her arms and tapped at her mouth, her face contorted in plea. Half-naked children with dirty legs and faces ran around in torn clothes with knots in their hair. Mangy dogs barked or fought, or slept to conserve energy. Amid the honking clanging din, furtive voices would find our ears (*Want to buy hasheesh, want to change money, want to buy rug, want to buy opium?*)

Jim and I landed with a nasty bump. Kathmandu is of the earth after all. It's rare to find life's dichotomies so apparent and in such close proximity. Despite all the luster and pomp, Nepal is an abjectly poor country, poorer than its neighbor India.

The next day, we traveled to the twenty-five hundred year old Swayambhunath Temple, famous for its main *stuppa*. A *stuppa* is a shrine with a dome-like top that cannot be entered like a building. Each side of the Swayambhunath *stuppa* bears the large smiling eyes of Buddha, kind and maternal, looking out in every direction across the northern Kathmandu valley. For centuries, these eyes have come to be associated with Nepal.

"Want to go up and see the monastery too?" Jim asked.

I shrugged my shoulders. "Sure, why not."

We climbed the steep white-washed stairs. The wind picked up and prayer flags on long streamers draped from the *stuppa* top flapped madly. Halfway up, the person in front of me hesitated, stopping our ascent. A gust of wind whipped my hair flat across my face. As I pulled it back, looking towards the temple floor, a crooked shadow—a passing blob of hair—caught my eye. I turned to navigate the next step as the phantom form registered in my head, giving me a start. I looked back to find it again, the wild Rastafarian head with the little stick body, so anomalous in this landscape.

"Jim, quick, look over there!" I said, pointing to the temple floor below. "Doesn't that remind you of Romeo?" The head stopped short, turned and looked straight up at me. It was Romeo, his face beaming.

I am not the fainting type but people have fainted for far less. Nothing in my life rivals this event. And placing it in the realm of coincidence only trivializes it.

When Romeo decided to leave Goa in 1984, about the same time we lost touch, he said he wanted to return to Africa. But a ticket back to Africa never came, and he found it impossible to stay in Goa. With a little money and the kindness of strangers, he traveled east, then north, across India with no destination in mind, taking in various attractions along the way. "I've always wanted to see Nepal," he told us, "so I decided to go to Kathmandu."

So here we were, Jim and I and Romeo on the other side of the world in the same city in the same temple on the same day. At the same time. It would all count for nothing if it wasn't precisely the same time. Chaos may reign in the universe, but our stars lined up like Haley's Comet in the seventy-sixth year.

And the light taupe pants in front of me on the stair, the man who hesitated—was he complicit? Romeo never saw us above. He was making a beeline for the temple gate when I spotted him. Had the man on the stair not stopped, had I not turned my head, had the wind that blew my hair in my face succeeded in blocking my view, Romeo would have slipped away. But a mere glance fielded that odd blur that was Romeo, no less blithe than a fly passing by.

Were the pieces as fragile as they seemed? Had all of us been complicit? Did talking and thinking about Romeo for more than seven months draw him to us? Or was it Nepal, this place that hears all prayers on the wind?

Jim and Romeo seemed initially impressed with our meeting but dispensed of it quickly. As we walked together, I was grateful they could chat about prosaic things. I could not; I hadn't come in for a landing yet. For me, it was a decisive event that still lingered, still held me close in its wake—as if that Rastafarian head parted my life down the middle. Everything had necessarily changed.

"Haha," Jim said, laughing. "And I can imagine how that went over." I marveled at their resilience, their robust conversation, their animated gestures. The earth had not shifted on its axis for them. What could I liken this to? Seeing a ghost? Being struck by lightning? Yes, it was something like that; being struck by a bolt of light. They laughed again. "So where are you staying? Let's have dinner together," Jim said.

Things are not as they appear; but I'd known it all along. Even as a very small child, I sensed it. I believed that the world was sweet and safe and predictable, like the folds of my mother's lap. But about age four or five, things began to turn on their head. The *exceptions* kept leaking out. Things like an omnipresent, all-knowing, all-seeing God. And miracles. And Santa Claus. And ghosts that floated in the night—all of them defying the laws of natures. Nothing was assured at all, as I'd thought. From what I could see, no one was really safe if the physical world bent its own rules. I was always wary that the world might forsake me as it had before—that if I looked at an inanimate object long enough, it might move on its own, or even jump.

With time, I saw that the sun came up and went down thousands of times. Inanimate objects never moved, ghosts never appeared and the physical world proved to be reliable. I began to relax.

But Romeo's presence set things asunder again. And yet, I wasn't really frightened by the prospect; at least here in Nepal. It was more like a door that had been ajar all my life had suddenly opened. I looked up to see the smiling eyes of Buddha on the *stuppa* follow us as we walked.

The clouds that veiled the Himalayas to the north an hour before shifted, exposing a full peak. The white snow mantle caught the sun like a mirror. A warm tingle moved down my neck and back. We are much more than our skin and bones and hair. Anything seemed possible now; reincarnation seemed possible in this place. I looked at this enigmatic little man who walked next to Jim and knew he was inextricably linked to us, as if we must have known him before meeting him sixteen years ago. To be sure, he was not just another person along our way. It all makes sense. The inexplicable affection I've felt for him all along.

At dinner, I resolved to stop saying "I just can't get over this" and proffer some convincing conversation. But my frustration spilled over when Jim and I returned to our hotel. "Has anything in your life ever rivaled this?" I asked.

"No," he conceded, "but just because I don't go on about it doesn't mean I'm not impressed too."

The next morning, the three of us ate vegetable *dhosas* at our farewell breakfast in Kathmandu. Romeo showed us an article about the UN High Commission for Refugees in the *Kathmandu Post*. Forty million refugees or displaced people span the earth, it said, many who have been adrift for generations. But the true figures stagger the imagination. People like Romeo who left home to make a better life are neither refugees nor displaced. They don't figure into these numbers; they weren't forced to leave their countries, yet they can't go home. Their repressive governments rarely welcome them back after they leave. The home Romeo once knew two decades ago no longer existed. Add to these numbers the yawning Diaspora who choose to live and work outside their country because they can't possibly make a living at home.

Since our farewell in Kathmandu sixteen years ago, with no money to scrape together to make the trip home, Romeo visited and over-extended his visa in Thailand, China, Vietnam and now Cambodia. Once while settled in Vietnam with some income, Romeo had saved the money to return home to Kenya. But this was the Eighties, when the political situation wasn't safe. For twenty years, Kenyans fled the violence and political instability in their country. Romeo no longer dreamed of returning home. He shrugged his shoulders. "I wouldn't even know any one. Where would I go?"

He has lived in Cambodia for eight years and earns money teaching English to locals. Cambodia has become home. And

Jim's work with an international relief agency takes both of us to Cambodia every year or two.

At sixty-something now, almost seventy, a year after he almost died of *dengue* fever, Romeo surprised us again. He has a girlfriend, though he goes to great lengths to deny it. "No, no, no, it isn't true, who told you that?" he laughs.

She's a country girl from the border of Vietnam and relatively young for Romeo—in her forties. An owner of an Indian restaurant in the backpacker alley of Phnom Penh, she delivers beautiful homemade meals each day to his room and fattens him up. "It's nothing. We're just good friends," he assures us a little too much.

The three of us watch the last rays of light disappear on the horizon, the din in the FCC now reduced several decibels. I turn to speak to Romeo but stop short, his distant vapid stare evaporating my all-is-right-with-the-world beer bubble. No matter what goes right in his life, it seems Romeo will be forever displaced.

In an instant, he recovers and jumps off his bar stool, clasping his hands. "So, shall we head off, then?" he says in his chipper English accent. I remember now how he detests goodbyes, how we could never find him in Kenya when it was time to go. He is more or less stuck, though; he can't hide now. We all sit on the river wall, snacking on vendor peanuts and watching the boats go by on the Tonle Sap river.

The night is glorious. "Uh! I really love the night," I say aloud. "For some reason, I feel more alive at night. How about you?" I turn to Romeo.

"Yeah, yeah, me too actually," his voice trails off. And then he is present again. "Yeah, I know what you mean, Ann," he says, convincingly this time.

"Really? I didn't know that about you. I wonder why we both like the night." No response. Romeo prefers not to unearth things subterranean.

"Maybe it's because it's a full moon tonight," he says, smiling.

"No, I've got it. It's because, you know, we're *related* and all."

He laughs, a rare, full-bodied laugh, and points his finger. "OK, OK," he says in his silly kidding voice he uses with children. "Now stop it, don't start that rubbish again." That's how you get Romeo's real opinions.

Just when everything seems perfect, photogenic, Romeo rises, mumbles something about having to go. He retrieves a small bag from his coat jacket and takes out a heavy silver bracelet with Arabic motifs. He remembers that I wear silver bracelets on my arm. It's truly exquisite, probably antique. How can he afford this? "It's wonderful, Romeo. It must be Arabic. Is it from Lamu?"

"Yes it's Arabic but from Zanzibar."

"And you've carried it all this time?" Probably traded for a backpack or something substantial. "It's so elegant. I really love it. You know I'll always treasure it."

"Well, I'm off then," he says, hugging me quickly and giving Jim a handshake. We grab our things and follow him to the street for fear we'll miss his departure. He hails a motobike and climbs on, putting his head down and turning to wave as they zoom off. You gotta give it to Romeo and Emily Post: they never tarry when it's time to leave.

Jim and I can't leave just then; the air is too electric, too welcoming. Everyone revels in the perfect temperatures, the humanity in the air. One of those pristine nights engraved in the psyche. The snack *wallahs* move about slowly, tingling their bells. Kids run by; families sprawl across the grass and eat ice cream. The stars appear in full force, though the moon is still at large.

The night endears itself, draws me to it. Since we first took breath, we have known this rich rhinestone cover that tucks us in at the end of the day. Like adoring luminaries, these beads of light follow us wherever we go in the world. How can we be homesick?

A silver haze washes the earth when night descends; colors soften and sounds ring truer. Shadows and street lights relent to the harsh glare of day and recast the landscape, making all things as new. The night renders every town and city in the world beautiful. When we look up, the silver haze works on us too, stilling the heart and giving it sanctuary. And for a few charmed moments of the day, for people like Romeo and those in the Diaspora of displacement, night is home.

INDIA: CHARMING DEITIES I HAVE KNOWN

No matter how dark the night, somehow the sun rises once again and all shadows are chased away.

David Matthew

The lines between countries can be fuzzy. India envelopes Nepal on three sides, so it's no surprise that many Nepalese people are of Indo-Aryan descent, particularly in the temperate and subtropical areas. Since we travel to India, our bus from Kathmandu to Varanasi, India, bulges with passengers of Indian descent. I feel like I'm already there.

Jim and I purchased a ticket on an express bus with a scheduled stopover-tour in Lumbini, Nepal, birthplace of Buddha. Every banyan tree and *chai* shop south produces more riders until it seems our seams will pop. This bus is no express. And I find it hard to believe all these people en route to Varanasi plan to stop at Lumbini for a tour.

My answer comes soon enough. A *Birthplace of Buddha* sign whisks by. "Whoa, whoa," we bang on the side of the bus, as the locals do when they want to stop.

A collage of straining faces peer back at the foreigners. Foreigners entertain the people of the developing world every day; it's our job. In certain countries like India, we experience the vagaries of fame; we're virtual movie stars. Talking, eating and, especially laughing, fascinate. Nose blowing ranks very high. Climbing out of this sardine can over heaps of junk while wearing a skirt should prove spellbinding.

The bus has stopped. "Isn't there a stopover in Lumbini?" I yell to the conductor up front who looks at me as if I'm making this up. Everyone turns to the conductor. He consults the driver and yells back.

"Oh, verdy sorry, madam, not today. We must get the parts in India straight away."

"Since we paid for the Lumbini tour, can we get off here to get our money back and pick up another bus?" I yell back. Heads ping-pong back to the conductor.

"Sorry, madam, no more buses to Varanasi today. But no problem. We give you the money. I'm coming, I'm coming." Jim and I sigh collectively. It looks like the trip to Buddha's birthplace isn't in the stars. And since the back of the bus looks like a battlefield of bodies and bags clear up to the front, we can forget the refund too.

At ten o'clock in the morning, people wipe their faces and fan with anything that moves air. Most sit indifferently and let the perspiration overcome them. In the dry season in March, the Ganges plains are as hot as the earth gets, scarcely traversable, much less inhabitable. By afternoon, the hell with the dust; all windows open wide in search of some air, the plains billowing in like little dust devils. The Ganges defy the laws of physics. In other places on earth, I recall, moving air brings relief, at least the sensation of a drop in temperature. Isn't that why we open windows when we move? But the Ganges plains are a blast furnace; the window only delivers the heat more quickly, like a furnace fan that sucks any semblance of moisture out of you. We all cook on slow bake like *naan-roti* bread in an oven.

Jim stands to give an old woman his seat. I soon stand for a woman carrying a young child. The others on the bus don't seem to notice the women. Need isn't delineated in a country teeming with abjectly poor people. Whether you're old or young, disabled or pregnant, everyone is in this together. And the Hindu religion assures its millions of supplicants that life unfolds precisely as it should. If your life is difficult, it is meant to be difficult. Hinduism is the glue that holds India's delicate balance together.

Just the same, the two women we give our seats to brim with grateful smiles. The bus stops for the night—we don't even know where, we don't even care where—and rise in the morning to do this all over again. The second day is hotter and dustier. And we've stood since we first got on.

By late afternoon, all of us are uniformly light-skinned and light-haired—the women's colorful saris and the men's shirts and *dhotis* (the male, cotton sarong) cast in the same white-beige likeness. We will arrive in Varanasi in another six hours, we are told. In the Indian way, peaceable but pushy, Jim and I vie for a sliver of space to call our own. With a firm grip on the ceiling bar, shoulder bag wedged on the seat rail, Jim's arm over my head, my leg pressing against his, we reconfigure each hour and hold fast to our spot. I long to pop the little man in the white *dhoti* whose bony elbow has jabbed me in the ribs for hours.

I turn to see a face with a chin where eyes should be, upside down, only inches from my watch. "It's 4:25," I say.

"Verdy nice watch," he says, smiling.

"Thank you," I say, remembering that people on the street have a fascination with watches. Actually, men on the street. Little has changed that way; we rarely meet and talk to women. Everyone takes notice of your watch first, and the assumption is that Westerners wear expensive watches. For some reason,

I feel a responsibility to dispel this myth. "Actually it's just a cheap watch," I say.

"Ohhh," he nods, a bit nonplussed. Then I feel stupid and, worse, unfriendly.

"But thanks for asking," I smile, remembering that he never asked for anything.

The advent of evening works like salve; everyone gives up the good fight. The bus is quietly anticipatory. Our warm fleshy cocoon and mingled smells have become oddly familiar, almost comforting. The roads must be improving as our bounces and shifts narrow. Jim sleeps standing up while holding on; it just isn't normal. This two-day journey merits an entry in the annals of really tough rides in Asia. For everyone else, it's just another bus trip.

Kerosene lamps flicker along the roadside, telling us that a major urban center comes soon. The effect is magical, a presentiment of things to come in the most sacred of Indian cities. Something resembling a cool breeze passes through the bus and wakes us up. Life is as good as it gets again.

A new energy fills the bus; everyone readies their belongings and springs to their feet. Before the door opens we are thrust forward and become like different shapes of clay pressed into one. A man yells reproaches. Crowd control has never caught on in India. I see the headline in the cheap Indian dailies—yet another bus accident, except this bus doesn't drive off the road. We reach our destination and, with doors still closed, the front page photo reveals an abstract sculpture of entangled faces and arms.

Sandwiched between a woman and my bag, the head of the little man in the white *dhoti* is bent at a right angle to mine. Quintessentially unflappably Indian, he smiles and laughs a silly laugh, saying something in Hindi. The single most confounding thing about people in India is how they always manage without complaint, and often good humor. Against all odds, there is even joy. Since we're all going to be crushed to death anyway, I feel nothing but affection for the man in the white *dhoti* now.

The bus stops and the waiting bicycle rickshaw drivers spot Jim and me, their eyes following us closely. Since so many people in India make their living on the streets, tourists are most vulnerable, especially those with blonde hair who blend in like a light bulb. To add to the mayhem, the rickshaw drivers climb up into the open windows to negotiate a ride. The irony of the Indian daily article widens: The life is drained out of all of us. We are long-gone with eyes closed, but the rickshaw drivers continue to negotiate a ride to a hotel.

With a surge, we are birthed from our metal womb and plopped *en masse* out the door, fresh offerings at the altar of the rickshaw drivers. Travelers don't consider themselves tourists. Some of us have been traveling for months or years on a very different budget than a vacationer. But the distinction is hairsplitting in India, moot. The limp wet money we carry in our money bag under our shirts is still, comparatively speaking, a veritable fortune to them.

Before we can catch our breath, five rickshaw drivers have stuck to us like pasty rice, yelling and shoving. I have no strength to haggle. Jim raises his hand like an auctioneer. "How much to the Yogi Lodge?"

Most rickshaw drivers in towns, we've learned, know most places. "Yogi Lodge no good," one yells. We know this pitch: he knows a better place and the better place is his cousin's hotel. He could be right. Yogi Lodge provides "very basic accommodation," our guidebook says. But the Yogi has waxed legendary since the Sixties. Even if for a night, we have to try it. The Yogi Lodge is where we go.

"So how much?" Jim asks again.

And the bidding begins. "Twenty rupees," one says. "Eighteen rupees. OK, fifteen only, good price!" "OK, OK, final price, fourteen!" another says. I retrieve my guidebook-bible which reports about a two-kilometer ride to the Yogi

Lodge from the bus stand, a six rupee fare in most Indian cities. Granted, prices can be higher in towns and, since Varanasi is a highly touristed town, the fare may be more.

A wiry little man with no shirt cuts through the others as cool as a prophet parting the sea. The haggling and shoving stops, and the group falls silent. He is more dark skinned than the others, gray haired with an ultra-short cut, older than all his competitors by decades and shorter by a foot. But just as fit. I prefer the older drivers actually; I suspect they're more trustworthy.

"Twelve rupees, madam," he says calmly, with a dark red smile, his front teeth missing. He's a clever one, seeking out the madam.

"How about ten rupees?" I say. The words seem to crush him. Most rickshaw drivers were Thespians in another life.

"No, no, madam," he says with a troubled brow, his head boggling madly. "It is verdy far for ten rupees only—maybe four or more kilo-meters." He shows me the fingers to prove it. That shoots my theory about older drivers. Of course, he is full of beetle nut and his ghoulishly red lips and gums prove it. And what a mess he is, like a little kid, red beetle nut juice all over his white *dhoti*. He can certainly use the fare to eat; he's so thin.

"I think ten rupees is a good price," I say.

"Madam, the hotel is not two kilometers only......," he begins.

"OK, fine, how about eleven rupees?" This is craziness; we're talking about cents here; why am I doing this? His head makes a slight bob to the side, coupled with closing eyes, signifying a slow grudging yes.

"So eleven rupees then?" Another bob of the head, eyes closed. "And we go to the Yogi Lodge, right?" He collects our bags with the speed of an adolescent, hops on his seat, feet poised on peddles, with eyes sparkling. That's what it is: his smile, the thing you've got to love about this little guy. In the end, the hard bargain is a charade; I already know he's going to get a nice tip.

We wave to the competitors who turn with the weight of the world on them and move off. We marvel at our good fortune; this has been a record short transaction. By Indian standards, Jim and I are an easy haul, just ourselves and a shoulder bag each. For a few rupees, rickshaw drivers transport great towering loads up and down hills, whole families and children, pots and pans, tires and metal.

Our driver's age and small lean body belie his strength. I doubt there's an ounce of fat on his frame. I'm thinking he's around my father's age, in his late sixties. With each pedal, he groans and labors for our benefit.

Nighttime in India is India at its best. For a few golden hours, the earth relents to the day and people come out to shop again. Everyone moves slowly, in relaxed strides. The quiet seems almost odd; five different Indian songs aren't flooding the street at once. Sounds are crystalline. The bell of our rickshaw *cling-cling-clings* its way through the lumpy streets, echoing off the storefronts. We slip in and out of people and pushcart *wallahs* and cows gravitating towards home. A warm breeze stirs and jasmine wafts on the air. Because it is *Ramadan*, sweets shops still bustle, the only places open late for Muslims who break the fast at sunset. The shop lights guide our way.

Everyone senses it, savors it, the richness of the day's last moments. Except our driver. He cuts off a pushcart selling *chana-dal* that apparently meanders too slowly. *Cling-cling!!* This guy is ruthless. He nearly hits a cow that throws up its head with big brown eyes flashing, bolting as quickly as his boney frame can carry him. The cows in India are unusually congenial and polite.

"Excuse me, could we go more slowly?" I yell forward. "Slow is good!"

As we move along, an odd sound, a kind of drone that competes with the din of the streets, averts my ear. I realize it's our driver. With hands waving and head bobbing, he carries on a brisk conversation with himself. Then nothing. He lifts his head as if testing the air and leans back. "Madam? Sir?" Jim and I look at each other and laugh; he's been talking to us.

"Sorry, sorry, could you repeat that?" Jim says.

He's off again in a nanosecond, his voice rising and falling in complete gibberish. "We can't hear you back here!" I yell. "Could you please speak more slowly?" Does he even hear me? I wonder.

I lean forward. He is talking about children, his children? "One, two, three, four, five, six, seven." His fingers pop up and down on the same hand. Then the third round. Thirteen in all! he exclaims as if he himself is surprised. (*Is this really the first time he's counted his children?*)

"Oh my goodness, you have thirteen children?" I ask.

"Yes, thirteen," he beams. "Oh, and grandchildren too!"

"Isn't that wonderful!" I say as Jim and I gaze incredulously at each other, bracing ourselves for the grandchild count.

He twitters on, head boggling. His name is Shiva, he tells us, and his namesake is the Hindu god of creation and destruction. "Do you know of Shiva?" he asks.

"Yes, of course we know Shiva," I say. Wrong answer; his face falls. But never mind, he's off again, showing us how Shiva the god danced the dance of creation and—with arms flailing, no hands on the handlebars—he danced so fast and so hard, the darkness shook and all the planets and the stars in the heavens formed!

As we scale a small hill, Shiva's back lifts and heaves, every muscle tight and glistening in the night light. He sits down to enjoy the brief respite of the descent and turns, hardly winded. "And madam, sir, you? You are married?"

We know this answer. "Yes, of course."

"And how many children you are having?"

"No children just yet," I say.

"Excuse me, madam, sir, NO children?" He shakes his head. "Ohhh, I am verdy verdy sorry," as if there's been a death in the family.

Silence reigns, lovely unbroken silence. I fear this is more tumultuous than the dance of creation. We've pulled Shiva's world out from under him and rendered him speechless. I must remember to adopt my nieces Audra and Blair for that answer next time. The rickshaw makes a sharp turn and Shiva cranes his neck to take me in fully, to see precisely what a barren woman looks like. I flash him my prettiest, winning smile, no doubt disappointing him again.

We soon stop at the hotel, and Shiva jumps out and disappears through the front door. In the darkness, we strain to make out the name over the door. *Yogesh Hotel*, it says. Shiva returns and begins to unload our things.

"Shiva," I say, "I think we have the wrong place. We wanted the Yogi Lodge, remember?"

His head boggles quickly. "Yes, yes, this is it all right. Yogi, *yogesh*, it's all the same. A *yogesh* is a young yogi. This is it all right, fifty rupees a night only." He continues to unload our bags.

"But if it's all the same, why didn't our guidebook just call it The Yogesh Hotel?"

Jim consults the map. "Is the Ganges River close to here?" he asks. "And the Golden Temple, how close is that?"

"Yes, sir, I am knowing my home, Varanasi," he says with wounded pride. "The temple and the river are straight away," he says, motioning with a sweep of the hand down the street.

"But the Yogi Lodge has been around for a long time. Look at this. This is a new hotel," I say. Shiva looks pained, as does Jim now. Quibbling over the age of a yogi at such a late hour seems fruitless. And Shiva knows it.

Of course, he asks for *baksheesh*. You know, for the children and grandchildren and all. He gets more rupees out of the deal, shaking our hands, thanking us profusely, and speeds down the street with a rattle that would move the universe.

The next morning, Jim and I grope along the streets in the predawn night, guidebook in hand. Sunrise brings the worshippers to the bathing *ghats* on the Ganges River as they make their early morning *pooja* rites—prayers and offerings. We walk and walk to discover that we are about a kilometer from the river, not two blocks at all.

Our first day suggests that Varanasi is as touristy as India gets. The most touristed sites tend to bring out the worst in a place. Many who approach us are commission men—have some angle or something to sell. Some get straight to the point, which we come to appreciate. Some befriend us, walk with us, then casually slip in the sell. Everyone assumes they're the first person to ask us to come, just for a minute, a minute only, nothing to buy, please, looking only, having a *chai,* in their marble shop, their uncle's silk shop, their cousin's essence shop. With such large families, one wonders, how many cousins can a person have? Battle fatigue makes it tough to make way for the sincerely friendly people who just want to chat.

Even the holy men try to shake us down. At a local temple, the resident priest accosts us, bowing with prayer hands. "*Namaste, Namaste*" (hello, I bow to you), a garland of flowers finding our necks, blessings, blessings, more prayer hands and bows, and finally, the extended hand for *baksheesh.*

Sadhus, the very eccentric-looking, wandering holy men of India (OK, crazed-looking holy men) always hang around temple sites too. "May I take your photo?" I ask my first *sadhu.* A slow coy turn of the head, eyes blinked closed, means *oh, all right, I suppose,* despite the fact that that's precisely why he's there.

As soon as the camera shutter blinks, out comes the open hand. Reluctantly giving in to photo-taking is a *sadhu's* bread and butter. Fair enough; he gave me a great picture. I smile and give him a few rupees, a generous donation by any beggar standard. But holy men don't come cheap. He complains loudly in Hindi for everyone to hear, pointing to his hand. I raise the donation to keep the peace and receive a blessing to boot.

As we make our way back to the hotel, we find the Golden Temple. Rounding the next corner, we pass a sign that says: *Yogi Lodge*. The Yogi Lodge we wanted. Jim and I smile. The proprietor is obviously no one in Shiva's extended family; no finder's fee here. To be honest, it looks pretty tired. OK, it's a dump.

At our hotel, we meet two guys, a German and Aussie, who sit on the veranda, empty beer bottles cluttering the table. We tell them about our hotel mix-up story for conversation. They throw their heads back and howl, hitting their legs. *Was it that funny?*

Both arrived on the late bus, independent of each other, over the two nights preceding our arrival. And both asked the rickshaw driver to take them to the notorious Yogi Lodge. "All the same!" their driver told them, "a *yogesh* is a young yogi." Can we guess the driver? It was Shiva, the creator-destroyer.

"But how is it possible we all picked Shiva when there are so many other drivers in Varanasi?" I ask. "What are the chances?"

"Maybe Shiver was the only one willing to come down in price," Myles, the one from Australia says.

"That Shiva is very clever, you know. I like the old blokes," Frans, the German guy says. "I like to give dem de help because I am thinking de tourists, they are not using dem so much." He laughs. "Guess I am wrong." We were all wrong.

"I think this is how new businesses market themselves in India," Myles says. "They put the word out to the drivers, the people moving the customers. Bring a new customer, you get a cut."

I figure Shiva is doing OK. Three overpriced fares from three rides with *baksheesh* thrown in, then *baksheesh* from the hotel owner times three again. Perhaps he's actually done us a favor. In the end, we have to admit, the Yogesh Hotel is nicer than the Yogi Lodge. OK, a lot.

During our remaining three nights at the Yogesh Hotel, Shiva is not to be found by night or day. No one has seen him. I was hoping to see him again.

When we pay the bill, Jim asks the manager, "Do you know Shiva, the rickshaw driver? Could you give him a message when you see him?"

"Shiva?" the manager says. "You mean the old chap? He is not far. You can tell him yourself. Come," he says, motioning.

He leads us out the back door to a courtyard. Past the walls of the courtyard, along a scratchy path and down a rise, we enter a small colony of tenuous houses surrounded by permanent housing on all sides. Bamboo poles support a collage of pink, blue and clear plastic walls and roofs and lean-to pieces of wood, cardboard and tin. The grand fig trees overhead protect the squatters most, lending grace and redemption to an otherwise squalid corner of Varanasi. A small shrine bears a picture of the god Ganesh with flowers and incense that burns at the foot of a banyan tree. A scruffy, bony dog finishes off the food in the offering.

Drying clothes catch the sun peering through the trees, on snatches of makeshift line, on low-spread limbs and flat on the ground. Women in colorful, worn cotton saris wearing plastic bangles move about, washing clothes and stirring pots on small open fires. An old woman approaches us on the path, bearing a huge mound of tree branches on her back. Bent with her load, she stops to watch, more interested in us than her burden.

Another woman comes behind her, this one middle-aged, bearing a homemade yoke of recycled tins filled with water, her sari torn and dirtied, a kerchief on her head. Bare-bottomed toddlers and barefoot children run and squeal, their legs and pants covered in the same soft brown colors of the baked earth. A little girl about four or five years old carries her infant, bare-bottomed sister on her back in a cotton sari-sling. Both of them look up with large *surma* stares, the thick charcoal around the eyes meant to lend a cooling effect and ward off evil eye.

Another young boy with blackened eyes gapes as if we are aliens. When we near him, I see that black flies sit on his lashes. Oh, this bothers me! Flies in India are so lecherous, children give up resisting them. I flap my scarf in the air until they are all gone, for the moment anyway, making him smile.

"Is there a public water faucet close by?" Jim asks the hotel manager.

"Yes, a pipe about fifteen meters beyond here." He points to where the woman with water came. A man dressed in a light sports jacket surfaces from under a plastic tarp, adjusting his collar and hair. The arms of his jacket are a bit short and his white shirt too tight at the collar. He stops to let us pass.

If I saw these people on the street, I wouldn't take them to be poor. These must be the "working class poor" I've heard of: people whose means fall short of basic necessities. I wonder how many office workers in India surface from shantytowns each morning? And how they manage in the rainy season. A wind storm could lift up this whole place.

"Does anyone know how many people live here?" I ask the manager.

"Oh," he sighs, "I doubt it. Maybe the census ministry. It changes every day and it only grows." He looks around and shrugs. "Hundreds, maybe three hundred or more?" A lot like guessing *nankhatai* cookies in a jar.

Our guide stops and pokes his head through the opening of one of the more sound-looking structures, a small corrugated steel house. He speaks to someone in Hindi, then walks around the back where an old dirty hammock hangs between two trees.

There sits Shiva on his deity mount of a large tree stump, crossed-legged with excellent posture, looking out across the small wooded clump. You might mistake him for a meditating yogi, if you missed the bulging wad of beetle nut in his cheek. He turns to us, an ear to ear smile, his bloody red teeth resembling a vampire who has just finished off his last victim. He raises his eyebrows, then his finger to be sure he has our attention, points to a white spot in the patchwork of stained blotches on the dirt ground, moves the wad in his mouth to the side and hoicks a mouthful of red liquid precisely to his mark, followed by a bizarre peal of laughter. We're even impressed and clap.

He jumps up with prayer hands. "*Namaste, namaste.*" He seems genuinely delighted to see us. The hotel manager waves goodbye and returns to work. Shiva introduces his wife, who is smaller than he is, as tall as a child—a perfect miniature couple. She is a good-looking woman with silver streaked hair pulled back in a knot, a jasmine flower in her hair. Dulled by age, her cotton sari is turquoise with a paisley border, but still beautiful. Even poor women have nice saris and bangles on their arms; only abjectly poor women, like the untouchables who sweep the streets, have tattered saris and no bangles.

"*Namaste.*" She bows her head with prayer hands, small yellow-gold pendants dangling from her ears, and colorful plastic bangles on her arm. The earrings were probably part of her dowry, worn all her married life. Shiva pulls out cooking oil tins for us to sit on while the wife returns with sugary milk *chai.*

"So what you are doing at my home?" he grins, folding a new wad inside his cheek, his short gray hair standing up on end.

"We are here to ask if you can take us back to the station for a 6:30 bus?" Jim says.

"Ohh, verdy sordy," his smile lines turn down with drama, "today not working. But I find another driver for you!" This surprises me. I never pondered it actually, but I assumed poor people always work, that they never make enough money to take off.

"Where have you been? We haven't seen you for days," I say. I can't resist. "All your traveler-friends who you brought to the Yogesh Hotel are looking for you!" He looks at me for a moment, then nods and smiles.

"I am good, no problem," he says, looking down. "Resting only."

"So business must be good then! Excellent!" Jim throws up his hands. "Relaxing is good!"

"Yes," Shiva says, "watching the children, enjoying the trees. Very beautiful here, yes?"

I decide to brave my way; I am too curious about this. "So Shiva, do rickshaw drivers save money from their rickshaw fares?" He recoils, twisting his face into a grimace, waving his hand as if at a bad smell. "So you don't save your money?" I ask.

"For what?" he asks, shrugging his shoulders.

"You know, for difficult times." His head boggles again; I've set something off.

"The difficult times? Every day the difficult time. All the same. Where are poor people putting the money? In the house? No. You see my house. In the pocket? The thief takes the money, pffttt," he says, pantomiming a hand in the pocket and flinging his hand. "Today I have the money," he nods emphatically and taps his leg, giving us another red toothless grin. "Tonight for the dinner: *chana* and *puris*." He smiles cleverly, takes a drink of *chai* and nods. "Good!" and clinks our glasses.

As Jim and I scurry up the path towards the hotel, I realize we never thanked Shiva as we'd planned. "The next time we pass a beetle nut *wallah*," I say, "I'm trying that existential blend that Shiva uses."

The rest of our ascent is quiet, laden in thought. As crazy as he may sound, Shiva's onto something. Something earth-shattering, actually. Our beetle nut-hoicking rickshaw driver-yogi turns everything we hold dear in the West on its head. The words of this simple little man dog me still.

Jim and I wave to the Yogesh Hotel manager and walk to the street. "You know, you gotta love Shiva's pluck," I say. "I'm thinking he'll be just fine, what do you think?"

Jim laughs. "Are you kidding? I'm thinking he'll be better off than most of us!"

We both take a deep breath and muster the courage to begin the feeding frenzy to find another rickshaw to the bus station.

THAILAND: UNHOLY MATRIMONY

The night is not crowded like the day, the night is filled with eternal love; take this night tight in your arms as you hold a sweetheart.

Rumi

Jim and I talked about marriage once at home when we weren't moving. Marriage seemed rather superfluous, we concluded. The only logical reason to get married was for children, which weren't an issue yet. And then the idea didn't cross our minds again. Moving through different cultures, mores and customs change with the wind. Customs from home start to look pretty relative too, meaning societal pressures to marry are less apt to follow moving targets.

For a long time, my mother told her friends: "Oh, Ann Louise and Jim are just good friends." She loved Jim from the start, but she especially loved the idea that a big strong male companion protected me wherever I went. She was always careful, I noticed, not to inquire about living arrangements. Too treacherous.

After a couple of years, her storyline grew worn and tattered. The relationship topic was buried six feet under. Both our God-fearing mothers—mine Methodist, Jim's Catholic—quietly gave up on their hopes of marriage, resigning themselves to our misguided ways.

Jim and I have settled in at the "hill station" of Kodaikanal in the Western Ghat mountain range of Tamil Nadu—for two weeks, longer than our usual stay. Hill stations are mountain resorts first developed by the British, who desired to take refuge from the searing temperatures of the lowlands. Kodaikanal sits high atop a six thousand foot escarpment. The earth rises up vertically like a plateau, so the plains below seem more accessible, more expansive and grand. I have never seen anything like it. Signs posted along the upper edges, often inconspicuous among the trees, warn trekkers to be cautious of the vertical drops hundreds of feet down.

It's the rainy season in southern India. From the same vantage point each evening, Jim and I perch ourselves high above the plains like Zeus in his heaven. Tonight, in complete dryness, we watch four separate electrical storms many miles apart, their jagged, white fingers stretching across the sky—an extraordinary light show. Maybe it's the headiness of this beautiful landscape that stirs the mortal within. Maybe it's the romanticism of the colorful wedding processions that often pass us in the streets, the groom on a white horse going to meet his bride.

Whatever, the idea finds me like a flower pollen six thousand feet up that lodges itself securely up my nose. "I just realized we've been together for nine years," I say aloud.

"Yeah, it has been that long," he says.

And then the small detonation: "Wouldn't it be magical to get married in India? We could just do it and announce the news back home—no costly ceremony, no decisions about locale or who to invite."

Jim looks as if the rock promontory under us has shifted. "Whoaa!" he laughs. "Let me put this on for size for a minute. What brought this on after nine years?"

"I don't know. I just thought, why not? You can chew on it if you want."

But every hour or so, just to be annoying, I ask him, "So, have you decided?"

To be annoying back, he replies "decided what?" That night he says, "I do like the idea of a marriage certificate in Sanskrit."

Two days later, we both awaken to the prospect that we might be married this day. We visit a local government office in Kodaikanal, where a clerk tells us we must advertise our intention to marry in the local newspaper for thirty days before we can marry. "Foreigners must do this too?" I ask.

"Yes," he says, "everyone." And it would have to be in a city where legal notices are published, not Kodaikanal.

"Why do people have to wait thirty days?" Jim asks. The clerk shrugs.

"To make the intention perfectly clear? To give other interested parties time to contest? Who knows. I am not making the laws," he boggles his head curtly. Ironic, how colonial bureaucracies often outdo many times over the legacy left behind by their oppressors.

"Is this a requirement everywhere in India?" I ask. The clerk ignores me and begins to stamp a pile of papers, pad to paper, pad to paper, his hand a blur. He stacks them unevenly upon another pile of papers against the wall. I guess this means we're finished. We stand there waiting, apparently invisible.

He finally raises his eyes, drawing his face in a bored, vapid response, nodding his head to the side slowly, closing his eyes. An Indian yes. "Yes, it's a requirement everywhere in India?" I confirm. He closes his eyes more slowly with a tip of the head:

another yes, and we're torturing him and keeping him from his work.

So forget marrying in India. As we leave the office, Jim makes an audible "phew." I look at him. "That was close," he says, and laughs hilariously.

The next best place to marry, we decide, has to be Thailand. Americans poured into Bangkok for R and R during the Vietnam war, probably getting married in droves. Thailand should be easy. I like the idea of a marriage certificate in Thai script even better. An Indian one would probably be in English anyway.

We continue to tour India and Burma, fly to Bangkok briefly, then head overland into the far reaches of Thailand. A man we meet on a bus tells us about a place called Mae Hong Son in the northwest province—heaven on earth, he says. So why not? We go to Mae Hong Son, eager to get off the beaten track.

West of the Golden Triangle, where Burma, Thailand and Laos meet, the landscape gives way to verdant blue-green mountains contrasted with young-green rice paddies that line the valley floors. Our bus snakes its way on a hilly dirt road to the small capital town of Mae Hong Son, nestled in a valley close to the Burmese border.

Many hill tribes color the province, but mostly the Shan people inhabit Mae Hong Son. The architecture of the *wat-*temples and pagodas resemble those we've left behind in Burma. This is because Burma, we learn, once ruled these parts. The Burmese and Thai border shifted and stretched amid countless border skirmishes over time—the days when the mountains were home to the small black elephant used in battle. Later hunted out, the few remaining black elephants were put to work in the logging industry. Today, they're relegated to the circus and carrying tourists. Looking a little silly dressed up in costume, they may be safer, but a warrior might find it a bit of a comedown.

Jim and I find a small guest house in town and strike out for the hills. Dressed in layers—sweaters are too bulky to carry in Asia—we climb to a temple perched high atop a hill to watch the sunset. The view from Wat Doi Kong Mu takes in the valley, the mountains and beyond. The lush green jungle stretches as far as the eye can see. The air is almost crisp. The windy river and lake below reflect the last of the evening light while the little houses hugging the lake cast their incandescent lights along the edge. A fine mist slowly settles over the valley. Our friend on the bus was right; this is indeed yet another paradise on earth.

Making our way home down the hill, we see a building on another hill that resembles a church, an anomalous silhouette in Buddhist Thailand. The next day, we explore the hill and find a small, very plain white church—so unassuming there's no cross or sign. An almost unnoticeable sign on the side facing the hills tells us it's an Anglican church. A footpath leads parishioners to the door; many little footpaths meander up the hill from the valley below. A long stand of flowers graces the front yard. A Brit lives here, no doubt, probably the pastor. "I'll bet he rides a bicycle and walks a little dog too," Jim says.

I'm enchanted with this place. "Hey, why don't we try to get married here? Even if we can't get the marriage certificate here, we could have the ceremony." My idealized picture of this ceremony-to-come blooms faster than the contraband poppies in the valleys beyond. "You know, this would be very romantic. It looks like a little mission church."

Where we married wasn't a big concern. We were prepared to go the Buddhist route, being in a Buddhist country. But here's this perfect little import instead.

"You *know* this little church would play so well with the mums," I say. "Something of a gift for living in sin all these years. A wedding ceremony delivered by a missionary in a lovely little mission church in the hinterlands of Thailand would find an esteemed place in their hearts. It's difficult to imagine a scenario better than this one, Jimmy."

As we look around the building, my heart sinks. Everything looks too quiet; no one stirs and the doors are locked. We return later that day to find the same thing. No one seems to know anything about the church. "How do you say *church* in Shan?" I ask an acquaintance who speaks some English. He doesn't even know the word church. I slip by one more time that evening on my own.

The next morning, we must leave behind the wedding ceremony of our mothers' dreams. As our bus bumps down the road, the locusts in the trees whirl and scream their goodbyes. Some of us hold our ears. *EWWW-WEEEEE-EWWW-WEEEEE*.

"You know," I tell Jim to make myself feel better, "it wouldn't have worked anyway. My mother wouldn't approve of an Anglican church; it sounds too Catholic. And your mother too; an Anglican church sounds too Protestant."

On the way south, we look into getting married in Chiang Mai, but the government office we need is in Bangkok, they say. One month after the whole marriage idea germinated in India, we arrive in Bangkok, the city that doesn't sleep. At eleven o'clock at night, people eat and drink in cafes along exhaust-filled streets like it's noon. We take more than an hour to travel by bus about one mile across town to Kao Sern Street, the infamous travelers' guesthouse area.

When we rise on the morning of September 2nd, I know this is the day. In the middle of the rainy season, the sun shines, the sky's clear. How auspicious can you get? We set out for a district office two hours across town, where we're redirected to another office ten or so blocks away. We walk for another half hour (Bangkok is not a pedestrian city) and wait for an interminable lunch break to end, to be told we must first report to our Embassy.

In another hour, the Embassy confirms that Thai marriages are legal and binding in the US and, no, we don't need any special papers from them. The Consulate recommends two district offices where we can obtain a more "expedient" marriage. Bangkok traffic inches and stops, inches and stops, during a torrential monsoon downpour. The door of the first district office is locked, closed for the day. We arrive at our hotel after dark—dejected, demoralized and soaked.

The next day, very early, we arrive at the second, closer district office where, we're told, we will need a translator to conduct business there. Everyone speaks very passable English, but never mind, we still need an official translator. We're sent to the TAT, Department of Tourism, for a translator, another five blocks away. The lady at TAT laughs and directs us to a travel agent (close by!) who calls district office number one that was closed yesterday.

"Do you think someone is trying to tell us something?" Jim smiles a crooked smile.

"STOP it!" I wail, already punchy. "You're not funny."

"Sir, madam, the district office says you don't need a translator," the travel agent says. We look at each other in disbelief. Is our luck really changing? This may be the day.

"September 3rd, I like that. It's easy to remember," I say. An hour-plus later in traffic on a bus, we enter the halls of district office number one, best district office! Our clerk reminds me of a Thai Danny Devito, diminutive but wide by Thai standards. The true irony is we could desperately use a translator. He stumbles and fumbles with English, protracts the simplest explanations and makes little sense in the end.

But we get his drift. We need two witnesses and a two thousand baht fee to get married. He must be quoting it wrong. "Two thousand baht?" I repeat.

"Yes," he nods.

"Two thousand, as in this two thousand?" which I write on paper. He nods yes. Jim and I look at each other. "How can a poor Thai person possibly afford seventy-some dollars for a marriage license?" I ask. He reddens and sputters. No understand.

After our eleventh bus ride in two days, we enter the TAT office again. With smiling, blushing faces, they all congratulate us in unison. "No, no, not yet," Jim says. "But we want to ask you, is it true that it costs two thousand baht to get married in Thailand?"

"Two thousand baht? Who tell you this?" the woman asks with wide, indignant eyes.

"You tell the police!" the boss-man intervenes, with more emotion than we've ever seen in Thailand. He guides us to the door and the three of us walk out onto the street. He's fast, and hot. We run after him down the block and across to a police station, grateful that one thing in this city we need is close.

Speaking in Thai, our advocate tells our story to two uniformed policemen sitting behind a counter. The younger one jumps up and pronounces: "We go!"

Jim and I stand there, not knowing what to say. Jim raises his hand. "No, really, that isn't necessary." The policeman continues walking outside to his police car, motioning for us to come. We follow, grudgingly, looking like bad children.

"What are we doing?" I ask the policeman who I suspect knows little English. He motions. Hurry, hurry, get in. We get in the back seat slowly, too slowly for our friend. Before the door is closed, we pull off with a screech, our siren screaming like the European sirens. *NA-NAAAA; NA-NAAAA; NA-NAAAA!!* Our circling lights bounce off buildings.

Horror turns to maniacal laughter. Bent over in the back seat, we both gasp for breath, laughing. "Oh, my GOD, what have we DONE, Jimmy? Please, let me just wake up from this soon."

I try to envision the next scene at the district office, which promises to be more macabre. We'll charge into the office, the officer will say "OK, where is he? Which one told you?

Show me! Show me who told you!" Oh, please, will we have to actually point out the guy? I'm thinking about the honor code in traditional societies, the idea that dishonoring yourself or your family is worthy of suicide. But do people think that way in Thailand? Japanese students in school have committed suicide for less. Is this confrontation going to push our civil servant over the edge?

What's all this sirens-blaring-racing through the streets of Bangkok about? Is a petty white collar offense worth all this fuss? Why are we really doing this? To impress the *farangs* to show our zero tolerance for corruption? "At least we're getting back to the district office about as fast as we'll get anywhere in Bangkok," Jim says, laughing.

The dreaded moment comes. We pass through the front doors and walk straight towards the right place; the officer seems to know where to go. Heads turn as the officer's brisk steps echo in the hall. Jim and I follow tentatively, distancing ourselves. We spot our man, and the police officer goes straight up to him, making the customary greetings—right hands shaking, with the left hand holding the right forearm. Does he know he's our man? We aren't consulted about a thing, save a few sidelong glances. And Danny Devito isn't the least bit ruffled or embarrassed.

This whole charade must be about saving face, protecting our clerk from shame. Whatever; we are glad. The climate has changed altogether. Jim and I seem superfluous. On this good note, we slip out. No one seems to notice as they talk. How do you tell a story to which you were participant but not privy?

On the street, we let out long weary sighs. A passing woman turns and looks at us in alarm, making us laugh. "Now where were we?" I ask Jim.

"I'm afraid it's too late to do any more business today," he says. Still empty handed, still unmarried, we need to find ourselves yet another bus to go home.

On September 4th, we sleep late. So what's the rush? When it's meant to happen, it will happen. Even with a fresh night's optimism under our belts, we're wary. We enter the third district office the TAT told us about the day before. The first clerk we consult nods his head towards the woman sitting at a desk (no pointing in Thailand).

"*Sa wat dee ka.*" We greet a solicitous, middle-aged woman in white blouse and long dark skirt. She understands our request immediately. Retrieving a Thai marriage certificate, she asks precisely how we pronounce our names, so she can spell them phonetically in Thai. She elicits the help of two co-workers to witness and sign. Handing the certificate to Jim with two hands, she bows and breaks into a full grin. That fast.

"But isn't there some kind of ceremony?" I ask. She looks puzzled. "Isn't there more?"

"No, no more. You make offerings to temple with family." So by twelve noon, we're half married. Which is progress.

We decide to marry at the Wat Traimitr in town, the Temple of the Golden Buddha, a modern temple with a solid gold ten thousand pound ancient Buddha, the most valuable Buddha in the world. We buy offerings outside and move to the altar. The interior is small and unassuming. So as not to look too amateurish, we've taken careful note of everyone else.

With prayer hands, we kneel and bow to the ground, laying the cream-colored lotus flowers on the altar, light the incense sticks and add them to the altar, bowing again. Our vows are impromptu—all in all, a perfect ceremony.

Like the other supplicants, we affix very thin gold foil pieces to the gold Buddhas lining the exit. We're completely married now. I have to admit: I do feel different; Jim probably more so. Even though he wasn't present at the temple, we consider a Dutch friend Frans as our "best man." Probably more accurately our only man. Frans has traveled the same route with us since Burma.

We make our way to the main post office, rehearsing the big phone call to the mothers. They're both home, first try. We tell them only that we're married—quite enough to digest to start. They're shocked but pleased. All the details will come later in a letter, we say.

It's easier to stretch the truth when you write. The real story is simply out of the question. My mother would never understand. Telling her we took our vows in a Buddhist temple conjures up images of a livid Moses (Charlton Heston) in *The Ten Commandments* coming off the mountain to find his followers worshipping pagan idols. All she would hear is we married in a pagan temple. ("No, mother," I've told her countless times, "Buddhists don't worship Buddha, because they don't think he's God.")

And I'm sorry; I'm just not ready to give up that lovely little white church on the hill which was meant to be our church. If only we could have reached the other side of its door. God knows, I tried to find that pastor who undermined everything, shirking his responsibilities by going on holiday or some such place when people needed him.

Jim wasn't dirtying his hands. So I wrote the mother-letters. I told my mother that a Methodist missionary married us in a quaint mission church in a little town in the hills of Thailand: it was so beautiful, she would have loved it. We got our marriage certificate in Bangkok. I told Jim's mother that a Catholic missionary married us, (if there is such a thing), in a quaint mission church in a little town in the hills of Thailand: it was so beautiful, she would have loved it. It was a bit hard to mail them.

Of course, they were both elated because they got the marriage ceremony of their dreams.

May God have mercy on our souls. OK, on my soul.

VIETNAM: ENEMIES IN ANOTHER TIME

The night is bright, with a starlit sky, I sit and think, as time passes by. Oh starry night, with a moonlit sky, take me away, and tell me why. Give me a reason, for love's end, give me a reason, for why I lost a friend. I sit and think, all night, about the things, that all went wrong, starlit sky, give me a reason why.

Anonymous

A window bangs open on the bus. I brace myself for the sound that doesn't come: that first person who hangs out the window retching, setting off a chain reaction. I try to lose myself in people-watching. A woman in front of us holds a scarf to her mouth. The driver downshifts, and all heads bob forward.

We climb another turn, heading south in the central highlands of Vietnam. The bus lugs and strains under its weight. Fat, squat buses like our own pass us going north. Tired and worn, they spew black exhaust and inspire little confidence. But I love these buses. The mere sight of one makes me laugh; they resemble a child's drawing of a bus more than a real vehicle. The grill even looks like a smiley face.

My seatmate speaks some English and tells me these buses operated in the Seventies at the time of the American war. The parts are homemade today. Presumably, he meant to impress me. "Ohhh," I say, smiling. Of course, they call the Vietnam war their American war. American war would be most correct; it was always our war.

Jim and I sit in the last seat that runs, bench-like, across the back—the worst possible place for his motion sickness. We don't talk much on hilly bus trips, as he must concentrate on holding his stomach at bay. Even if he wanted out of here, he couldn't possibly navigate the blur of colors and bags and vegetables that was once the aisle.

Our little-bus-that-could rounds a corner, the pivotal corner that separates the central highlands from the southern lowlands below. My heart bottoms out as if on a roller coaster. The land falls away so dramatically from the road, I hold my chest. The coastline rolls out beneath us, lacking only a crescendo of violins. Never have I seen such a spectrum of land from a road. Only a plane could provide a greater vista.

Jim and I lean towards the window, bending over our sleeping seatmate. The view spans many miles north and south, softened at the edges by the humidity. Along the shore, reefs hide just below the transparent blue-green waters of the South China Sea. A long, shell-white beach catches the sun—the famous China Beach, my guidebook tells me. Inland, the lush yellow-greens of the rice fields hold the sun like a chartreuse light. I look around to see the locals' reaction. Some peer out blithely, but most look forward or sleep, their heads jostling with the bus as it inches its way to Hoi An.

Hoi An evokes an illustrious past with some of the best nineteenth century French and Japanese architecture in the country. A major international seaport for centuries, Hoi An once rivaled the thriving port of Malacca in Malaysia. But the river mouth silted up, taking the sea and its ships with it. A sense of lost glory lingers still and Hoi An is now an unassuming river town.

We feel invisible when we first walk into town. The din of the urban streets that carried us along and wrapped us in community in Hanoi evades us here. The town is disconcertingly civilized, devoid of blaring horns and children playing, makeshift retail stands, women washing dishes on the curb. A rickshaw slips past. The driver turns to eye us closely for any signs we might send his way. Three bicyclers pass. In Hanoi, we couldn't see the other side of the street for the bikes, much less cross.

The trees that line the streets of Hoi An accentuate the beauty of the French shuttered house fronts. In all of Vietnam, we have not experienced such a mild mannered place and move instinctively towards the market on the river. *How curious,* I muse, *that I miss the din.* Ordinarily, we would welcome the calm.

We've learned to live with small uninvited entourages trailing behind in places like India. Curiosity we don't mind; any visitor likes to feel that the locals take some interest. But the Vietnamese response is unique, and no doubt complex. Outside of the business-friendly people, we see two types. The grovelers, I call them, who completely confound me, seeking us out and proclaiming with thumbs raised: "America number one!" And they are often men old enough to remember the war, and who live in the north, not just the south. Since we're inclined to keep our citizenship mum in Vietnam, the grovelers blindside us every time.

The first time we walked the streets of Hanoi, looking obviously American, I fully expected someone to run up and push us away, and say "Get out, get out!" When first asked if we were Americans, I thought, *Oh no, here it comes, the barrage of insults.* I guess I couldn't imagine why they wouldn't be hostile.

In fact, people were nothing but courteous. Maybe even too courteous.

"Don't forget that an entire generation has passed," Jim said.

"Not for them," I'm betting.

We also get obliviousness from the Vietnamese—people scarcely taking notice at all, as if we walk the streets of a bustling Western city. This reaction I can understand, though it's quite anomalous in developing countries, especially one that recently opened its doors to foreign travelers. At least in the beginning, tourists should be novel.

"I get the same thing," a German friend told me. "It isn't just Americans. I think the Vietnamese are very proud people and probably just sick of foreigners."

He's right, of course; they have to be. When you consider the history of Vietnam—that they've lived under someone else's thumb for twenty-some centuries—a vassal of China for centuries, a French colony for another hundred years, an occupied territory of Japan through World War II. The US was involved well before French independence in 1954, and then we staged one of the world's nastiest civil wars for another twenty years.

In 1975, free of foreigners at last, Vietnam was destitute. Sovereignty was about all the people could call their own. As if the war didn't cripple them enough, a twenty-year embargo hogtied every sector and cut the country off from the world, never enabling the people to get back on their feet.

Jim and I walk across the seventeenth century Japanese covered bridge as a bus of Japanese tourists with beany-copter-type orange hats shuffle past us with their guide, enveloping us in their din. Cameras flash like fireworks. They take photos of every blessed person in the group, blocking local traffic. Even to us, it feels like an invasion.

Two shopkeepers stand at their doors watching. In a camera blink, I see how the Vietnamese must see us—funny looking foreigners, interlopers, all of us enemies in another time who brandish cameras now, streaming back by the thousands, wearing too few clothes, disrespecting their sacred land still. We're the foreigners they've never invited, but alas, need.

Or perhaps they don't give it a thought at all; they've moved on.

As the sun sets that evening, Jim and I stand on the Cam Nam bridge close to the market enjoying the river. A small Vietnamese man with a pleasant smile and graying temples approaches us. I take him to be in his mid-sixties. His name is Monsieur T, he tells us, probably condensed to make it easy for Americans who travel in large numbers in Vietnam. While fellow countrymen aren't generally well traveled in Asia, former military people making peace with the past seem to hold the number one tourist spot.

Dressed in a threadbare white shirt with gabardine pants and leather belt, Monsieur T looks more like a civil servant from colonial Vietnam. He chats with Jim in English then asks if we'd like to take a boat ride down the river. His English is very good. "No, so sorry, we're tired and go back to the hotel now," Jim tells him.

He walks with us to our hotel, delighted to learn Jim speaks some French. As often happens, I trail behind like a coolie. I use the snippets of time to be alone and browse in the vendor stalls.

Jim and Monsieur T cut a comical pair from behind, Jim towering above with animated hands flying. When we part ways, Monsieur T and I haven't exchanged a word. "Well, it's obvious, he isn't interested in a woman's opinion on anything," I say to Jim.

Monsieur T waves goodbye and yells, "maybe tomorrow you take boat?"

The economics of a four dollar, one hour boat ride comes down to a relatively small outlay of money for a tourist and enough money to live on for maybe one day for Monsieur T.

If he garners three or more boat rides a day, he rises to the middle class. The problem for all the boat ride hawkers is that four dollars goes pretty far in Vietnam. A tourist can rent a small motorbike for the day instead or put down half the cost of a very decent local hotel room. From the Vietnamese point of view, the cost is downright steep, precisely why Monsieur T isn't approaching them. If a middle class Vietnamese father decides an evening turn in a boat sounds like a good idea, his entire extended family comes in tow. For these two American travelers, we just don't care about taking a boat ride.

"It turns out," Jim tells me, "Monsieur T was educated in French schools, later became a civil servant under the French, and also worked for the Americans."

"So he has to be more like seventy," I say. "Do you think he's a Francophile?"

"No and yes," Jim says. "He was careful, almost defensive, about telling me he wasn't, yet he went on to say in so many words that life was better then. Everything worked better then."

"But not with the Americans?"

"He didn't say anything at all about Americans."

"Hmmm, curious. So what does he do now?" I ask.

"This boat tour guide thing, a huge step down in his mind, from what I gleaned."

"So what else did you talk about?"

"He told me about life in Hoi An before and how economically depressed it is now. And then," Jim says, smiling, "how beautiful it is up the river at sunset."

"Boy, he just doesn't give up."

Early in the morning, the store owners open their shops by lifting flat horizontal planks, one on top the other, that line both sides of the front wall until the full width of the storefront is exposed to the street—an age-old design that proves effective against rising floodwaters from the river. Only the door and door frame remain when all the planks are gone.

Above the doorframe, a piece of wood with a yin-yang symbol surrounded by a spiral design (called *mat cua* or "watchful eyes"), protects the residents from harm. *Yin-yang* may be Confucian but watchful eyes sound animist to me. I love this about human culture; nothing under the sun is discrete. Everything evolves out of what came before.

As we near the bridge, my eye catches Monsieur T's white shirt. He leans on the railing, his shoulders hunched over with head down, surveying the water as if in deep thought. He looks much older. A sadness rises in me. There aren't many tourists here now and boat guides seem to be the job-by-default in Hoi An. We keep walking, and he doesn't lift his head or notice us. Two requests to ride a boat stop us before we cross the bridge. I look over my shoulder to see that Monsieur T still hasn't budged.

Every blessed time we venture out of the hotel, we bump into Monsieur T. We pass him again that evening. He chats with Jim while I walk around the market. Jim says he enjoys his company.

The next day, surprise, surprise, he's on the bridge again. I turn my head just as he looks up and greets us like old friends, speaking in English. Would we like to take a boat ride today? We need only to tell him and he'll arrange the boat right away—which means he doesn't even own the boat. If he has to pay someone else for the boat, what does he make? "No, actually, we have plans to tour town today. I'm sorry," I tell him. "And we just aren't interested." Isn't it better in the end to dash someone's hopes instead of giving them false hope?

He smiles broadly, a bit forced. "Enjoy your tour then!" he replies. Oh, the burden of wanting to help everyone who needs help.

"He took that pretty well," Jim says after we leave.

"I doubt it," I say.

At the end of the second day, we conclude that Hoi An has been lovely, but we'll be bored silly if we stay another day.

We decide to continue south, and find seven other travelers in our hotel to share the cost of a minibus. After much negotiation and altercation with a minibus owner, we pay a hundred dollars, eleven dollars each, for the long trip to Nha Trang, to set out early in the morning. Prearranged minibuses or vans coordinated with other travelers are the main mode of transport now, except for our short bus ride to Hoi An to experience a cartoon bus.

On our way back to the hotel, we see Monsieur T. "Please, let's cross the street and go around him," I say to Jim.

"No, come on. Let's just say goodbye. We may not see him again."

This time, Monsieur T speaks to me in English. He even reads my mind. "I am sorry, I prefer French to English, which is why I don't use English so much."

"No, actually," I say, "I think your English is very good." He asks where we go. We tell him we'll probably wash up and find a place for dinner later.

"I am wanting to ask you, can you come back to my house for a cup of tea before dinner?"

We are both silent for a moment, our answer too long coming. I'm really bushed; my eyes say *please no* when my face meets Jim's. "We're really tired," Jim says.

Monsieur T continues, beaming: "Today I am saying to my mother, I will bring my American friends home to meet you. She wants to meet you and make Vietnamese tea for you." His mother? How old could his mother be? And I never knew they grew tea in Vietnam.

Jim shoots me a look as if to say, *Oh come on, what's the big deal?* "Of course, we can come," I smile weakly.

We walk for blocks; will we ever get there? I thought Monsieur T lived close to the bridge. I lose count of the turns through a maze of alleys, wondering how we'll ever find our way out. We must ask our host to escort us back out when we leave.

The afternoon is very hot, the air, oppressive. "At this rate, we'll arrive at the house drenched," I say to Jim. Water droplets fall on us. Monsieur starts to run, giggling. We all look up to see wet clothes hanging between the buildings overhead. Monsieur T giggles harder, like a little kid, making me laugh. He's a different person when he laughs. We turn, cross a courtyard and leave our shoes outside the door, entering a large dark kitchen with high ceilings.

My eyes adjust to the light to see that the walls are blackened with years of cooking and grease, everything a nondescript gray. Large iron pots hang on the wall and a wok with oil sits on a mammoth antique stove. We pass shelves lined with little porcelain Chinese-style cups and, down a hall, a room with an old sofa where they apparently live.

We ascend a very steep staircase (*how can short people manage such steps?*) and enter a large room equally nondescript with utilitarian chairs and tables. The floor creaks loudly under our feet as if no one has walked here for days. A tinge of mold hits my nose and makes me sneeze. There is no rug, only blackened wood with worn foot trails across the room. The room lacks any color, the walls a time-worn blah with nothing to adorn them. No, I see a single crucifix hanging on one wall. I have read that Hoi An was the first place in Vietnam exposed to Christianity.

Curiously, though, just under the cross, a small red Buddhist shrine champions the only color to be found in the room, the corner and wall blackened with smoke. Are they Christian or Buddhist?

Then I discover the windows. Such lovely windows; they carry the room by themselves. Five in all, taller than two Monsieur Ts, they are huge, simply exquisite, reaching up the wall with great panes of old glass and shuttered on the outside. Two are closed securely. The three open ones are virtually opaque, the glass is so dirty, opening to balcony rails. Decorative Chinese-type lentils adorn the tops, probably mahogany wood darkened with time. This has to be one of Hoi An's historic family houses. Oh, what I'd like to do with this room. I'd thrust the doors out, open the shutters to an afternoon breeze, scrub the glass and bring in the full sunlight.

Monsieur T extends a hand towards two wooden chairs and pulls up a third. He walks to the back of the house and speaks in Vietnamese. These ceilings must be twelve feet tall. As I continue to mentally renovate the room, I hear footsteps sliding across the wood.

His mother scurries in, just a breath of a woman, bent over and white-haired, weighing no more than a young girl. Her demeanor is completely disarming: she wears a plain blouse and dark print sarong with little stick-like ankles appearing and disappearing from under her sarong. She smiles warmly to us, bows slightly and extends her shaking hand, jabbering something in Vietnamese. Monsieur T's voice changes when he addresses her, measured and slow, almost sweet. Coupled with the giggling incident in the alley, my opinion of him has risen tenfold. "She says you are welcome in our home."

Jim says, "Please tell her thank you very much." Monsieur T speaks to her again, and she nods and leaves.

He tells us this home has been in the family for more than a hundred and fifty years. His great grandfather, a shipping merchant when Hoi An was still a successful port at the beginning of French rule, built the house. Monsieur T watches me. "You like the house?"

"Yes, very much. It's lovely." We are actually warming up to some semblance of a real exchange.

"What would you pay for this house?" he asks. I smile, a little perplexed. He can't be serious. He told us himself, the house is a family heirloom; surely he cannot sell it.

I smile. "Oh, I know it could never be for sale." And the subject thankfully drops like a stone. "May I look at the shrine?" I ask him. He nods and extends his arm.

The shrine is plainer than most I've seen, with a small bronze happy Buddha and used incense sticks sitting in urns filled with sand. Pictures unevenly line the wall, but a framed photo with an old curled picture of a young couple sits on the shrine shelf. I look closer without being obvious. The woman is stunningly pretty with piercing dark eyes. She takes my breath away, especially because I sense she is dead. And then I feel a great sadness; that haunting irony that grips me when I gaze upon a dead person in a joyful moment.

These images remind me of the countless shrines in the alcoves outside the temples, the poignant reminders of the Vietnam war. Every day people tend to them with care. Candles illuminate thousands of photos, mostly of men, that climb the walls and stretch on and on as you walk down one side of the temple and up the other—this being one mere temple in a country of hundreds of temples.

I examine the photo again, suspecting the man could be our host with dark hair. I turn casually to compare his features. Yes, it's definitely Monsieur T; he is very handsome too. He meets my gaze as he and Jim talk.

"That is my wife," he offers. "She died in the war at age thirty-five." I couldn't possibly brave the other questions that come. How could he gaze upon the beauty of this woman again and again? What kind of a hole does this make over thirty-some years? And the other irony: the wife of a Vietnamese working for the Americans is killed in the war. How does he reconcile this? And why did he stay after so many fled?

We cannot fathom what other people endure. When someone colonizes your country, occupies your life, you are a prisoner with a semblance of freedom—not restrained in irons, but imprisoned nonetheless. Relationships become muted, no longer black and white. Your prison guard protects you, feeds you, even becomes your friend. Sometimes, life judiciously renders you blind, almost forgetting, allowing you to get on with the business of living.

The feeble little mother lugs in a tray carrying a blue and white Chinese tea pot and cups, worn and stained with wear. Has this poor women brought these heavy things up the back stairs? Monsieur T jumps up to take the tray. We drink and chat some more. He speaks only of nieces and nephews, no children. His family spans the earth as a result of the war.

"Does anyone else in your family live here?" I ask.

"No, just my mother and myself."

And it strikes me. That's what is missing in this house, a full generation after the war. An ancestral home in the family for a hundred and fifty years should be bustling with people and children. Instead, it is devoid of life, unsettlingly still.

There is a sister in Holland and a younger brother in the United States, Monsieur T tells us, in Arlington, Virginia. "Oh, yes," Jim says. "Arlington isn't far from Baltimore where we live."

"Oh," Monsieur T jumps up. "Could you take a letter and mail it in the US? Sometimes the mail is not good in Vietnam." Of course, we tell him. He leaves the room to retrieve an addressed airmail envelope, which he hands to Jim. "And when do you go home to the US?" he asks.

"Only a couple of weeks," Jim says. Was this possibly the reason we were invited here? Is he worried it might get lost in the mail?

He leaves the room again and returns with another tray of blue and white bowls. Jim and I look at each other. "Something for your dinner since you must be hungry," he says. "Simple Vietnamese noodles." The soup is noodles and broth with greens, the Ramen noodles that feed the world. We eat to be polite.

Our end of the room dips in shadow as the sun descends. Monsieur T rises and looks at the clock on the wall, as he wears no watch. He fidgets, making me feel like our stay is suddenly over and we're meant to leave.

Then he does something odd. He turns and talks to Jim in French, speaking quickly. I catch the words "sun" and "water." Jim looks at me and blushes, as if I'm following all this, and says in English, "No, no, I'm sorry. We are very tired and need to get back to our hotel."

Oh please, no, don't tell me he's still pushing this damn boat ride? So this whole tea idea was a pretext for that?

A kind of desperation edges into Monsieur T's voice, who apparently tries to reason with Jim again. "I'm sorry, tomorrow isn't possible either," Jim says. "We leave early in the morning." I watch as our friendly little tea disintegrates into tannic acid. Jim valiantly remains calm.

Monsieur T's complete demeanor changes; he sits erect, his face ashen, disbelieving. He squints as he speaks in French again, sternly now, not in the charming host voice at all, but with a kind of desperation. He asks a question. Jim hesitates and asks a question back. I know him as well as anyone and search his face, which is red clear back to his ears. He takes his time, measuring his words—not angry, but flustered. Looking down, Jim counters with another question. Why are they doing this? Monsieur T nods, still rigid, watching Jim carefully, his breathing labored. Jim digs into his pocket and counts out some Vietnamese *dong* bills and hands them to him.

"Please, somebody, tell me what is going on!" I finally say aloud.

Jim turns to me and says with as much precision as possible, "Monsieur T is asking us to pay for our meal."

I am dumbstruck. "But why?" The light catches a bead of perspiration running down Monsieur T's cheek; he blots it with a white handkerchief.

Jim continues, methodically. "I told Monsieur T that we cannot go on a boat trip tonight. Then he pointed out that he fed us a meal. I said I thought he was being hospitable, you know, the way people are sometimes to other people."

I feel blindsided, as if I turned and an object came sailing across the room and caught me in the face when I was smiling. No one could have seen this coming, even dreamed it up. This is one for the etiquette books. Twist someone's arm to come for a cup of tea, add Ramen noodles, chat them up and get to know them better while arousing their sympathy, twist their arm again to take a boat ride, and, when they don't relent, make them pay for all expenses surrounding the ruse.

Monsieur T blinks like a great bird. I'm guessing he spoke in French to somehow minimize the impact. If everyone didn't hear, it wouldn't seem as impolite.

"Madam," he demurs, sitting up, "Jim has offered to pay for the meal. He has asked me, would I like to receive money for the meal, and I am saying yes." Monsieur T's version, for the record. We all sit motionless, realizing that words cannot fix this. Jim moves to stand.

The mother waddles in. She removes the heavy tray, nods and smiles sweetly to Jim and me. Monsieur T stands and fidgets. Surely, this is not the way he wanted things to go. "Do you still want us to deliver your letter?" I ask. He hesitates, then puts his hand out to retrieve it from Jim, standing there like a stiff, in the way, to add to the unease. I want to thank him, like you do out of habit when you leave.

"We can let ourselves out," I say, feeling the need to say something, to somehow smooth everything over. How can you share conversation and tea without saying something afterwards? It's Monsieur T who has broken all the conventions, conventions that ironically underpin life here more than most parts of the world. I finally say nothing, not knowing what to possibly say.

We somehow get ourselves down the steep back steps. My face is still hot, a veritable beacon of light as we bump through the back alleys lost, the shadows growing by the minute. I try desperately to sort this out, to understand what happened. Over the years we've traveled, there were people aplenty who invited us to their home or became our fast friend, hoping that we would later buy a rug or a guide or a scarab. We grew to expect it and usually smelled ruse before it got out of hand. No one, but no one, had ever gone to such lengths. Was this protracted acquaintance really for the sole purpose of breaking us down to take a stupid boat ride? Was it about getting even or something like that, humiliating a couple of Americans? I couldn't even guess.

We walk in silence, getting lost in the maze of streets. My thoughts race madly; I trip over my own feet. "So how much did you pay him for our so-called meal?" I finally ask Jim.

"Five thousand dong," he says. "That's what he asked for. Fifty cents." Which is the going price for soup on the street. If that doesn't beat all. Even by Vietnamese standards, five thousand dong is nothing, very little money.

His face keeps coming back to me, the last moment I gazed upon him as we left. Instinctively, I hesitated and turned to him for some final exchange. He couldn't reciprocate. With jaw clenched and head down, he bore the side of his face to me. In the end, it bothered me most that we left like this.

We finally find our way back to the main street, the sound of the road crunching underfoot. I am exhausted.

At 6:15 the next morning, we pass for the last time across the bridge in our rented minibus with the others. I wish everyone was talking. I don't even want to look. Of course, he isn't there; it's too early. But I'm relieved he isn't. I still hold the image of him staring into the water there, so sad.

Jim and I are quiet in our thoughts, rekindling again the last minutes with that very enigmatic man. We ride for a number of miles, bumping along, staring off into the landscape. The minibus hits a big pothole that registers from my tailbone to my head. I put my head down and hold my head with both hands. "Are you OK?" Jim asks.

"No, not really," I say.

And then someone breaks the silence in front which somehow enables me to speak. "Monsieur T and his mother were really struggling, weren't they?"

Jim and I face forward, not looking at each other. "Yeah, I think they were," he says quietly.

We ride for a while longer and then I burst out. "Uh! I wish so MUCH that we'd just taken that damn boat ride! Lots of boat rides!"

Jim doesn't answer. And then, "Yeah, I know. Me too."

CAMBODIA: THE YOUNG GREEN GRASS

Night, the beloved. Night, when words fade and things come alive. When the destructive analysis of day is done, and all that is truly important becomes whole and sound again. When man reassembles his fragmentary self and grows with the calm of a tree.

Antoine de Saint-Exupery

I tear a bite from my baguette sandwich and sip the thick Khmer coffee. Jim and I sit at a small restaurant on Wat Bo Street in Siem Reap, Cambodia, home of the ancient Angkor kings. We stare transfixed at the rain that pours off the tin roof in sheets. It is April, 2001—supposedly the dry season.

Our waitress approaches the table, holding our check. Rigid and blushing, devoid of expression, she bows slightly and delivers it to Jim with two hands. Dressed in a school uniform and quite pretty, with dark shoulder-length hair curled up at the ends, she looks to be eleven or twelve. Probably the owner's daughter.

The check is an endearing sight, if ever a check was endearing. As if from an English primer, the deftly-written letters are large and deliberate, the same hand used on our menus. We pay ten thousand *riel,* about two and a half dollars for everything with a small tip. I smile at her. "This is for you. Thank you for being such a good waitress."

She looks down, her eyes flashing wide with a fiercely suppressed smile of pride. "Thank you, madam," she says with flushed cheeks.

"And the English lettering is very good. Did you do that too?" I know I'm not helping the fits of blushing. She nods and purses her mouth, the trace of a smile this time. But she grins to herself full tilt as she turns to leave, a little skip in her step.

Since we view the Angkor temples for a week, we find ourselves at the Cheese Sandwich Restaurant every day. Other days, we meet waiter number two, the equally reticent younger brother. By the third day, we're accepted, earning smiles of recognition from them both.

The kids wait the tables, and their mother waves from the pass-through window to the kitchen, a one-woman red-faced marvel serving up multiple meals over a single steaming wok. Her shy smile confirms her motherhood, an older version of her daughter. A husband never surfaces, but this is common, we find. Many men have gone missing in Cambodia.

With time, we elicit some information from our blushing waitress. Her name is Chenda, and we're surprised to learn that she is fifteen years old. Cambodian children are smaller than their American counterparts by about three to four years. She looks to be twelve in size, though she's too clever to be twelve.

Chenda and her brother attend Khmer school by day and English class at night. Their mother covers the morning and early afternoon shifts alone. At 3:05 p.m. sharp in a cloud of dust, the children tear down Wat Bo Street on their bikes, straight into the shop, past the tables and into the kitchen.

Work begins again. But they love work; they happily sacrifice their childhood and grow up entirely too fast, all for a glimpse of the mysterious foreigners. And to practice their English.

The poorer kids along the ancient monuments tourist track depend largely on their wiles to make a *riel*. Jim and I call them the souvenir children—the postcard children, the scarf children, the drink children, who brighten the paths leading to the ancient Khmer temples in Siem Reap. For some reason, they're mostly girls and a group of five converges like clingy little beggars as we approach.

"Madam, madam, scarf for yoouuuu!" One raises her arm draped with fabric. "Madam, buy scarf from me," a weak little voice asks. She's a doll; this is really tough. "No, I'm so sorry, sweetie." I smile and keep walking. They don't miss a step keeping up. Most of these kids' families probably need the money very badly. Cambodia is as poor as the world gets.

The first girl with dark, intelligent eyes, the wheeler dealer, skips ahead. "Look, madam," she says, holding up an armful of scarves. "Beautiful scarves for youuu. Many scarves of different colors." I know I'm in trouble when I tarry or talk.

"Oh but, mademoiselle, I haveee Khmer scarves already. Too many scarves!" Unamused, she cocks her head with a piteous face. She's quite a beauty with a lotus flower in her hair. "But madam, please buy scarf from meeee! I am very poor."

I've already bought scarves for all the women in my life and then some. "I'm sorry, sweetie. I just can't, but I loved meeting you. Bye." I stop to shake their hands to conclude the conversation. A bit surprised, they find this hand-shaking quite curious, as if I give them a gift. And then they're still on my heels.

"Is madam from America?" the lotus flower girl asks. "American madams always call us sweetie!"

I laugh aloud. "Really? How interesting. Yes, I guess I'm guilty. I'm American."

As if on cue, with thumbs pointed up, they chime, "America number oneeee!" All over the world, children flash these regrettable exports and parrot Vs for victory or peace or whatever; they don't know. We smile blithely and sign them back. At least we're communicating. We approach the temple entrance which they can't cross, setting off a last frenzy of drama and outstretched arms. Why is it we don't find these children a nuisance after the hundredth plea, the pleas that wear thin in other countries?

The Bayon is Angkor's signature temple, with four-sided towers bearing more than two hundred relief faces of the Bodhisattva deity, Avalokiteshvara, looking out in each direction, his sensual full-lipped half smiles the embodiment of peace. The hundred-plus temples of Angkor make up the largest temple complex in the world, the nucleus more than two hundred hectares. The Angkor kings reigned from the ninth to fourteenth centuries. I never appreciated the breadth of their empire, which was huge, blanketing most of Southeast Asia up into China.

More than anything else, I love the fluid architectural lines throughout Southeast Asia—the ubiquitous winged motifs and curlicues that accent roof lines and headpieces. Much like the sensual *apsara*-dancers who curl their fingertips when they dance. For years, I attributed these motifs to the Thais, though they originated with the Khmers, influenced by the Chinese before. But then all things in Southeast Asia are influenced by the Chinese.

Jim and I settle under a great fig tree to read our guidebook, the same tree whose massive gnarled roots snake through Angkor's temples, lift them off their foundations and crush their roofs. The German and Japanese antiquities conservators have opted to let them be. To remove them would destroy the temples. The roots both undermine the temples, but secure them in their tentacle hold as well. Like a Jules Verne movie, giant octopus arms overpower many jungle temples. People flock in droves to Ta Prohm, Cambodia's most photogenic temple to bear witness to this curious marriage of art and Nature.

Our lovely fig tree looks harmless enough and shades us from the blasting afternoon sun, though it seems we aren't meant to have a relaxing moment alone. Some new little girls spot us and come charging over with their wares. "Oh, please, no," Jim moans. They ignore "mister" and snuggle and cling like favored nieces, fascinated by everything and missing nothing. None of them seems older than ten or eleven.

"Ohhh, how beautiful... madam's earrings... madam's rings... madam's green eyes...madam's hair! And oh look, a little red heart on madam's arm!" Even my moles are scrutinized. They all lean in to examine it closely. "Madam, what is it?" the smallest one asks.

I laugh. "I call it a little red heart." Being close like this seems remuneration enough. They forget the hard sell and just act like children.

But we're highly expendable, it turns out. A Japanese tour bus pulls up, and the souvenir children hop up and run, swarming the steps. I hear one of them make her scarf-spiel in Japanese. The Japanese woman declines and the girls smile and wave, "good luck, madam!"

How can they be so happy? You would never know their country has suffered such a devastating civil war. These are the offspring of the survivors of the holocaust. Surely the after-effects of the war, the random Khmer Rouge skirmishes in the countryside that destabilized the country for another decade, affected them growing up. Through the Nineties, Jim and I waited to come here. Only since 1999 has real security returned. These children have got to carry some remnants of Cambodia's terrible past.

The past is ubiquitous in Cambodia, like incense on the wind. I feel it most keenly here in the countryside. On a glorious sunny day, when you can almost forget, it's there, rising from the earth on the humid air: what's gone missing. The fathers and husbands and brothers, the professionals and doctors and teachers, anyone who wasn't a peasant—they all went missing. And then the present day reminders—the locals with missing limbs, the booming prostheses business, the signs to keep on the paths, to watch for land mines.

The earth knows everything and holds the loss still—the scale of it, the more than two million people killed in a country of only seven million. The earth knows all of it, where each land mine remains. Each particle of soil is rife with the knowledge of Cambodia's unspeakable past and made sacred by it.

At the same time, Nature implores the land to forget. If you listen closely, you can almost hear the jungle grow, turning the soil and erasing the past. Siem Reap could never have been anything other than a verdant paradise, you would say.

And next to us, entreating us to buy yet another handmade Khmer scarf are these candescent faces— like the young green grass that pushes up through the monsoon mud and prevails against all odds. More than anything else, these smiling, imploring faces that hold no memories are Cambodia's hope.

While Jim attends a conference for work, Romeo, our friend from Kenya living in Phnom Penh, joins me for a short trip to Sihanoukville (known as Kompong Som locally), on Cambodia's southern coast. Kompong Som is pleasant and easy-going but not a place you would expect to return to many times.

Again, souvenir children find Romeo and me at Ocheuteal, the most touristed of the five beaches in Kompong Som. This time, their wares are fruit and candies and snacks. Three young girls and a boy share the shade under our cabana. Transfixed by Romeo whose small, wiry, African darkness is so anomalous in Cambodia, they ask too many questions. "Is that man your husband? Where is he from? Where is your husband?" They hound us to buy something in between, giving up and taking off before long.

A boy about eleven or twelve with a mop of straight dark hair approaches. "Madam, madam, how are you today?" And answers himself, "I am fine, thank you very much." He doesn't want to sell me something at all; he wants only to speak English. "Madam. What. Is. Your. Name?" He giggles, so pleased with himself. His eyes catch the light as the wind brushes the hair from his eyes. I say my name and remove paper from my journal to write.

His name is Ra. He writes his name in Khmer, and I show him how to write it in English. "Madam, madam, look." He writes HELLO, and I write THANK YOU.

After an hour, he lifts the rattan tray filled with cellophane bags back to his head and is off. But he reappears in the afternoon and we play English class for another round. His eyes sparkle with enthusiasm; there's an unusual sweetness about him. Two younger children nose their way in, following our scribblings carefully.

We soon draw a crowd, the natural laws of Asia. Like a magnet, a small group always draws more unto itself. A hodgepodge of faces, young and old, block our light and breathe down on us. "Go, go, go!" Ra yells with arms outstretched, enjoying his own authority. And then we're quickly back to work, and no one has left anyway. All of them are hungry to learn and most of them, I learn, aren't in school.

As the sun drops into the ocean, the children make their way home, complaining about their poor sales for the day. Ra's sales have to be bad, though he doesn't seem to care. I hope his parents won't be angry. Romeo and I leave the beach and are surprised to find Bono, our morning motodriver, still there. He smiles and waves. We never asked him to wait or return, but he's probably here for us. Everybody's a motodriver in Cambodia, and getting a fare is very competitive, so it's worth his while to wait most of the day for a sure-fare with a foreigner.

I go alone to Ochheuteal beach the next morning. Romeo doesn't enjoy the children who come around like clockwork.

Ra is missing today. "Where is Ra?" I ask his friend Pros, who takes English class at the premier English school in town and is the most accomplished of the English speakers. His facial structure is quintessentially Khmer, the classic image of King Jayavarman himself—which is to say, ubiquitous in Cambodia. I see Pros in every Khmer temple and every Khmer sculpture.

He points up the beach now. "Ra is coming."

Ra comes running to fill more pages of my journal. I draw pictures to show him new words. "Madam, madam!" He shows me a drawing of a tree he replicated from mine. There's a bit of artistic talent there as well. He wears me out with the English lessons.

I give him the pages containing his handiwork, some clean sheets and a pen, a small treasure in Cambodia. "Now you have homework. You can write words at home. And show your mother your hard work."

He puffs up a bit, smiling a large chipped-tooth smile. "Thank you, madam."

With Pros' help as interpreter, I learn that Ra is fourteen years old and not in Khmer school. He attended school briefly years before and dropped out due to lack of money. Many families can't consistently afford the fee charged for the teacher, twenty-five hundred *riel,* or fifty cents a day, much less the cost of clothes and supplies. Ra's father is dead and his mother is sick (Ra points to his head). She and Ra's younger brother also sell on the beach each day.

Would Ra's mother support the idea of his going to school again? I wonder. In the end, a decent job for one family member would support all of them much better. Poverty makes it difficult to see past the moment. "Would you like to go to school to learn English?" I ask him.

"Yes, madam!" he chirps. Through Pros, I tell Ra that I will pay for him to go to Khmer school and English school. "What does he think?"

They talk. Pros says, "He says he would like it."

But I need his mother's permission first, her blessing. Now that I've raised Ra's hopes, she may well dash them. So we drive to town and Ra retrieves his mother. She looks frail and tired, older than I'd expected. I wonder what she's witnessed these last twenty-some years. Though Cambodian children look younger than their age, the years play catch-up later because adults look older than their age. So I'm guessing Ra's mother is fifty.

Stiff and blinking, with hands clasped tightly, she looks unnerved. In all fairness, meeting with some foreigner about your son would set most people on edge. Under large tinted glasses, I see one eye doesn't move with the other. This is what Ra meant when he pointed to his head—she is probably blind in one eye.

Bono and Pros explain my intentions. She listens carefully without looking at me. The voice that surfaces belies her demeanor. Not shy but forceful, her voice rings strident and opinionated as if making a speech. My heart sinks. Even when she turns to me, I can't glean the answer; her face is completely devoid of expression. Then Pros translates. "Ra's mother says thank you, madam. She is very happy."

"But ask her for me, Pros, can they manage with less money with Ra not selling on the beach?"

He asks and replies, "She says they will do it, madam. Ra can sell in the afternoon."

"So the answer is yes, we can definitely enroll Ra in school?" I ask.

"Yes, Madam, she says yes. She is very happy." Though her face remains expressionless. But I am very relieved and take her hand in both of mine, trying to convey my thanks. Handshaking is not an Eastern custom, but Cambodians understand it. Emotion tears at her stoic facade as she wipes her good eye from the side of her glasses.

When Bono takes me home that evening, I ask him to retrieve the boys at the beach and bring them to my guesthouse in the morning.

Early in the morning, Bono pulls up with Pros and Ra in tow and another motobike and driver for Romeo and me. Ra's eyes dance; he understands that something very big is taking form. Riding around with foreigners instead of selling at the beach is pretty cool too. Not to mention all your friends seeing you and asking a hundred questions.

We go to an international private school first. But the headmaster is out of town. Come back another day, we are told. Bono takes us to the Psar Leu Primary School in town where Ra attended school before. Children in white shirts and navy blue shorts and skirts crowd the gated courtyard during recess. This makes me realize that Ra is going to need clothes for this new venture.

The din of the school courtyard is wild. Children climb on the fence and trees like little monkeys. When our entourage enters the courtyard, we are immediately more fascinating than recess. *Voila*, the screaming and playing stop, and a courtyard full of curious faces and uniforms follows us.

On the other hand, the adults in charge don't seem to notice us. Bodies squeeze into the school office doorway as we ask to see the headmaster. The "head mistress" is at home for lunch, we are told, but we can visit her there. "At home, it's OK?" I ask.

Yes, they assure us. How nice that the school is run by a woman. And how nice that she's so flexible, though I can't imagine she'll appreciate a visit. Bono gets directions and we're off.

A fifty-something, attractive woman receives us in her courtyard, dressed in a dark skirt and white blouse. She is lighter complected than most Cambodians. Carrying on school business at home must be normal. With an all-business head mistress manner, she purses her mouth like people with unstraightened front teeth.

She invites us inside. Typical of most urban Cambodia middle-class houses, the main living area is open by day to one side, a few wooden chairs arranged on a cool stone floor. At night, motobikes or cars are brought inside, a metal wall pulled down and locked. Pairs of shoes sit at the entrance, though our hostess insists we needn't remove ours. Of course, we do. As if we're invisible, she never acknowledges Romeo or me, though her eyes constantly find Romeo. The houseboy returns from the store with special tea and a roll of toilet paper.

The red Chinese religious shrines tell me the family is Chinese. Many Cambodians use Chinese shrines as a cultural observance more than a religious one, but Madam Horn's many Chinese decorations, and her name, confirm her ancestry. About ten percent of Cambodians are Chinese and often assume entrepreneurial and professional roles.

Before we can speak, Madam begins to fuss, rail actually, at Pros, whom she obviously knows. She scolds him for dropping out of Khmer school, he tells me later, a decision he made to attend English school instead. There is no anger in her face, but her voice rings untrue in this country—brash and loud. Not once in weeks have my ears heard a raised voice in Cambodia. The five of us uncomfortably endure the onslaught until it plays out. Pros lets her have her full say, then responds very calmly. As I've suspected all along, this child is destined to be Cambodia's next deity-king.

When Madam is finished, I nod to Ra and Pros to jump in. They scramble to their feet as if to make a presentation to the teacher in class, repeating the request in Khmer, which must sound pretty polished by now. Madam Horn speaks no English, but asks countless questions of Pros and Ra in Khmer, in an almost combative tone. How could she possibly have so many questions? I fear we will go school-hunting again.

But like Ra's mother, her voice belies her answer. Pros suddenly turns to me. "Madam says Ra can come to the primary school." And many ages can be found in all the classes. He can attend Khmer class in the morning and English class in the early evening at Psar Leu.

The black cloud lifts as quickly as it came. Madam headmistress's demeanor changes. She now relaxes and seems genuinely pleased. Tea lubricates our unease and the two of us exchange some personal chitchat through our premier translators. She is married, with grown children living elsewhere, and will retire in six years. I am married with no children, I tell her. No, this is not my husband. Further questions come to a screeching halt. All I care is that she seems committed to education and has the children's best interest at heart.

I am shocked to learn the cost is only two dollars a month for Khmer school and another two dollars for English. I will fund Ra for six months to begin, to see how things go, and handle all the finances at school in the morning. As we leave, she shakes Romeo's and my hand and, through Bono, thanks me warmly, expressing her pleasure that Ra will attend school again. Not until that moment do I feel a real rapport.

The big deed done, we all stand smiling at each other in the courtyard. The jubilant Ra recognizes this as a milestone. Though he basks in the moment, school has to be a complete abstraction. The odds are against him and he will be a large risk. School makes demands he's not used to; he has no study skills or discipline. He'll do things he hasn't done for years. And as supportive as his mother seems now, her needs will always come first. There are no illusions. Developing countries don't provide Social Security programs for old age. Children are their parents' chattel and security for the future. If mum gets sick or needs more money, Ra is another statistic. No, not even a statistic, because no one is keeping track. And in time, he will be torn. Selling on the beach is more fun. But poor kids in the developing world do prevail sometimes, uneasily—and mostly if their parents want them to. Ra just might.

"Back to beach?" Bono asks.

"First, can we go to the market to get clothes and notebooks for school?" I ask. Romeo begs off as he has to take the afternoon bus back to Phnom Penh. He gets another moto, and Bono, Pros, Ra and I ride four astride to town, where we pull up to the central market entrance that teems with locals milling about.

Scores of little stalls roll out a complete discount department store in increments. But few customers move about. Merchants dust their wares, shoo flies, stand leaning against walls and sit full force in front of electric fans. We approach the packaged foods aisle, where colors jump out at us in blue and pink cellophane wraps. Then the jewelry stalls, the stalls and stalls of shoes, the towering housewares, the clothes, everything under the tropical sun for sale.

We pass a lady painting another lady's fingernails—polished nails for sale, just like at home, something I wouldn't expect to see in Cambodia. People hang on our attention on both sides of the aisle, inviting us to come in. "Yes madam, have a look, please." Of course, no one assumes my friends are buying.

We lose our way and retrace our steps to find the stationery area. Everyone springs to action again, certain we're back to buy this time. We negotiate the price of notebooks and pens and pencils, make a purchase and move to the inner sanctum. As smooth as polished rock, the dirt floor opens into little gullies and rivers of water to be navigated. The oxygen thins as we move inward and scarcely exists in the middle. The dry heat sucks the moisture from my face. How can these people possibly work here all day?

We stop at a shirt stall. The proprietor jumps like a man shocked by a live wire, fawning over our every need. He pulls white shirt after white shirt out of loud, crinkly plastic packages. Then it hits me. New shirts aren't the way to go. Ra will look like a clown if he shows up for school with spanking new clothes.

And Ra seems to read my mind. "Madam, madam, come." He tugs at me as we move to the used clothing area that fills a huge open quadrant of the market. Clothes piled in mounds on flat wooden platforms follow one after the other, no doubt, the final stop of St. Vincent de Paul's overseas shipments. The shirt piles, the pants piles, the skirt piles. Everything Ra picks up he likes, regardless of size, and holds it up for my approval. "Madam, look! Good!" he beams.

"But we can't buy them unless you try them on first," I say with Pros translating. In quick order, we find three nice white shirts that fit and move to the shorts pile. I must look as bad as I feel. The sweet lady proprietor gives me water from a thermos, sits me in a chair and turns her fan directly on me. Ra and Pros look unruffled.

She hands Ra a sarong to wrap around his legs to try on the shorts. Extremely modest, he pulls up the shorts over the sarong which bulge inside like fat lumpy scarecrow legs. Pros covers his mouth and giggles, making me realize how truly contained he is most of the time. I love to see him laugh, which makes me laugh. I don't think I've ever seen Pros laugh. The lady has a great throaty guffaw and she makes us laugh more. Over and over, she plies him in Khmer and shows him how to do it. We all double over to see Ra's expression, a sheepish look with cheeks blazing, as if paralyzed. The woman and I smile at each other, finally understanding the problem. We turn our heads.

By the time we find three sets of shorts that fit, I'm certain I have lost weight from the heat. We buy some flipflops, the shoes of choice everywhere in tropical Asia, much more quickly. Used clothes, new shoes and school supplies for a year cost less than eight dollars.

Ra carries four plastic bundles with an expression of unbridled bliss. Christmas in Cambodia at a hundred and ten-plus degrees. "Madam," he touches my arm, unable to look me in the face. "Thank you."

And then I realize Pros must feel left out. We find a T-shirt table and have the most fun there. More than anything else all day, the boys are most smitten with their very cool T-shirts, which they assume to be American.

I'm famished. They must be, too, so I ask Bono to choose a local restaurant, simple fare, nothing fancy. I want to do something more for Bono and Pros, my faithful translators and supporters. We sit in an outdoor restaurant with tables that line the main road in town. We all order a fried rice dish, and I can't believe my eyes when the waiter delivers our food. Each plate is a virtual mountain of rice and veggies, as large as I've seen in Asia times two. These people eat modestly; this was not at all what I'd envisioned for lunch. By any standard, especially Asian standards, this is obscene, enough food to feed all of us for days.

The chairs are too low or the tables too high, but Ra and Pros sit with chins just clearing the table top. They chew slowly and politely as if under some edict to eat, a last supper. They are not having fun; this is not a special treat at all. Perhaps they've never eaten in a restaurant before? I try to add some levity, make small talk, ask questions, tell jokes—anything—to no avail. No one seems to be listening; my translators aren't translating.

WHAT is going on? There's little eye contact. They don't even talk among themselves. If only I'd suggested the market we just left, where all the food stalls are true local fare and less daunting.

"Please, it's OK guys," I tell them. "You don't have to eat all this food. It's too much." But they chew and chew like little cows masticating their cud. As if to attain Buddhahood, they eat every blessed grain of rice until only little slicks of oil remain on the plate. I can't even imagine where those skinny little bodies put all that food. I'm almost grateful to see Bono leave food on his plate.

"Why don't you take it home with you?" I ask. He blushes. What am I thinking? It's not like they have refrigeration. "You know, I mean to share with your family," I add, smiling.

Maybe this is like India, where it's a sign of privilege to leave food on your plate; only poor people eat everything. "You know, in America, we always take food home if we can't finish it. Nobody thinks anything of it." He still registers nothing, perhaps not comprehending. Now I'm blushing. We head out quickly in the hope that I will stop embarrassing everyone and ruining an otherwise perfect day.

The day before returning to Phnom Penh, Bono takes me to the beach for the last time. I fear I'll miss seeing the boys, as I didn't tell them my plans. One of the girls sees me and goes running off. They soon come, Ra smiling broadly, Pros with his usual poker face, both donning their new T-shirts.

And then I realize the eternal problem of helping only one or two. Every kid on the beach should have a new T-shirt and be put in Khmer and English school. And every kid on the beach knows that Ra will go to school soon, that he and Pros went shopping and lots of clothes were bought, and that we all went to dinner. Word of mouth communication is quite efficient on this beach.

Bono unloads my parting gift, four large cellophane bags of peanuts containing twenty small packages each. Designed to establish Ra and his family in a little microenterprise venture, the hope is to increase daily sales to ensure Ra's success in school.

The young beach vendors desperately need coaching, precisely why sales are so lean and competition is so fierce. They all sell the same few things, the same pineapples, the same papayas, the same chips and sesame candies. The quantities they sell are too large and not user-friendly. And then they ask too much money. For two dollars, the same price as a meal, you get a whole sticky, dripping pineapple. Tourists prefer smaller snacks and like to part with smaller sums so they can help more sellers.

I got this brainstorm to buy shelled peanuts for Ra because no one sells peanuts on the beach. If he sells them for five hundred *riel,* only twelve and a half cents each, more tourists will buy them and he'll make a nice profit—three hundred percent. I try to explain the economics to Ra, setting it out on paper with Pros translating. The girls and cousins gather round, fingering the merchandise. Bono shoos them off and puts the peanuts back in the bag. At least twice.

It's not going well. "Do you think he understands?" I ask Pros.

"Ra understands," Pros says.

"Do you understand, Pros?" I ask my star pupil.

"Yes," he nods, perfectly deadpan.

"Are you *sure?*"

"Yes, madam," he says unconvincingly. No lights are going on here. Even non-materialistic kids like these would get excited if they understood how fantastic the profits could be, and how easy it would be.

"And the important thing," I say to Pros, "is for Ra to save ten thousand *riel* from his sales to buy the packets again." More vapid looks.

"Just save this," I say to Ra, leaving the paper in the hope it might all seep in after some math classes in school. As a last-ditch effort, I ask Bono to please go over it with Ra some more. But I doubt Bono understands either. I've run out of backups.

"Ra, where is your mother?" I ask. He leaves and she appears with him, winded and smiling a half-toothless smile. We have achieved a kind of sisterly status. She produces a wrapped gift with foil paper and yellow ribbon, a feast for the eyes and so anomalous and garish on a beach in a poor country.

Most Cambodians give gifts in hand-woven boxes, but this is meant to be special—the way the foreigners do it. A long white, crocheted scarf with fine handiwork is inside.

"Mother, mother!" Ra points to his mother to tell me she has made it. She retrieves the scarf and shows me how to wear it across the shoulder and chest.

"Like Buddha," Bono says.

"Ah, yes, the scarf of Buddha," I say. Hugging in public is not common in Cambodia, and the only kissing I've seen is mothers kissing babies. But I just can't help it. I hug Pros and Ra and his mother, and kiss them on the cheek.

Ra's mother turns and blots her good eye, speaking to Pros. "She wants to thank you very much, madam," Pros says.

I don't want to leave them. In only three days, this spot of sand on the map precisely halfway around the world that meets the ocean and catches the sun rivals home—a place that will always draw me to it. And with that comes a new fear for the safety of my friends. That the unpredictability of this place, far less predictable than anything I could know, might harm them in some way.

My wishes are that the lesson in economics will see the light of clarity, that the peanut venture might work, that Ra and his mother will be financially stable and he can remain in school. Success is very delicate here.

I still see the vacant looks of Ra and Pros, the image of a flustered Bono beating off the kids from the peanut bags.

Bono readies the motobike. I look back to see them all waiting patiently to see us off. The girls grin impishly, already waving. What was I thinking? Of course, they'll rip those bags open and eat the peanuts as soon as we're out of sight.

I sense it still, even here: the knowledge of this earth, the loss of this place. But I also sense that this little knit of family and friends will prevail. Not easily, but they will. Because they have before against all odds.

Our motobike zigzags its way across the sand to the beach road. I turn to take my last mental snapshot, straining to see the faces of my guys and the girls, Ra's mother and friends. But they evade me, eclipsed by the sun. I throw them a kiss, something I showed the younger girls how to do one day. The women stand with prayer hands to face. And those adorable, silly girls mimic me back, throwing kisses with exaggerated pirouettes in the air. Ra and Pros wave.

There is no missing Pros who stands tallest along the line. His long slender arm sways slowly against the light, back and forth, strong and staid like the fig trees of Angkor.

Postscript: When I returned home from this trip in 2001, friends loved the idea of sponsoring a Cambodian child in school too. The second year's entrance class was six girls and a boy. Few children could look more proud in their uniforms their first day of school. But none of these children, including Ra, lasted more than two years. Their inappropriate age placement probably contributed most. Even with each other, thirteen and fourteen year olds simply cannot attend class with six year olds. In 2002, I formed a formal nonprofit organization, the Cambodian Children's Education Foundation. Children are no longer recruited from the beach but in close cooperation with school administrators instead. We have an outreach worker too—Than, who works with the schools. Attrition rates have dropped dramatically. The foundation has grown slowly and cautiously, presently supporting two partner-schools in Sihanoukville and forty-two Cambodian children in Khmer and English instruction. A generous gift of ten thousand dollars from the John and Mary Geisse Foundation of Ohio funded a computer lab for Antaraktvib school students and many sorely-needed computers, copiers and supplies for the office. Kids hungry to learn computer skills and surf the Internet can now enjoy affordable instruction. I return every year or two to Cambodia. Large fancy hotels are inundating sleepy little Kompong Som and I scarcely recognize it. Some day, I will settle in for a few months, drive around on a motobike myself and teach English to the next generation of Ras.

Half the proceeds of *1089 Nights* provide educational assistance to disadvantaged students in Cambodia; $24 supports a child in Khmer school for one year. If you'd like to help, please write: The Cambodian Children's Education Foundation, PO Box 104, West Friendship, MD 21794-0104.

INDONESIA: THE STORIES WE TELL OURSELVES

Learn to reverence night and to put away the vulgar fear of it for, with the banishment of night from the experience of man, there vanishes as well a religious emotion, a poetic mood, which gives depth to the adventure of humanity.

Henry Beston

Our route taxi whisks us from the airport towards Ubud, the traditional center of Bali. Few people stir at nine at night. As we near the city of Denpasar, a wonderful light show unfolds. Larger-than-life statues rise up in floodlight, theatrical and macabre, one after another. The gods that populate Hindu life in Bali grace office buildings and roundabouts, rushing by like a video in fast-forward.

Jim and I crane our necks. "Could you go a little slower, please?" I ask our driver. It's December, 2004, twelve years since our first visit to Bali, and we're smitten all over again.

I recognize Saraswati, the goddess of music and the arts. But I don't recognize the demons. I look for my favorite, Barong, everyone's favorite, the veritable patron saint of Bali, who protects all Balinese households. His formidable appearance—always dark, open-mouthed, teeth and fang-bearing —wards off evil spirits. But beneath that nasty exterior, he's actually a sweet, playful demon. "What in the world took us so long to get back here?" I ask Jim.

Our driver, Wayan (WHY-ahn, meaning first-born), stops at Hanuman Road in Ubud for the drop off. Across the street, brilliant spotlights illuminate the inner compound of a temple, a cloud of insects swirling above.

As I open the car door, my heart flipflops to hear a *gamelan* orchestra again—the slow and deliberate beat accompanied by a soulful flute. *Ting-ting-ting-ting.... ting-ting-ting-ting.* The pace will build. Ever so slowly, it will rise faster and faster, and crescendo to a feverish pitch and come crashing down at the end. "Do you think it would be OK if we had just a peek?" I ask Wayan. Slipping into the play with a local seems infinitely better.

"A peek?" he asks.

"Sorry, a look inside," I say. He nods and smiles, cutting the engine. The three of us scale the steps over the raised threshold and pass through the double golden doors to the temple.

Ah, so here he is! Center stage we find Barong in his hairy, beasty glory, confirming that we're really in Bali. He dances in a circle with a wild red and yellow-haired demon, the gamelan orchestra tapping out his steps. As they turn, large sagging breasts tell us the other demon is an old woman and a very ugly one with long red tongue, yellow teeth and fangs.

I look around. Mostly locals fill the stands, very few tourists, and no one even notices us. The children are transfixed. Some people cheer, I guess for Barong.

"This is the Calonarang dance," Wayan says, "where Rangda and Barong fight. Rangda is queen of the *leyaks*."

"Who are the *leyaks*?" I ask.

"The witches," Wayan says. "The red and yellow hair and tongue is the fire. You see the followers of Barong fall to the

ground? The power of Rangda is so great, even Barong cannot
save them."

A little boy one tier behind us watches with a dour face,
as if he wants to cry, but he's afraid he might miss something.
This is no Disney production.

The music mounts, followed by the deafening crescendo.
Rangda and Barong fall to the floor. Wayan yells over the
music. "They fall down in the trance." A drum booms and my
chest vibrates, signaling the end. The actors rise and run off
the stage: a rather anti-climatic end.

"So the forces of darkness won?" Jim asks.

"No one wins in the Balinese play," Wayan says. "Rangda
is the Goddess of Death. She can never die. But the fight
between good and evil makes everything right, back in the
balance again. When there is the balance in their world, there
is the balance in ours."

"Do children growing up on Bali learn these things in
school?" I ask.

"No, they learn from these plays and their parents. The
Balinese play tells the story of our culture. They are the same."
Wayan seems very clever. As we talk, we learn that he studies
at a university in the Netherlands for part of the year.

"When I am little boy," he says laughing, "the first time
my father is taking me to see Rangda, I am very afraid. I am
crying. She is very ugly. Sometimes now in my village, I am
Barong."

"You mean you perform as Barong in plays like this?" I
ask.

"Yes, but very hot inside the head!" He grimaces and laughs.
We sit and watch the crowds empty.

"Today is Kajeng Kliwon Day," Wayan continues. "We
dance the Calonarang on this day because the *leyaks* come out
and make the bad magic and cause trouble."

"Really? I'm so grateful we caught Calonarang, even for
only a few minutes," I say.

"Kajeng Kliwon day is every fifteen days," Wayan says.

I repress a laugh. "You mean the witches come out every fifteen days?" He nods. "So that's why people are so busy making offerings in Bali?"

"Yes, there is no rest from the *leyaks*," he smiles.

"Do you make the offerings to the *leyaks*?" I ask Wayan.

"Me?" He hesitates. "I make the offerings, but I do not believe in the *leyaks*."

"So you make the offerings to cover yourself just in case?" I smile.

"Yes," he says with a little chortle. "For me, it is really the tradition. The Balinese rituals are beautiful."

He's such a good-looking kid with dark hair and beautiful white teeth; if only my niece Blair could meet him. Since I'm on a roll, I ask: "Do you think most Balinese believe in the *leyaks*?"

He hesitates again. "Many still believe. But it is changing."

Wayan drops us off at a traditional *homestay*, a bed and breakfast of sorts, where the Balinese open up rooms for tourists within their walled family complex. Our night watch-lady fiddles to unlock the double doors. A Barong face on the threshold overhead greets us, welcoming but menacing. As the doors part, the night light catches gold flecks that reveal a traditional Balinese compound. Few places in the world rival the beauty of this culture.

Seeing is difficult. But the mere suggestion of the place takes my breath: the grandeur of the outlines, the luxuriant sweeps of the rooftops, the architectural detail, the rich sense of history. As we move, the light of the streetlamp catches the gold, worn but elegant, threading its way along an edge.

The young woman opens the double doors to our room. In contrast, our abode is Spartan, though clean and cheery. This is fine, we tell her, content to sleep on the street at this point. Jim removes the wooden bar that wedges the doors to the porch. We step outside and look down upon a stand of small shrines used for offerings for this family. Fuchsia bougainvillea climb up the porch. Gardens fill each open space, sending out sweet jasmine in the air. There is no place else I would rather be right now.

As we lie in bed, an odd distant voice cries out in the night. "What is that?" I ask. It sounds like a frog; perhaps a night bird. Or a child's cry. "There it is again."

"I don't hear it," Jim says.

"Are you serious, you can't hear that bizarre cry? It's disconcerting, actually."

He listens carefully. "It's probably a frog in the rice fields," he says.

In the morning, we bathe from a traditional *mandi*, a huge clay pot about four feet tall filled with water that is ladled over the body. A bit cool. Then we strike out to take in the new Ubud.

So much has changed and so little has changed since 1992, when we first visited Bali. The tourist shops that dotted the center of town on Monkey Forest Road have multiplied more than the sad-looking Balinese dogs, their owners equally as hungry for a sale. Bali's tourism still struggles after the nightclub bombing in 2002. And November is the off-season. Too many shops sell the same handicrafts and clothes and silver.

The owners implore us to come in to look, and hover a little too closely. "Yes, madam, for you we have morning discount." At other shops, we find the first sale discount, the good luck discount, and the Merry Christmas discount, in a Hindu culture no less.

As we walk, we navigate the little offerings of color on the ground that protect shops and home entrances, Hindu statues, and key junctures, such as bridges and road crossings. Offerings at public shrines are awash with pink and yellow flowers and smoking incense sticks, piled to overflowing. The whole of Ubud, it strikes me, is like a vast open-air temple. And the women are the caretakers of these ancient rituals, keeping them alive each day. For hours, they sit in small groups on the roadside and make the offerings that others will buy, talking easily with hands moving. Few activities in Bali are solitary. People are always together, it seems.

We return to find Made (MAH-dee, meaning second-born), one of our *homestay* managers, readying an offering at a small shrine under a fig tree in the courtyard. Watching this process is the best part. He picks a few flowers around the courtyard and prepares his modest offering on a tray. Flower tops or petals are most commonly used for offerings, along with rice and fruit. Bougainvillea pink seems mandatory. Other custom-tailored additions complete the mix—cookies, candies, cigarettes, money—whatever the supplicant sees as a sacrifice.

The painstaking preparations, the offerings, the lavish festivals, the paintings and plays—all these rituals lift up beauty to the gods. Preparation and ritual are one. As much as the rice they eat, the love of beauty sustains the Balinese people.

Made lights the incense and splashes water from a shallow bowl. With upturned fingers, he flicks his hand once, twice, thrice. He's really good—moving with the same flourish and timing as a *legong*, the young girl dancers who once performed for the king in his court (and now, with the purchase of a ticket, every night in town). I wonder if Made is a dancer too; I must remember to ask him.

Everyone in Bali is an artist of some sort; there are few artier places on earth. The simplest eating places, *warungs*, serve meals with a color and flair befitting of a magazine cover. Locals who work one job by day transform into musicians or painters or dancers by night. The place runs amok with art galleries and museums. Artists from all over the world flock here in the hope that a bit of Bali's inspiration might rub off.

But as Hindu as Bali appears, you quickly realize that it's only nominally Hindu. The visible pantheon of deities imported from Java in the tenth century provide a rich cultural folklore, but the Balinese brand of Hinduism is largely animist. As Wayan confirmed, supplicants are very much focused on appeasing evil spirits or eliciting help from the gods. Everything the Balinese do—the offerings, plays, festivals and funerals—are an elaboration of protection.

Spirits have apparently found Bali to their liking for centuries. The night writhes with forms of questionable intent. People enjoy a kind of night vision, seeing things the rest of us don't. Or perhaps can't. The only recourse if you're Balinese is to make the spirits happy or confuse them into going elsewhere. And to be safe, this means regular offerings.

Since today is an auspicious day, the new moon, the owner of our *homestay* plans a special ceremony. Naturally, auspicious days are as frequent as the spirits are persistent. Every community has its own temple and calendar. So if you wait on the corner for any length of time, a religious procession will pass you by. The *ting-ting-ting-ting* of the xylophone and flute signals the arrival of a mini-gamelan orchestra before you see it. The men and women wear lavish traditional sarongs, the men with the ceremonial headbands, the women bearing headdresses of tall fruit bowls. You automatically know it's an auspicious day.

So the matter of sealing off an "unprotected" doorway and consecrating a new one is what the fuss is about in our *homestay* courtyard. It seems one of our family's entrances lacks the all-important inner wall. In a properly designed, traditional Balinese house, if you're a spirit, you enter the exterior doorway and come smack up against another wall. Since you can't navigate right angles, the inner wall stops you. Being of lower intelligence, presumably because you're dead, you become confused and leave. Even the doorways to the lavatories in the very modern airport, I noticed, have inner walls.

A stone mason has readied the new doorway for days. The extended family gathers now in their best dress. Before the Dutch "civilized" Indonesians, the women wore colorful sarongs and were bare-breasted. Now they wear sarongs with sheer, see-through blouses and dark bras underneath. The black thatch-roofed family shrines where offerings are made are decorated with gold and white ceremonial umbrellas. The shrines are wrapped in silk aprons, yellow and red, and checkered black and white cloth, the traditional fabric of Bali. The uninviting demon-guards made of stone, (who we know are actually benevolent), flank the doorway and wear the same fabrics.

The old entrance is closed off with a low masonry wall. Spirits are apparently short and not good jumpers either. The women make offerings at the family shrine and burn incense. The young cousins play some kind of leapfrog game on the grass. Dressed in white, the priest rings a bell, says prayers, makes incantations and places chalk marks at key spots upon the new entrance wall. The stone mason participates too, digging up the earth around the exterior wall at the new entrance and dumping a pile of yesterday's offerings with the dirt.

Balinese tradition rests as much upon fooling the spirits as appeasing them. All the guests at our *homestay* can rest easy because our family has crossed their Ts.

The next morning, Jim and I sit under a small thatched pavilion on the edge of the *homestay* eating a leisurely breakfast. Made is running behind on breakfast orders. He's an unusually nice kid, about eighteen or nineteen. Keeping up with managing, cooking, room-cleaning, errand-running, generally making fourteen demanding guests happy twenty-four hours a day, six days a week, pays two hundred thousand *rupia* a month, less than twenty dollars. Wages include housing, if you call sleeping on a grungy mattress rolled out on the office floor a room.

Our French neighbors, Louis and Antoinette (real names, a marriage apparently destined to be) and American and

Venezuelan expat friends, Mellissa and Gorge, join us at the table. Made delivers our egg *jaffles*—a waffle-type dough filled with egg—fruit and Balinese coffee, and sits down with us. We discuss the wall-closing, wall-opening ceremony of the day before.

"Very important!" Made tells us, about paying homage and performing a proper ceremony. "See restaurant there?" We follow his gaze to our side; the restaurant appears to be closed. He lowers his voice and leans in. "The restaurant go on top rice paddy before the harvest. Not making the offering." He lets that settle in, sitting back. "And see? No business!" He waves his hand with a glint in his eye that makes us believe him.

I look again as if to find something barely perceptible loaming there. It is odd; the restaurant next door seems to be doing perfectly well. *Please, that's ridiculous*, I tell myself. As warm and humid as the day has become, I feel a chill and cross my legs. Everyone eats in silence.

But what a waste, to sacrifice a rice field ready to harvest for a restaurant with no business. For hundreds of years up until only twenty years ago, Ubud was nothing but rice fields, each field picked off one by one by restaurants and guesthouses. Like the farms at home. Farming can't compete with developer's prices.

As we eat, a racket assembles next door. Dump trucks loaded with stone back up to the rice field, garbling Made's words and spewing exhaust fumes. We turn as one raises its load high, thousands of pounds of stone crashing down. Melissa instinctively jumps up in alarm. A cloud of dust passes through us. It seems like sacrilege, a sea of white pebbles consuming young green rice plants and burying them over.

"So what's this going to be?" Mellissa yells angrily over the truck to Made.

"Parking lot," Made says.

"What about this one? Did he do all the right offerings?" Antoinette asks.

Made nods."Yes, he is making the offering before the harvest."

"Now Balinese are making offerings for *parking lots*? Who is the goddess of rice paddies, Made?" I ask.

"Dewi Sri."

What's become of the deities in Bali? How could Dewi Sri consent to a parking lot, even if the proper rituals are performed first? Surely, all of it displeases her. For centuries, she's enjoyed great favor—the myriad rice paddies have assured her rule of the place. But now in Bali of all places, we have the prospect of a world where gods are expendable. And worse, no longer immortal when the rice paddies are gone.

Forget the offerings to the menacing little spirits. This is a goddess. Isn't anybody worried about Dewi Sri's disapproval? In the name of progress, she's been asked to descend her regal mount to accept offerings for eateries and parking lots? The tackiness of it all—that a goddess could come to this. It's too much, the prospect of Bali denuded of its rice fields and Dewi Sri on the dole.

Jim asks for another cup of coffee. We need to change the subject. I turn to Louis the Frenchman, the nature expert. "I've been meaning to ask you, what is the animal that makes that odd sound at night? You know a very strange cry, like a frog or a bird maybe?"

"It's the lizard, I believe," Louis says. "Not the gecko, a bigger one."

Made pipes up. "Oh, but sometimes it's the spirits."

Antoinette makes an audible puff of air, a French puff. "What kind of spirits?" she asks.

Made becomes self-conscious and giggles his silly giggle you can hear day and night around the place, his eyes twinkly and rounded like commas. I want to hug him, he is so sweet. He epitomizes the Balinese people for me—warm and gentle and easy. He drops his smile, fingering the table. "Sometimes I am fear," he says. "The people walk on the ground, but the spirits float all over the night." So much for changing the subject; there's simply no getting away from the spirits in Bali.

"Do you see them?" Antoinette asks. All eyes bear down on Made. His eyes narrow as if they sting, measuring his response. He smiles his inimitable smile, nodding.

"Yes, you see them?" Antoinette confirms. He nods again. She isn't ready to let this go. "You see them *all* the time?"

"Just at the night time. Sometimes. And when my father was dying."

The owner's wife walks past and waves to us, a tray of morning offerings in hand. She asks Made to do something and continues towards the tree shrine, deposits a few offerings and flicks her hand. "Spiritual" has taken on a different meaning this time in Bali. Before, I'd thought Bali was the most spiritual place I'd ever seen. Frightened and superstitious, maybe—but probably not spiritual.

I often make long walks from town at night, spirits notwithstanding. The exodus of living souls starts after the sun sets. Most people are well-rooted at home by the time the color has left the sky. It's about 9:30, hours after sunset. The rise and fall of the *ting-ting-ting-ting* melody of the *gamelan* orchestra carries from the royal palace's courtyard. As I pass the front gate, tourists and *Ketuk* dance performers and musicians file out, talking in quiet tones. The farther I walk from the palace, their numbers diminish, until I'm finally alone with a few dimly-lit street lights.

It could be the middle of the night, the street is so quiet. I round a corner. As the shops thin, the clouds of yellow vapor from the business district give way to another light, a cool gray light that guides my way and blankets the road and rice fields beyond. The moon is high in the sky, glorious and full. Jim would probably say it waxes or wanes a day short of full; he can always tell.

A moon shadow moves beside me, then behind. The air is soft, a welcomed respite from the cloying humidity of the day. Frangipani lilts on the air, and I feel supremely content. This night is a refuge to crawl in, as perfect as nights on earth come.

The road bends and the trees move and play with the light on the ground, giving it back in patches. A cylinder of light moves in the air, maybe ten yards away, its form pulsing and quickening as I approach. What is it? A plastic bag in the wind? A twirling top? I think of Made and stop, breathing shallowly, straining to make it out.

Is this what Made sees in the night? If only for a moment, I want to be graced with Balinese eyes. A motorbike rounds the corner. Its headlight reveals hundreds of large winged bugs crashing against the air in the moonlight. Of course! I smile, breathing more easily, a simple explanation.

Forms that writhe in the night are the stories the Balinese have passed down through the centuries, like a family heirloom—an ancient lens on the world that sees black magic in the night. Some of us see the night as good magic. Or simply the time of day when the earth turns away from the sun.

"Not all Balinese fear the night," a local painter assured me. "It's the poor and uneducated who believe these things. When the standard of living improves and education is universal, they will be free to enjoy the night."

A muddle of voices greets me just before I enter the spanking new threshold to the *homestay*. Jim and the others are quite awake, confirming that another world lives inside the walls of Ubud by night. As we go up to our room, Made slips me a flyer—a good place for massages, he says.

I realized later that I'd gotten my wish. Thousands of miles away, Jim and I sat outside at night on the deck of our Baltimore home. In our world, the night is innocuous and predictable; if there are spirits here, they must be content.

Sitting there, I realized that I did see with Balinese eyes in Bali. But I looked in the wrong place—in the night—because that's where I expected to see the spirits. I never dreamed I could see with Balinese eyes in the starkness of day.

The next morning, the morning of the day, I decide to treat myself to a traditional Balinese massage and try Made's recommendation. I follow the sign up the staircase, enter an open courtyard and find a woman sitting at a desk who jumps up, as if surprised to see me. There are no other customers I can see around. My masseuse comes out and greets me with prayer hands. In her thirties, she has a bright, winning smile, her dark hair pulled back with a jasmine flower.

But my traditional Balinese massage is not wonderful. Three times I try to explain "easy, easy" with my hand, "no need to work so hard."

She smiles each time, a little too solicitous. "Yes, as you like, madaaaam," and continues to tenderize me. Shortly before the end of our hour, she gets the message.

Tipping in the developing world confounds me and elicits passionate debate among travelers. I want to tip poor people especially. But I don't want to transform kindness into expectation and corrupt people in the process. In this situation, I suspect my masseuse receives less of the fee than the owner. Poor people often put up with yawning inequities just to make a little money. I give her five thousand *rupia*, one dollar, separate from the six dollar massage. "Ohhh, madam, thank youuuu!" she exclaims, wringing her hands, a burst of emotion I have never seen in Bali.

Now that we are fast friends, she makes a furtive glance towards the door and bends close to my face to whisper. "Madam, business in Ubud veryyy slow. Please, you have friend, you want massage, you call me this number. I come your hotel. Before, I work in Kuta. Business veryyy good in Kuta. Not good in Ubud."

"OK, good, thank you, I'll remember that," I say in a normal voice that sounds loud. She gives me the card of the shop with her home telephone written by hand. I remember Kuta well, a world away on the same island, a happenin' beach scene brimming with tourists and snakes. Where the night club bombing occurred in 2002. Everybody's a masseuse in Kuta, hounding you all day long for a massage on the beach.

The shop owner and masseuse wave me off. Nice enough people, but not a place I can recommend enthusiastically. Feeling newly present in my own skin and smelling of sandalwood oil, I slink to a coffee shop that caters to Westerners.

The next day, for a solid hour, I can't take it in. I discover my passport and thirty dollars are missing from the small zippered compartment inside my pocketbook. I must be mistaken. It wasn't stolen. I must have left it at the bank. I re-check all my belongings, the same pockets, two times more. I realize I haven't used my passport since we came weeks before. Jim changed money, not me, and my pocketbook has always been with me. When could my money and passport have possibly been stolen?

Thievery in paradise won't compute; nor the rest of it that rises to the surface. My mind takes leave of it, keeps circumventing the inevitable: The only time my pocket-book wasn't with me—the only place was the massage place. Clearly the only time.

I replay the massage two times over in my mind, each moment held up to scrutiny. And a few things are odd. The lighting in the room was very sedate for the middle of the day, with curtains drawn. To create a mood, I assumed. Then my masseuse asked if she could move my pocketbook and jewelry—to a place out of my view.

The oddest thing of all: she left the room three times. The last time she'd brought a basin of warm water to sponge the oil off my body. Perhaps she prepared the water during the other two absences? Or went to the bathroom. Even masseuses have to go at inopportune times, yes?

No, not likely, I counter myself, choreographing the entire scam. Everything was completely staged from the moment I walked in that place. She removed my pocketbook from the room the first time, left it with the owner to take her time fishing through everything, deciding what to take, what not to take, then returning it after the second exit. I still had my Balinese *rupia*. Clever enough. They knew I might miss those. I would pay in *rupia* and notice immediately if they were gone. But how did they think they could get away with this and hope to stay in business? Is this why their price was cheaper, to lure tourists in? Did they really pull this off with any frequency?

Over and over, I see the masseuse's vulnerable, disarming smile, not the smile of a conspirator. But she acted so oddly—fawning her thanks—so excessive and unBalinese. And the strange whisperings. All atypical, I suspect, because of her unease. Perhaps this was her first time. The vulnerability I saw was probably sheer terror after the deed was done. Those moments as I paid her were the most difficult, laden with the possibility of discovery.

It's too late to go to the Consulate today, I decide. Jim and I sit on the porch of our room overlooking the rice paddies as I try to cool my ruminations. The sun sets behind a cloud and the lizard-spirit cries its strange guttural cry. Can a visitor who breathes the air of another country for weeks, who drinks its water and eats its food, become as its people? Is Bali making me see things that aren't there?

The next day, the US Consulate says I can't get a new passport until I report the event to the police.

"Do you want me to go to the police with you?" Jim asks.

"No, no, I want to do this alone."

Even as I wait in the police station, I don't know what to believe or what I will say. But I have to make a convincing report. A cadet-type underling with limited English skills pecks the computer keys, typing ten words a minute as the ceiling fan rustles his papers. He stops to retrieve the papers that fall to the floor.

I tell him how cleverly and methodically these women ripped me off. I'm certain of it now myself. As I look into the air and recall the events, I am so convincing.

The chief enters the room, sits on the desk and swings his leg up, reading the finished report. "Madam, did you report the lost passport to the massage place first?"

The question sends me straight up in my seat. "Well, no," I say, smiling uncomfortably. "What would they say if I returned? 'Oh yes, forgive us, here's your passport. We accidentally took it when you were here?'"

"No," he looks up, perfectly deadpan. "You might have accidentally left it there."

I blush profusely, a wave of contrition washing over me. Another story altogether. What if he's right? What if I've implicated innocent women trying to eke out a small living? "OK," I say calmly, "I'll go there and let you know if I find it."

But reason returns as I walk down the street from the police station. This is a colossal waste of time. I never used my passport or touched my passport in Bali. The chance that I'd accidentally left it is almost nonexistent.

I have no desire to face those women again and couldn't dread this trip more. I climb the very high steps to the massage room. The masseuse greets me warmly, like an old friend. If she's acting, she is very good. I tell her I must talk to the owner who looks up from her chair as we walk across the courtyard. "Hi. I wanted you to know I just filed a report with the police. I discovered my passport was missing after my massage yesterday."

My face is hot. She turns without looking at me, collected, calm, as if not hearing. "The police chief just called," she says, she knows about the report. Her stoicism astounds me. But the masseuse is not composed. All the lines in her face are drawn taunt with the weight of my story. Her concern lies solely with my quandary, my lost passport, not the implicit allegation I make against them.

"Ohhh, I am so sorry, madaamm." Surely, she doesn't really understand what's going on. Or she's a drama queen.

With no trace of anger or emotion, the owner says, "Your passport is not here. I would have told you if I found it." I want to believe them as I look into their faces. I do believe them. They are the same genuine people I met yesterday. I don't know what to think. I thank them and leave.

The owner's monotone voice still sounds in my head as I descend the steps: *Your passport is not here. I would have told you if I found it.* How could she have told me? And how could someone accused of something they didn't do be so calm?

I can just see them up there now. They breathe easier, maybe even hold their mouths laughing so I won't hear. *Boy,* they marvel, *it was tense there for awhile.* But they're so glad it's over, relieved nothing has come of it. The little inconvenience was well worth it. My passport probably bears a new photo and name already. They should both get an academy award.

Made waits on his motorbike. A light rain presages the daily afternoon downpour. He says he didn't really know these people; he just distributed the flyers someone gave him. He seems too defensive. Could Made possibly be involved? Or the police captain?

How bizarre that I thanked the women when I left. No, that was OK, I tell myself. If they are innocent, it was the right thing to do. I am so confused. *What are they: guilty or innocent? I have to know.* But I may never know. Perhaps Made is right; perhaps there really are spirits to be reckoned with in Bali. No place is exempt from thieves. How could I have let my guard down? How could I have thought otherwise?

Made and I ride home in silence. In the evening, the offerings have browned at the edges, littering the streets. No longer beautiful. Stepped on, ridden over, the mass of crushed pink bougainvillea petals return to the earth. The strays have eaten what was edible. The Balinese live in the moment, then let it go—like the temporal prayers carried in each offering, that ride on loops of incense smoke and are gone. Poof.

I ask Made to pull over so I can buy some offerings. "I have to do this," I tell him. We stop again at the large shrine that intersects the two streets above our street. He watches as I add my flowers to the mound of color and petals heaped up through the day. I light my incense off another. A small faucet drips under the shrine. I cup enough water in my hand and flick once, twice, thrice like a *legong* dancer. Made smiles approvingly.

The next few days, I am not admitting it to myself, though it colors everything. Ubud has become tainted for me and has fallen from grace—much like Dewi Sri through no fault of her own. Everything seems less genuine. Even Made's giggle seems a little less true to my ear. The Balinese are just like people everywhere on earth. How could I have thought otherwise?

Jim and I travel back and forth to Denpasar to complete the necessary paperwork and photos for the new passport. The day before our plane departs, we count our remaining *rupia* to assess our finances. He has gone downstairs in search of Made to get some change. I dump the contents of my pocketbook on the bed. The lining hangs down. A weight comes from inside the lining. My hand touches the object, not wanting to confirm the outline.

I feel inside the zippered compartment. And then I find it: a hole in the lining to the side. I reach through and retrieve my passport, the loose papers and the thirty dollars. I realize that the *rupia* didn't slip through because the currency was too large.

I moan like a tortured *leyak*, holding my head. I see the faces of the young women again. I am at least grateful they were true. I bury my face in my hands and sit, catatonic. *How can I ever face them again?* I can see them now. The masseuse will console *me.* (*Oh madam, I am sooo happy you have found your passport!*). The owner—the cool, collected one—she may not forgive me.

I bound into the air. "I'm going out for a bit," I say to Jim, who walks past me at the door. "I'm going back to see those women and the police chief."

As I descend the steps from our room, Made's silly giggle emanates across the compound. And everything is set straight again.

EPILOGUE: THE MOONLIGHT ON MY BED

All night I could not sleep, because of the moonlight on my bed.
I kept on hearing a voice calling. Out of nowhere, it answered
"yes."

Zi Collection, Chinese folk songs, 6th-3rd century B.C.

In all the world, there is not a finer love: travel. It takes our breath away, shows us places we couldn't dream of, gives us new eyes and new ways of looking at things. It holds up a mirror to our country, to our culture, to ourselves. It shows us what matters, makes us forever young and dulls the mortal beat. And it loves every one of us in equal measure. Surely it is divine, because few things can touch us so deeply.

I was like a lovesick teenager after I discovered travel, sleep-walking through my days until I could go again. The career track held little sway. Jobs were dispensable, largely a means to an end. Paltry two-week vacations, standard fare in the US, only meant greater job turn over. My resume became a work of fiction, riddled like Swiss cheese holes with gaps in time. I chose this lifestyle at a personal cost. I could never forsake travel, I said.

But things change in matters of the heart. Other suitors intervened. I loved them just as much. I missed travel and always dreamt of moving. But before I had known it, I'd grown roots, deep into the earth. Setting out again meant ripping myself from the folds of my nest and family and friends.

Jim and I both took travel for granted; we neglected it for years at a clip. I'd have never believed it. Graduate school, jobs, home ownership, mothers, animals have a hunkering down effect. Today, I marvel each time we set out; that we actually accomplish leaving. The challenge of a mere one-month vacation stretches out like a yawning abyss.

Last year, I joined Jim in Cambodia for a trip to China, marshalling the services of no less than twelve friends and family in order to pull it off. The "fill-in team" looked after my elderly mum; fed, medicated and read to our aging special needs cats; watered the plants; retrieved the mail; filled the birdfeeders and delivered me to and from the airport—replete with backups and Plan B.

"Aren't you excited about your trip?" friends always ask. It's a natural enough question to ask. But I'm rarely excited. Convinced we've picked a bad time to go, I'm usually trying to figure out how I can get a refund on the airline tickets. "But you always think it's a bad time," Jim says. "Is there ever a good time?"

My head and heart remain at odds. The sweet residue of all the trips that went before, that live with me always, get me out the door. They never let me down.

I go through the motions of getting ready like an automaton. I finally tear myself from the house and lock the door, countering the tug of the cocoon as I load the car. When I leave my driveway, I know the slow decline of the animals has already begun.

Thousands of feet high and twelve time zones later, I anticipate my arrival, suspended between two worlds but not present in either. When we're almost there, I know the metamorphosis is imminent, though you couldn't call it excitement yet.

The plane lands in Phnom Penh. As I descend the stair, the heat smacks me in the face like a wet rag and tells me I'm here. Jet travel is still like space travel to me: I cannot fully fathom that I'm on the other side of the world. My heart races when I see my first Cambodian face.

The hall leading to the street teems with strangers vying for space, many who hold signs. Written in Khmer, I know they all carry my name. Exhausted and light-headed from lack of sleep, I come back to life again. I am smiling like a fool; everyone I pass smiles back.

Jim soon collects me and our car disappears into Phnom Penh's streets. Motobikes weave in and out before us. The one next to us, deserving of a photo, carries three girls and a giggly baby. The girls are beautiful with broad candescent smiles. Most vehicles are motos, locals going wherever, and drivers in search of fares. No one seems to worry about time; the rush of the wind is enough. The traffic expands and compresses, but the cars always have their way. Shops and cafes and rows of frangipani trees whiz by.

In a few brief minutes, I'm transformed, emotional, happy to be nowhere else. Everyone at home must fend for themselves. I open the window to be closer to the street, letting the humidity displace the air conditioning. I want to climb outside, to be swallowed up by the energy of the streets.

I've never quite understood it—that these streets make me feel complete. How are they different from the crowded promenade at Baltimore's Inner Harbor? I've picked it to the bone; I have to know. I need only to look around, the answer is clear, not hidden. In the developing world, the streets remain the lifeblood of the city. The energy is vibrant and tangible. Everyone takes from it, pays homage to it day and night.

Souls have poured their lives into these streets for millennia; pushed their handcarts across the lumpy holes, peeled their fruit and sold it into the night—the skins grinding into the earth for generations. As they do now. So much living has been pressed into this dirt, connecting us to our beginnings.

A world of dichotomies usurps the senses—sweet smells and foul smells, vibrant colors and colors blackened with dirt, bells tingling on the wind, horns honking to wake the dead— all hours, never sleeping. As squalid as the streets may be, the cadence is primordial, as old as the first city.

The city streets at home were like these streets once, their pasts entombed in cement now, their vendors banished to indoor shops, their stories like wandering ghosts.

In our lifetime, these cities will change too; we will scarcely recognize places like Phnom Penh. They will eagerly follow in the West's footsteps, make all the mistakes we've made. It has already happened. Cars will crowd out everything like weeds, displace the vendors, gridlock the streets. The rise and fall of the music of the streets—voices bartering, laughing, arguing, communing—will fall silent.

It was Shiva, the creator-destroyer from India, who got Jim and me off on this discussion about why we don't travel more. "If a simple beetle juice-hoicking rickshaw driver in India has it all figured out, why can't we?" Jim asks. "Instead of saving his *baksheesh*, he took off and enjoyed it with his family the next day. He lived one day at a time with no regrets. When is a nestegg large enough? The problem is, we never think it's large enough. You and I have always been ready; we can live more simply, travel more, do all the things we've always wanted. But we're afraid. Because of this disease that plagues us, this American obsession with security that doesn't exist."

"Yes, the whole idea is very compelling," I say, blushing, just as I said the last two times. Jim is right that we are afraid;

I am afraid. "But Shiva was a little scary too. Living for the day is living on the edge, especially here in the West. Where would all of us be if we lived like Shiva?"

"I have no doubt, he is not without a safety net," Jim says. "You forget the strong sense of community he has in India, that all people in the developing world enjoy, and that we've lost in the West."

"These are things that can't be forced, Jimmy. I just can't do this now. Maybe later." And then we fall silent.

But this time, this isn't the end of it. Jim pulls out his big guns. "Yesss," he says slowly and deliberately, "but that's what my parents said. And your parents. And theirs before them. They could have had much richer lives; but they were too busy working. They never really took the time to enjoy themselves because of money."

Like we've been too busy working. We turned a deaf ear when travel beckoned. We had to make more money than was needed each day and prove something to ourselves. Were we mistaken?

Even when we ignored it, the universe conspired against us, simply cranked up the volume. When we least expected it and in the oddest places.

We installed a skylight over our bed, a simple enough home improvement. When the final touches were made, we realized how colossal this idea had been. Like magic, the dead space that was a white ceiling came alive and moved, opening up a veritable camera lens on the world above our roof. What is it about a box with moving images that makes us want to watch?

We never noticed how our trees hug our house, how delicate but tenacious squirrel nests are in the wind. How the slow movement of the clouds can leave you floating and clear your head. How dramatically blue the sky looks against the golden autumn leaves.

Save a few cherubs, our Renaissance ceiling painting was no less grand than a Michelangelo.

By night, our monitor became a planetarium on the world, tracing the journeys of the moon and stars over my bed, demanding an audience. The low wispy clouds rushed by, as redolent as a clock ticking.

With Stonehenge-like precision, the moon's light followed a path across my heart in May. In early October, it rested directly on my face just after I'd close my eyes, illuminating my sleep.

I used to envy astronomers. Few of us enjoy such a charmed perspective, I thought—thinking in light years, focusing on other galaxies each day. Astronomers can't sweat the small stuff. Now I realize that they have nothing on us.

Because there are many lenses on the world, many charmed perspectives to be found. As much as any telescope, they open the heavens to us. A haunting melody, a beautiful poem, a mother's love, an evocative painting, a dizzying dance, a lover's kiss. They all summon us. "Hurry. Look," they say.

Travel makes me look most. My body syncopates with the earth; I rise with the sun and sleep with the stars. The indoors serve only to rest my head at night; the outdoors are my living room. My gaze is always focused out.

When I return home, I see my little piece of the world with new eyes. When the lens threatens to turn in, stuck in my own orbit again, the universe continues to beckon. The moonbeams alight on my bed at night, and say "yes." As long as we have the moon and the stars, there is no place left to hide.

I plop myself next to Jim as he types on his laptop, the last pages of *1089 Nights* in hand. He answers emails from the Philippines, using the evening hours to catch his colleagues who just begin work.

I sigh a mortal sigh, musing. "Well, I'm almost finished with my book. But the ending evades me—the right words—you know, like the times I struggled to describe the desert of Wadi Rum and my lovely man-bird on the train. How can I possibly convey what travel means to me, Jimmy? It's the last dab of paint on the canvas, the one thing left to seal our odyssey."

Jim sits erect and strikes a pious pose. With prayer hands, he bows. "Ah, my little grasshopper, you cannot! But you have passed the test and Buddhahood will be yours."

The Kindness of Strangers

by Ann von Lossberg
(with thanks to Rumi)

A silent groundswell of love
graces each path,
and runs deep,
feeding the soul.
Drink from it,
take your fill.
But replenish it again.

ACKNOWLEDGMENTS

Three mentors cheered me through the rigors of birthing a book—telling me over and over that I could do it, I must do it, I would do it. I have never basked in such lovely, dizzying affirmation. They are Carolyn Males, Ed Claflin and Arlene Uslander, themselves talented authors, editors and critics in the industry. Barbara Erakko Taylor freely lent her thoughtful opinions and support; Pam Taylor was my photography consultant extraordinaire. Various friends vicariously traveled the world with me as readers, provided invaluable feedback and spurred me on—Ann Bracken, Mikki Buchness, Renee and Rebecca Goldstein, Peg Hargreaves, Bob Krasnansky, Rosella Livi, Sharon Maben, Carole McShane, Claudia Mitchell, Patty Reed, Jennifer Seiders, Joan Shepherd, and Gary Smith. Friends and family participated in my focus group as well. Aref Dajani, Hind Abboushi and Tarek Abuata lent technical assistance about the Arabic language and Islamic culture. Mary Ann Wilkinson provided a writer's retreat when it was sorely needed. Stephen Weathers and the designers at iUniverse were so helpful and patient. Gayle Conard and Sandy von Lossberg lent nurturing sibling support. Most of all, I am indebted to Jim who first fueled my love affair with travel and who awarded me the much-coveted Hudock Promising Writer's Fellowship for two years running.

Ann von Lossberg is available for book club signings and discussions, in person or via teleconferencing. Contact 1089nights@gmail or nights1089@verizon.net to make an appointment.

Autographed copies of *1089 Nights* can be ordered at 1089nights.com

Printed in the United States
129971LV00002B/13-96/P